JFK's Ghost

ALSO BY DAVID R. STOKES

The Shooting Salvationist
Apparent Danger
Camelot's Cousin
Jake & Clara
Jack & Dick
When Good Samaritans Get Mugged
I Am Prodigal
The Churchill Funeral Plot
Make the Choice to Rejoice

JFK's Ghost

Kennedy, Sorensen, and the Making of Profiles in Courage

David R. Stokes

Guilford, Connecticut

An imprint of The Rowman & Littlefield Publishing Group, Inc.
4501 Forbes Blvd., Ste. 200
Lanham, MD 20706
www.rowman.com

Distributed by NATIONAL BOOK NETWORK

British Library Cataloguing in Publication Information available

Library of Congress Cataloging-in-Publication Data available
Names: Stokes, David R., author.
Title: JFK's ghost : Kennedy, Sorensen, and the making of Profiles in Courage / David R. Stokes.
Other titles: Kennedy, Sorensen, and the making of Profiles in Courage
Description: Guilford, Connecticut : Lyons Press, 2021. | Includes bibliographical references and index. | Summary: "Examines Joseph Kennedy's take-no-prisoners approach to advancing John F. Kennedy's political ambitions"— Provided by publisher.
Identifiers: LCCN 2020054203 (print) | LCCN 2020054204 (ebook) | ISBN 9781493057689 (hardback) | ISBN 9781493061426 (epub)
Subjects: LCSH: Kennedy, John F. (John Fitzgerald), 1917-1963. | Kennedy, John F. (John Fitzgerald), 1917-1963. Profiles in courage. | Kennedy, Joseph P. (Joseph Patrick), 1888-1969—Family. | Presidents—United States—Election—1960. | United States. Congress. Senate—Biography. | United States—Politics and government—1953-1961. | Sorensen, Theodore C. | Ghostwriters—United States—Biography. | United States—Biography—History and criticism. | Authorship—History—20th century.
Classification: LCC E842 .S824 2021 (print) | LCC E842 (ebook) | DDC 973.922092/2—dc23
LC record available at https://lccn.loc.gov/2020054203
LC ebook record available at https://lccn.loc.gov/2020054204

For David Thomas Vaughan (USN), who makes this author a proud Navy Grandpa

CONTENTS

Acknowledgments

I AM, FIRST AND FOREMOST, GRATEFUL FOR MY LOVELY WIFE, KAREN. FOR more than 45 years, she has been my wife and best friend. She has also been my biggest fan. Her love and unwavering encouragement continues to provide the wind beneath my wings. And our three daughters, Jennifer, Deborah, and Brenda, are just like her, filling me with so much gratitude. Don't get me started about our seven wonderful grandchildren.

Thank you, as well, to my literary agent Leticia Gomez, CEO of Savvy Literary Services. Her efforts brought this book to the attention of the good people at Rowman & Littlefield. I have also enjoyed working with Rick Rinehart and Meredith Dias, both with R&L.

Early on in my research for this book, I reached out to Evan Thomas III, a gifted and award-winning author and former editor at *Newsweek* magazine. His father, Evan Thomas II, was John F. Kennedy's editor for *Profiles in Courage* 65 years ago. Thomas graciously let me interview him, and he also provided a picture of his father. Thank you, Evan.

I am also indebted to Aimee Wismar, who works with Textual Reference at the John F. Kennedy Library in Boston, for her help with material from those vast archives—even during the time of COVID-19.

Finally, I am grateful to my parents who instilled in me a love for history and current events at tenderly young age. —DRS

CHAPTER 1

December 7, 1957

SENATOR JOHN FITZGERALD KENNEDY'S GLAMOUROUS STORYBOOK world, not to mention his celebrated and calculated climb toward the presidency of the United States, was about to experience a potentially catastrophic political earthquake. His grandest dreams, as well as those of his family and die-hard devotees, were about to devolve into a nightmarish scandal. But this wasn't about his long-rumored and carelessly chronic marital infidelity—nor did it have anything to do with his carefully concealed, but likely life-threatening, health challenges. No, this potentially career-ending issue involved the achievement Kennedy was, in fact, the most proud of in his entire life.

It was Saturday night in America. And, while some no doubt had exciting plans that would send them staggering into Sunday, for many citizens, the kids were tucked in bed and mom and dad were settling down with a sandwich, or a bowl of ice cream, or maybe some popcorn, to watch a little television.

Because of the infamous date on the calendar, they may have talked a bit about where they were and what they were doing that same day sixteen years earlier when the world was suddenly and dramatically changed by dreadful news from a faraway place called Pearl Harbor. Or maybe life had now become so routine that those turbulent days of war seemed part of a distant past. At any rate, there was a new international conflict to keep an eye on.

A cold one.

For the fully domesticated, television was becoming more and more of a centerpiece to home life. Living room furniture tended to be arranged around it. Advertisers and producers were always trying to come up with new ways to capture—some might say manipulate—the attention of the unwitting public.

This night was a case in point. The big gun during the ten o'clock hour in the Eastern time zone was on Columbia Broadcasting System (CBS): *Gunsmoke* starring James Arness as Dodge City marshal Matt Dillon. The radio version from a few years earlier had featured William Conrad in that role, but he didn't make the small screen cut. The corpulent radio man had the voice, but it was Arness who had the well-chiseled features.

Those whose dials were turned to NBC, and frankly there weren't all that many of them, saw funnyman Ernie Kovacs using his legendary skills trying to breathe life into a quiz show called *What's It For?* It featured inventors and inventions. But the show was on life support and would be replaced by *Ted Mack's Amateur Hour* by Christmas.

On ABC, however, there was something that actually had potential. A hard-hitting and cigarette hawking newsman with a staccato delivery had recently made the leap from a local New York show called *Night Beat* to a coast-to-coast offering titled simply, *The Mike Wallace Interview.*

It was the beginning of take-no-prisoners television news, and Wallace was its ascendant star. The format was simple: the host and one guest, sitting across from each other, having an animated conversation. During the show's brief tenure, Wallace had already interviewed an eclectic group of guests, from mobster Mickey Cohen, to feminist activist Margaret Sanger, to architect Frank Lloyd Wright, to blonde bombshell Jane Mansfield. And along the way, he had already earned a nickname—"Mike Malice."

This night the scheduled guest was Drew Pearson, whose syndicated newspaper column called *The Washington Merry-Go-Round* was among the most widely read in America. He was particularly interested in presidential power, and few journalists have ever had "so intimate an acquaintance with the men who held that power."[1]

At precisely 10:00 p.m., the image of a man clutching a cigarette in a Edward R. Murrow–like manner filled small screens tuned to ABC, and the broadcast began:

Good evening. Tonight, on the sixteenth anniversary of Pearl Harbor, we bring you a special interview from Washington D.C. We shall examine the dangers of another Pearl Harbor, a Third World War, with the most controversial correspondent in Washington, Drew Pearson. Drew, in a moment I shall ask you whether you think there's going to be a Third World War, we'll get your view on President Eisenhower's uncertain future, and I shall confront you with the charge made by two past Presidents of the United States, that you are a chronic and a vicious liar. My name is Mike Wallace. The cigarette is Philip Morris.

3

After Wallace told his audience that Philip Morris was the best smoke around and that, "No filter is needed, because the mildness comes from the tobacco itself," he and Pearson discussed Cold War tensions for a few minutes. Then the conversation shifted to domestic politics, particularly President Eisenhower's health. The President, who had once also loved his cigarettes, but quit smoking them in 1949, had been a sick man for a couple of years, beginning with a heart attack while playing golf in Colorado in September 1955. He recovered from that sufficiently to make a successful run for reelection, his personal popularity being more than enough to overcome any negative perceptions about his capacity to do the job. Then in June 1957, he suffered a stroke and remained in a protracted convalescence—far from public view.

Wallace quoted a statement made by Vice President Richard Nixon about how Eisenhower was "not in such a condition as to make it necessary for him to resign." If he shared the quote to bait Pearson, it worked because the newsman launched into a somewhat surprising defense of Nixon. In fact, he made a near-endorsement of the man he had more than once referred to as "Tricky Dick."

Wallace pressed, asking Pearson if he thought President Eisenhower should resign because of his health. Pearson didn't hesitate, giving his interviewer what would years later be known as a "soundbite" or "tweetable" quote: "Well, my prediction is . . . that, er . . . and this is a little bit not quite the way you stated it, but I predict that Mr. Nixon will become President of the United States, within approximately a year." Pearson went on to suggest that Nixon would be a "better" president than the great hero of D-Day and architect of victory in Europe a dozen years earlier. That should have been the part of the interview that would be remembered.

But it wasn't.

Their discussion of a Nixon presidency in the event of an Eisenhower resignation led seamlessly to speculation about 1960. Wallace curiously described Nixon as the Republican Party's "glamour boy," an odd observation seen in retrospect through the prism of so many unflattering Nixonian images. The host then suggested that the Democrats had a glamorous potential candidate of their own—John F. Kennedy, who happened to be tuned in that night.

The very mention of Kennedy's name seemed to strike a nerve in Drew Pearson. Before long, he was well into a lengthy criticism of the U.S. senator from Massachusetts, which he tried to temper with half-hearted compliments: "Jack Kennedy is a fine young fellow, a very personable fellow, but he isn't as good as that public relations campaign makes him out to be."

Then Pearson dropped his own atomic bomb: "He is the only man in history that I know who won a Pulitzer Prize on a book which was ghost-written for him, which indicates the kind of public relations buildup he's had."[2]

CHAPTER 2

"A Target on His Back"

EARLY THE FOLLOWING MONDAY MORNING, JOHN F. KENNEDY—JACK TO his friends—walked into his office on Capitol Hill—room 362 in the Senate Office Building. He greeted his secretary, Evelyn Lincoln, and asked her to place a call to Clark Clifford, the powerful attorney and influential Washington insider. Years later, she said, "Soon after I went to work for John Fitzgerald Kennedy I learned that if he wanted something done, he wanted it done immediately."[1]

Mrs. Lincoln, as Jack always called her, was his first hire when he set up the Senate office in January 1953. She would continue on as his personal secretary until November 22, 1963. Born and raised in Nebraska and the daughter of a congressman, Evelyn was well liked and enjoyed friendships with the other secretaries in the building. In fact, she regularly had lunch with the head secretary in a nearby office—Rose Mary Woods, who worked for Vice President Richard Nixon.[2]

Described as "pleasant, tactful, competent, and loyal," Lincoln was often frustrated with Kennedy's work habits and management style.[3] He grew to depend on her for personal matters. It was her job to know "whether his clothes had come back from the dry cleaners or whether the barber shop would be open at the time he wanted his appointment." She was forever trying to organize his cluttered desk, prompting Kennedy to bark at times, "How can you expect me to find anything? Why don't you leave my desk alone?"[4]

Kennedy had a fidgety way about him. Lincoln recalled how her boss could be "so ill at ease," and a bit unkempt, like when he was sworn in as a Senator in January 1953.[5] Back on that day, the short end of his necktie "was clear up by the collar and the long end down below his belly. And he was forever trying to stuff his necktie into his pants."

This was one of those days, following a couple of sleep-challenged nights.

A few moments later, Clifford was on the line. Jack rubbed his eyes and, with a sense of urgency in his voice, asked the lawyer to come to his office on an important matter. An hour later, the accomplished lawyer was seated across from Kennedy. He listened as Kennedy rehearsed what Pearson had said on Mike Wallace's television show.

"I can't let this stand," the Senator told Clifford. "It is a direct attack on my honesty and integrity." He wondered about a possible lawsuit against ABC, Drew Pearson, and Mike Wallace. But Clifford told him that pushing for a retraction would be a wiser course of action.

Then the phone rang.

Mrs. Lincoln told the Senator that his father was on the line.

Joseph P. Kennedy was a multimillionaire and the former U.S. Ambassador to Great Britain under President Franklin Roosevelt. He was also the driving force behind his son's successful political career. To say Joe Kennedy was a control freak would be a gross understatement. He kept his children on a short leash even well into their adulthood. His grip on them has been described as "something close to totalitarian."[6] Years earlier, Jack joked to a good friend, "I guess Dad has decided that he's going to be the ventriloquist, so I guess that leaves me the role of dummy."

From his son's first days as a congressman, Joe kept tabs on him with the help of a network of spies. One secretary kept a detailed log of visitors to Jack's office, sharing it with the old man. Joe also paid the man who ran Jack's office in the late 1940s to report on his son's activities. And then there was the maid in Jack's Georgetown townhome on Joe's payroll who reported to him.[7]

Joe Kennedy was very upset.

Even from where he was sitting, Clark Clifford could hear his angry voice. He was screaming at Jack, who listened stoically. He was used to his father's tirades, having endured them all of his life. After a few moments, Joe paused, giving Jack the chance to calmly say, "I will let you talk to Clark."

He smiled and handed the phone to the crafty attorney.

"I want you to sue the bastards for fifty million dollars!" Joe said. "Get it started right away. It's dishonest and they know it. My boy wrote the book. This is a plot against us!"[8]

Of all many honors he would receive throughout his life, none would make Jack prouder or happier than winning the Pulitzer Prize for biography in 1957. And, of all of the abuse he would receive throughout his life, none would make him angrier than even the suggestion that he had not really written the book that won the award—*Profiles in Courage*.

The Pulitzer came with its own inherent spotlight, one that, at times, resembled an irresistible target on Jack's back. The attention carried with it scrutiny of the sort he had not yet fully experienced on the national stage. And there was a measure of envy on the part of his political peers. Many resented all the attention he was getting. Soon rumors began to circulate—rumors that Kennedy had not actually written the book and that sales figures were being manipulated to ensure the book's continued placement on bestseller lists. The FBI even started a file, sensing Kennedy could be vulnerable to a fraud charge.[9]

If the rumors were proven to be true, all of Kennedy's hopes and dreams, as well as those of his admirers and boosters—not to mention his powerful father—would come to nothing. And there would never be that brief and shining moment in America remembered ever since.

Camelot.

The story of the writing, publication, and popular reception of *Profiles in Courage* is in many ways a window into the era of all things Kennedy to come. And as with so many legends, the myths were superfluous. Jack's actual accomplishments were significant on their own merit, with no real need for embellishment.

Jack Kennedy's rise to the pinnacle of political power after World War II is a compelling story of ambition, wealth, skill, and a measure of cunning. He was prone to sickness—near death on a few occasions— yet he won the White House in 1960 evincing the image of youthful vigor, or as Kennedy would call it in his Boston brogue, "VIGAH." He brought erudition, charm, wit, and charisma to the presidency in ways never before seen.

As president, Kennedy oversaw the largest economic expansion in the country up to that time. He started the Peace Corps, faced down Soviet leader Nikita Khrushchev over missiles in Cuba, supported reforms in South America, started the United States on its path to the moon, and laid the foundation for later reforms in civil rights.

He was also rock-star popular.

A few years later, Richard Nixon, Kennedy's generational rival, would win the presidential prize in 1968. However, *his* pathway to it was mocked as contrived and image-laden. There was even a best-selling book about it, called *The Selling of the President*—a cynical look at how Roger Ailes (of future *Fox News* notoriety) and many others purportedly manipulated the political process, as well as Nixon's image, en route to victory.[10] But Nixon's 1968 team had simply borrowed from the Kennedy playbook in 1960.

Not that anyone noticed.

Like all successful politicians, Kennedy brought a tight-knit entourage with him wherever life and work took him—men and women who would do just about anything for him. They covered for him at times and worked as one to keep the flame of his image burning bright even long after he was gone.

They still do.

John F. Kennedy won the coveted literary award three weeks before his fortieth birthday, and it was well timed. He seemed to intuitively understand how beneficial it would be to have a Pulitzer on his political CV. After all, the man he hoped to succeed as President of the United States in less than three years was nearly three *decades* older than Jack and had a long and celebrated career of hands-on leadership and high-level executive experience. In contrast, Jack had never managed anything more than a small crew on an ill-fated PT boat and his Capitol Hill office staff.

Hardly the stuff to match the architect of D-Day.

It was understandable that Jack was concerned about being perceived as young and inexperienced, not at all ready for the responsibilities of the presidency. He needed to add a measure of gravitas to his bio. The Pulitzer Prize was a shortcut to what biographer Robert Dallek has described as the "the stamp of seriousness" he needed to win high office.[11]

With the publication of *Profiles*, JFK's celebrity brand spiked nationally. The book was an instant bestseller and garnered stellar reviews. Because of his literary success, Jack also received several honorary college degrees. *Profiles* became a global publishing phenomenon and was translated into dozens of languages.[12] Its author was increasingly perceived to be an erudite man of letters. Portions of the book were serialized in mass circulation periodicals. Kennedy was inundated with new speaking invitations from far and wide, all of this with the 1956 Democratic National Convention scheduled for that summer in Chicago.

And John F. Kennedy had his eyes on the vice-presidential nomination.

CHAPTER 3

"The Idea of Courageous Leadership"

IMAGE WAS EVERYTHING TO JACK KENNEDY. HE CAME BY HIS PASSION TO create and manage his public persona, as well as his flair for it, naturally. It was in his DNA. And the production and promotion of *Profiles in Courage* would be his masterstroke.

His father had effectively molded his own image a generation earlier, first as an incredibly successful businessman, then as a motion picture mogul. He eventually became one of the wealthiest men in America, acquiring a net worth that would be valued in our day at several *billion* dollars.[1]

But Joe Kennedy got bored with business-as-usual and set his sights on politics, pitching his substantial tent in the camp of Franklin Roosevelt in 1932, during the New Yorker's first campaign for the presidency. Though he would be ever-wary of the ambitious Kennedy, FDR found him useful, first as the czar-like watch dog over the country's stock markets as Chairman of the newly created Securities and Exchange Commission (SEC), then with a much bigger prize—U.S. Ambassador to Great Britain at the time when war clouds were in full development over Europe.

Then Joe set his sights on the big prize—to succeed FDR as President of the United States in 1940.

But the elder Kennedy's temperament and arrogance ultimately undermined his image in ways that led to his political demise. With his personal ambitions in ashes, Joe shifted gears and began to live vicariously through his sons, particularly his namesake, Joe Junior.

Then came the mother of all game-changers—World War II. Jack became a hero, while Joe Jr. became a *casualty*. And it wasn't long before their father began to place all his hopes and dreams on plan B—Jack. The problem was that Joe's second born son was not the natural born leader that his late brother was.

The old man had his work cut out for him.

Beginning while Jack was still in college, the Kennedy public relations machine had already started to give him a makeover. The first step was to take an otherwise ordinary college research paper—Jack's senior thesis at Harvard—and turn it into a book. Actually, more than just a book, it would be a bestseller titled *Why England Slept*. Kennedy influence and money fueled its research, polish, and promotion propelling the young writer to a brief, but significant moment of celebrity.

Then, as fate would have it, and with Jack in the navy serving in the South Pacific, a tragedy, one in which Jack demonstrated his own heroic courage, became the stuff of legend. Joe Kennedy made sure of it. He saw to it that an article about his son's experience and exploits got the widest possible circulation. Money was no object. Then came campaigns for the House of Representatives and the U.S. Senate, all bankrolled by the old man's money and driven by his image machine, which included a network of powerful movers and shakers from business, academia, journalism, and politics.

But the biggest and most effective effort of all was the one connected with *Profiles in Courage.* Joe Kennedy not only helped with the promotion of the book, he helped to facilitate the awarding of the Pulitzer Prize. And when questions arose about the possibility that his son might not have really written the book, Jack's father went into full nuclear mode, mobilizing a well-oiled fix-it machine. He knew what it was to have a career derailed by a public relations disaster, and he wasn't about to let that happen to Jack.

He was determined that John F. Kennedy would become the President of the United States.

Kennedy, of course, won the presidency in 1960. Lurking in the shadows, however, were a few things that, had they come to light back then, might have spelled doom for him, the kind of political meltdown his long-time rival Richard Nixon would experience more than a decade later. The kind of fall that could have given much earlier birth to the cynicism many Americans expressed in the aftermath of Watergate.

There is some indication that serious political trouble was brewing for President Kennedy before his fateful trip to Dallas. Journalists and political opponents had been busy digging up dirt, including about a particularly damaging story about Jack's womanizing and his relationship with a possible East German spy.[2] He had watched with a blend of fascination and fear as a scandal played out in Great Britain in 1963, one that reached the highest levels of British power and threatened his friend, Prime Minister Harold MacMillan. It was called The Profumo

Affair. And Kennedy knew that he was perilously close to having something similar exposed about him.[3]

All these years later, in the wake of so much historical analysis of Kennedy, the prevailing wisdom suggests he would have had great political difficulty in our day. Truth be told, he would have indeed found things challenging in his *own* time had the public known certain things about him. The answer to the rhetorical question: "If the American people had known then what we know now, would Kennedy have become, or remained, President of the United States?" usually defaults to two specific issues—womanizing and health.

However, there was another potential scandal that could have threatened Kennedy's political career more than his girlfriends or the fact that he did indeed have serious health issues that betrayed his image as a healthy and vibrant leader. But this problem had been effectively handled thus far by Kennedy and his people, as were the others.

By cover-up and deception.

John F. Kennedy's race for the presidency in 1960 was built around the idea of courageous leadership. He presented himself to the American public as a man of action, someone who would get America moving forward again, implying that President Eisenhower, and therefore his Vice President Richard Nixon, the Republican nominee, had presided over a dormant nation stuck in place, or worse—the past. Kennedy said he had a futuristic vision to meet the challenges of the new decade. He also tended to frame the times as laden with conflict and crisis. And he was confident he had the kind of courage needed to lead the nation at such a dangerous moment.

In fact, he had written a book on the subject. He told friends that *Profiles* and the Pulitzer Prize it brought him were bound to be help to him with his run for the White House.[4]

If, as one historian wrote fifty years after JFK's death, "*Profiles in Courage* constituted, essentially, a deceit on Kennedy's part," and if that would have become well known in the late 1950s, Kennedy's image would have lost much its luster. It represented an existential threat. And, in what turned out to be a photo-finish election on November 8, 1960, the outcome would likely have been different. That is assuming

Kennedy would have even won the Democratic nomination that year in the first place.

Yes—*Profiles in Courage* and the Pulitzer Prize were *that* important.

Profiles examined the concept of *political* courage, with a specific focus on the U.S. Senate, where Jack Kennedy served in the mid-1950s, representing Massachusetts. The book dealt largely with eight Senators, men who hazarded their own careers though the courage of their convictions.

There was John Quincy Adams, the future sixth President and son of the second one. He chose the national interest over those of his own constituents in the case of a proposed embargo against Great Britain. Because of his stand, Adams lost the support of his party—the Federalists. He was even called a traitor.

Next up was a look at a trio of Senators who tried to save the Union from inevitable division. The book drills down on the Compromise of 1950 and examines the roles of three political giants: Daniel Webster, Thomas Hart Benton, and Sam Houston. The great issue of that era was, of course, slavery. As the country grew and added western territories— Texas, New Mexico, Oregon, Minnesota, Utah, and Arizona—there was no federal law as yet prohibiting slavery. And the Senate became ground zero for the emerging national debate. Millard Fillmore was in the White House, and he agreed to a plan chiseled together by Henry Clay and Stephen Douglas which allowed some of the territories to make their own decisions about being slave or free. The plan also included strengthening the already notorious Fugitive Slave Law, requiring people in free states to return escaped slaves back to their owners in slave states.

That was the great sticking point.

Webster supported the compromise, even though it went against the wishes of the vast majority of citizens in Massachusetts. He was widely denounced and died a couple of years later. Thomas Hart Benton from Missouri also supported the bill and was voted out of office then next year. Sam Houston's support of the Great Compromise went against the grain of the secessionists in Texas, those who wanted to leave the Union. The legislation also called for Texas to surrender much of present-day New Mexico, adding to Sam Houston's tarnished political image.

The courage shown by these men all included their tacit approval of slavery in an effort to save the Union from dissolution. So, while history has shown all three men to be courageous, they were also terribly *wrong*. Their courage was, at the very least, misplaced.

It is hard to imagine any political leader in our day—particularly anyone claiming liberal bona fides—applauding the "courage" of men who supported, for whatever reason, a law that facilitated the return of slaves in the North to their "owners" in the South. But in the mid-1950s, this seemed to raise very few eyebrows.

In the next section, *Profiles* dealt with issues after the Civil War. First, there was the impeachment of President Andrew Johnson, Lincoln's successor. Perceived as being too soft on the South, he was opposed and attacked by radical members of his own Republican Party. When he was on trial in the Senate, he was acquitted by only one vote—and that was cast by a Senator from Kansas named Edmund Ross, who suffered great political consequences for voting his conscience.

A decade later, Senator Lucius Lamar (D-Mississippi) faced his own dilemma over monetary policy—the issue of so-called "free silver." Lamar supported the gold standard, which put him out of sorts with his constituency.

The next part of the book starts with the run-up to the First World War. By then, Senators were being elected directly by voters due to the Seventeenth Amendment, as opposed to being appointed by state legislatures, as had been the practice since the founding of the Republic. Senator George Norris from Nebraska opposed President Wilson's policies and the potential for America to join the European war. It was a courageous effort, but a losing proposition. The final Senator in the book is Robert Taft (R-Ohio), son of President William Howard Taft, who spoke out *against* the highly popular Nuremberg Trials after World War II.

In his 1956 Foreword to *Profiles in Courage*, historian Allan Nevins wrote: "Senator Kennedy treats of a special kind of courage: the moral courage of a parliamentary leader who in behalf of principle confronts the passion of his colleagues, constituents, and a majority of the general public."[5]

CHAPTER 4

"One of America's Great Political Writers"

WRITING WAS IN TED SORENSEN'S BLOOD. EVEN BEFORE HE WAS BORN, his mother was leading a writing club for women in Lincoln, Nebraska. She wanted to develop a greater audience of women for great literature. She was a lover of language and studied the power of words to facilitate change. Her son would follow in her footsteps on both counts.

Annis Sorensen also shared her love for *storytelling* with her children, "instilling in them a common passion for prose." She especially encouraged her son Theodore "to explore his own capabilities with the written word." That was the beginning of the young boy's lifelong passion for writing. He would go on to spend his life working on his language skills and would eventually become "one of America's great political writers."[1]

He would also become JFK's ghost.

Ted's father was a wordsmith, as well, having served as the editor of the *Daily Nebraskan*, the student newspaper at the University of Nebraska. So, both parents instilled in their son a passion for the English language, "as a beautiful instrument of precision."[2]

Theodore Chaikin Sorensen was born on May 8, 1928 "in the middle of everywhere," at least that was what it said on a road sign in Nebraska.[3] Sorensen remembered it as "a wholesome place in which to grow up, the kind of small-town environment now seemingly gone forever." His mother, Annis Chaikin, was the daughter of Russian Jews and known in their community for her activism and work for causes such as woman's suffrage. She was also a pacifist. Her views were no-doubt shaped in large part by what her parents had experienced in the old country. It was a brutal world they left to come to America. She worked her way through the University of Nebraska as a maid, graduating in 1908 with a degree in classic literature, as well as Greek and Latin. She earned her master's degree a year later.

Unable to find a job that interested her in Nebraska, she set her sights on New York, ultimately landing a position with the Ladies Committee of the *New York Jewish Protectory and Aid Society*, where she worked as a probation coordinator for "delinquent Jewish girls."[4] While in the big city, Annis gravitated to other local pacifists in New York, people like the famous social activist Jane Addams and the Zionist Rabbi Stephen Wise, as well as "social work leaders and radical muckrakers."[5] Ted said decades later that coworkers were captivated by her "fresh stimulating views" and her "delightful disregard of convention, precedent, and authority."

After a few years, Annis returned to Lincoln and the University of Nebraska, becoming the executive secretary and editor of the *University Journal*. It was in that role, at one point, that she became acquainted with a strange story involving the famous car manufacturer, Henry Ford.

As a war in Europe threatened to draw the United States away from neutrality, and as President Woodrow Wilson took steps to shore up America's military forces (despite his stated policy of keeping the nation out of war), a strong peace movement took hold in parts of the country. The Detroit automaker became an outspoken advocate of pacifism and at one point threw his influence—and fortune—behind what many called a foolish political stunt. At a New York City press conference in November 1915, Ford announced that he had leased the *Oscar II*, a ship from the Scandinavian-American Line, and would load it with the leading peace advocates of the day.

The idea was to mobilize international opinion to end the war in Europe before more nations, including the United States, were drawn in. The press quickly dubbed it *The Peace Ship*, which was meant sarcastically. Newspapers across the country lampooned Ford "as a Don Quixote accompanied by an assemblage of Sancho Panzas."[6] The Evangelist Billy Sunday, then at the height of his popularity as a wave of patriotism swept across the nation, remarked, "As a winner of publicity, Ford takes the cake."[7] And one former U.S. Senator said, "In uselessness and absurdity it will stand without equal."

The ship sailed that December with great fanfare, but to no actual effect. Even Ford's good friend Thomas A. Edison thought the automaker had gone slightly mad. He visited Ford's cabin aboard ship just before it left. "I'll give you a million dollars if you'll come," Ford shouted into Edison's near-deaf ear. But the famous inventor shook his head and smiled as he walked away.[8]

One of the passengers on Ford's big boat was from Lincoln, Nebraska, and Annis Chaikin sought him out hoping for an article for the University Journal. His name was C. A. Sorensen. He was an active member of the Nebraska Peace Society and had been invited by a Unitarian preacher to join other peace advocates on the ship. In all, the "delegates" on the *Oscar II* included thirty-six students and twenty-eight journalists. C. A.

Sorensen almost missed the boat, his train having arrived in New York thirty minutes after the ship was scheduled to depart.[9]

Christian A. Sorensen's ancestors were from Denmark. His parents, as was the case with Annis, immigrated to America during the late nineteenth century. He grew up in rural Nebraska. Ted described him as "a country boy," and his mother as "a city girl from Omaha." But they were both well-educated intellectuals.[10] They eloped in July 1921. Christian was a nominal Unitarian, so the couple determined to raise their children in that faith, a Rabbi in Lincoln assuring Annis that "the similarities between Reform Judaism and Unitarianism would make it logical for the two religious groups to join as 'Jewnitarian'."

When Ted was born, his father had just been elected as Attorney General of Nebraska as a reform candidate. He was "an active prosecutor of the state's prohibition laws and a crusading anti-vice campaigner."[11] The Sorensens were big supporters of George W. Norris, who represented the Cornhusker State in the U.S. Senate. Ted grew up idolizing Norris, a politician who believed "an educated elite judged the best course of action based on their concept of the common national interest."[12] Ted's father actually managed one of Norris's campaigns. His admiration for the Senator seemed to create in Ted "an independent spirit that was unafraid to question the accepted wisdom or the views of his political superiors, a trait that served him well in his years as a public servant."

Although their socioeconomic stations were worlds apart, Ted Sorensen's family life was similar to Jack Kennedy's in one telling way—he grew up in a home where discussions of social issues, public affairs, and current events were frequent. The house was "filled with national news magazines," and Ted's parents—even his older brother—would regularly quiz him about the issues du jour.[13]

Ted had "a fierce commitment to racial justice" and helped to establish the first area chapter of the Congress of Racial Equality (C.O.R.E.). They managed to get the city's swimming pool integrated. As a young man, he earned a reputation as a serious and persuasive intellectual.[14] And like his future boss, Sorensen had a great memory, "mental and physical energy, intolerance for small talk, and directness of manner."[15]

CHAPTER 5

"The Second Son Born to Joe and Rose Kennedy"

FRANKLIN DELANO ROOSEVELT SAT IN HIS SUITE AT BOSTON'S RITZ Hotel working on a campaign speech he was scheduled to give at Boston Garden. He was the Democratic nominee for the President of the United States, and the 1932 election was just a few days away. Joining him at the Ritz were his son James and daughter-in-law Betsey. Betsey had brought a friend—a wealthy department store heiress named Kay Halle. Kay had "bright eyes, strikingly blonde hair, and abundant if sometimes guileless enthusiasms," historian Arthur Schlesinger remembered years later.[1]

Halle recalled the moment when Felix Frankfurter, then a law professor at Harvard, came in with another man. "He was unmistakably Irish," she remembered, "with his copper colored hair, and a beaming smile that exposed his shining teeth." Kay asked Frankfurter about his friend. He said, "Joe, tell them who you are."

"I'm Joe Kennedy," he said. "Mr. Frankfurter brought me with him because, though I've been interested in all sorts of businesses in Boston and California—in films and banking and though 'Honey' Fitzgerald, Mayor of Boston, is my father-in-law, I've never had the thrill of being a part of a presidential campaign. So, I put some money into Mr. Roosevelt's campaign, and I'd like to go along with you all and take part in the fun."

Kennedy had not only managed to survive the ravages of the Great Depression, then holding the nation and the world in its death-grip, but he had actually *thrived*. He made his money "by sharp dealing, by stock churning and bootlegging, and other maneuvers that were not always in line with Marquis of Queensberry's rules."[2] He actually increased his fortune substantially by waiting for stocks to bottom out and then snatching up bargains.

Earlier that year, Kennedy had played a vital role helping FDR secure the Democratic nomination, placing an early morning call to William Randolph Hearst at his San Simeon estate in California and persuading the media mogul to throw his support to FDR.[3] The key was the California delegation which had been committed to the Texan John Nance "Cactus Jack" Garner, who was then serving as Speaker of the House of Representatives. Kennedy urged Hearst to use his influence to make sure

California's delegates supported FDR, and in exchange ensured Garner the number two spot on the ticket.

With his overture toward Hearst, Joe Kennedy had high hopes for Mr. Roosevelt—and himself.

Kay Halle found Joe to be both attractive and charming. In fact, they would eventually have a love affair. But that night she was on her way out to visit Betsey Roosevelt's father—Dr. Harvey Cushing—at a nearby hospital, where he was being treated for an ulcer. Joe Kennedy asked to join them because, as it happened, his son Jack was in the same hospital.

Joe took Kay to Jack's room.

"He couldn't have been more than twelve or thirteen," she said.

Actually, he was *fifteen*, but he was thin and frail and looked much younger. "Jack was lying in bed, very pale which highlighted the freckles across his nose. He was so surrounded by books I could hardly see him. I was very impressed because at that point this very young child was reading *The World Crisis*, a history of The Great War by Sir Winston Churchill," she said.[4]

Kay's encounter with young Kennedy that night was the beginning of a relationship that would endure until Jack's death, and it highlights two themes that would come to define his life and career—passion for the written word and a never-ending fascination with history. Schlesinger would later reflect on Kennedy's attraction to the past: "History was full of heroes for him and he reveled in stately cadences of historical prose. His memory when he read was photographic. Situations, scenes and quotations stuck in his mind for the rest of his life."[5]

Jack's mind was sharp, but his body was a battlefield.

The second son born to Joe and Rose Kennedy, John Fitzgerald, was born on May 29, 1917, less than two months after President Woodrow Wilson took the United States into a war that he had promised to avoid. Jack was two years younger than his brother, Joe Jr. and found himself much of the time living in the shadow of his talented sibling. There was a definite rivalry there, "that admixture of love, jealousy, anger, and competitiveness had jelled into the seminal relationship in young Jack's life."[6] Jack was very sensitive and unable to see that his brother likely felt threatened by him, seeing his "potential far better than Jack saw it himself."

Joe Sr. also did everything in his power to ensure his children—particular the older brothers—grew up understanding world affairs. Jack seemed to take to this better than his older brother. He read the *New York Times* every day and had a "near encyclopedic knowledge of current events." He was described as "a fiercely intelligent young man who looked with wry bemusement at his life."[7]

That "bemusement" meant that Jack "was careless about his clothes, careless about his appointments, and careless about money. Worse yet, he was intellectually careless. He was living through the Great Depression, with millions unemployed and the roads and rails full of hollow-eyed wanderers, and yet he knew and felt nothing of what his compatriots were suffering."[8] He spent much of his time in the classroom daydreaming and barely getting passing grades. Teachers regularly noted that he didn't work to his potential. In fact, in today's academic environment he might be diagnosed with attention deficit disorder.[9]

Then there were his physical problems. In 1920, just before his third birthday he nearly died from scarlet fever. "Jack was a very, very sick little boy," his mother recalled in her memoirs.[10] She also believed that this early episode contributed to his ongoing vulnerability to a host of diseases. Jack certainly seemed to catch everything that came along—and then some. From whooping cough, to measles, to chicken pox, chronic bronchitis, and even asthma. Rose kept "an index file with notations of her children's medical histories." Jack also struggled with his vision at times and began wearing glasses as a teenager, something he was sensitive about throughout his life.

Photos of him wearing spectacles were very rare.

His siblings sometimes mocked him for being sickly. There was a standing joke his brother Bobby recalled years later—"When we were growing up together we used to laugh about the great risk a mosquito took in biting Jack Kennedy—with some blood the mosquito was sure to die."[11] One doctor familiar with his case suggested that Jack was also "born with a weak back."[12] In the 1970s, Dr. Elmer C. Bartels, who had often treated Jack years before at the Lahey Clinic in Boston, explained, "An unstable back is something you are born with and it doesn't maintain itself properly."[13] So later injuries, from football, and then the war, simply aggravated a condition Jack had since the day he was born, and would suffer from until the day he died. Pulitzer Prize–winning journalist Seymour Hersh said illness was "the most important fact of Kennedy's early years."[14]

But with all his health struggles, Jack remained a cheerful optimist, facing his challenges with great courage and never indulging in self-pity. He never expressed anything "about why the God his mother worshipped daily should have plagued him with these constant illnesses."[15]

He used his down time, whether in the hospital or while resting at home, for reading. This was Jack Kennedy's *real* education. His chronic childhood illnesses, and the attendant downtime, allowed him to retreat into a world of the mind, one infused with voracious reading. Jack would not begin to take formal studies seriously until his junior year in college, but his poor academic record before that masked his impressive autodidactic development.

CHAPTER 6

"The Muckers Club"

JOHN F. KENNEDY GREW UP SURROUNDED BY PRIVILEGE. HIS WEALTHY father saw to it that he and his siblings wanted for nothing, even during times when much of the world struggled to barely survive. Joe Kennedy presided over an empire of wide-ranging business enterprises. And he was a patriot. During the First World War, his public service as the manager of a Boston steel shipyard brought him into contact with Franklin Roosevelt, who was then serving as Assistant Secretary of the Navy. It was a relationship that would continue for a couple of decades.

Joe had married Rose Fitzgerald, the daughter of a Boston mayor, a local political legend in his own right. They had nine children. Rose was a devout Roman Catholic, while Joe was nominal in his faith, leaving the religious grounding of his children to her. Joe's work ethic and his tendency to stray from his wedding vows ensured that they would never be all that close to each other. At times, their union "appeared little more than an elaborate, exquisitely rendered masquerade." In fact, the only real thing they had in common was the children. The young Kennedys "were their mutual business, and when they were around them, there was usually some other agenda at work, some life lesson being imparted."[1] The Kennedy family was described years later by journalist Stewart Alsop as "a remarkable closed corporation," with Joe as its CEO.[2]

In 1928, Joe Kennedy purchased a palatial home in Hyannis Port, Massachusetts, along Nantucket Sound on Cape Cod. The three-house compound located on six waterfront acres "became as close to a spiritual home as the Kennedys would ever have." The family spent summers there and it became "the school in which more than anywhere else Joe and Rose created the emotional ethos of the young generation of Kennedy men."[3]

Joe's storied business brains enabled him to see trouble on the horizon after the family's first full summer at Hyannis Port. He saw impending doom for the economy, particularly the stock market, and pulled all his money out long before the crash in October 1929. He managed to insulate and isolate his family from the worst of the Great Depression, "while some of his less prescient neighbors were relegated to living in mansions without electricity and pawning their family valuables."[4]

When Jack was ready for high school, he followed his older brother to Choate, a private boarding school in Wallingford, Connecticut. Always overshadowed by Joe Jr., a star athlete and popular guy on campus, Jack found ways to make a name for himself. Because he was sickly and underweight, he attracted the nickname "Rat Face." Jack responded by acting out, and his rebellious behavior made him popular with some of his fellow students.

One time, Jack smuggled firecrackers onto the campus and planted them in a lavatory. After they had done their damage, he sat in the daily chapel conducted by Headmaster George St. John, who held up a "badly injured toilet seat." St. John then described the culprits responsible as "the muckers," which Jack took to heart. To the headmaster, such pranks were contrary to the spirit of the institution. He regularly admonished the students to, in words resembling some Kennedy would make famous decades later, "ask not what Choate does for you, but what you can do for Choate."[5]

By his junior year, Jack had attracted a loyal following and the group came to be known as "The Muckers Club."[6] One member of this clique was a fellow named Kirk Lemoyne Billings, who liked to be called "Lem." He and Jack became lifelong friends—likely the closest friend in Jack's life. Billings was "tall and personable and always ready to join in Jack's zest for fun."[7]

And he was gay.[8]

Jack and Lem didn't have much in common apart from the fact that "they were both second sons and survived Choate together." But there was something special about their friendship and Jack "clearly needed Billings and his loyal company."[9] So close were they that Lem took up residence in the White House when Kennedy was President.

Jack's father set up trust funds for his children. He saw life as a "giant feast" and wanted his children to be able to experience it the same way. The funds were "as much a part of that vision for his sons' lives as private school education and athletic competition, as well as part of his vision of what he thought a true man should be and have and do." Joe later told his good friend Bernard Baruch that the money would allow his sons to "spit in his eye" if they wanted.[10]

Beyond any doubt, Jack therefore grew up with a deep-seated sense of entitlement. He also had no problem letting others do things for him.

Chapter 7

"The Gathering Storm"

JACK PACKED RELATIVELY LIGHT, STUFFING THREE PAJAMA TOPS AND bottoms, seven handkerchiefs, sixteen pairs of socks, eight pairs of underwear, fourteen shirts, and four pairs of pants into his satchel. But he also brought his car.

A nifty 1936 Ford convertible.[1]

He and his good friend, Lem Billings, boarded the SS *Washington*, one of the largest and fastest American vessels competing for market dominance with the Germans and British, for a trip to Europe. It would be a life-changing experience.

By the summer of 1937, the world was lurching toward its rendezvous with war. Japan was well into its military incursion into China, Spain was engulfed in a full-throttle civil war, and Mussolini's Italy was firmly in control of Ethiopia—all things that spelled doom and demise for the League of Nations, the largely ineffectual global network created in the aftermath of The Great War. And Nazi Germany, fresh from its unchallenged occupation of the Rhineland region, was preparing for its next expansionist move—the annexation of Austria.

Jack and Lem got off the ship when it stopped at Le Havre, France, and waited for the car to be offloaded. Then, sans top, they motored through scenic Normandy, staying the first night at a little inn in the town of Beauvais, about forty-five miles from Paris. They reached the City of Lights the next day, where they spent their time in typical tourist fashion. They managed an excursion into Spain, even though the at-war nation was marked as not approved on their passports. Watching their first bullfight, both young men were less than impressed by such heartless cruelty—Ernest Hemingway's popular romanticism notwithstanding.

Along the way, Kennedy experienced his first political awakening. He not only saw a continent in the midst of dynamic change, but he also learned some things about himself. When he and Lem made their way to Mussolini's Italy, Kennedy got his first up-close and personal look at the political ideology called fascism then taking hold in much of Europe. Years later, Billings would reflect on the fact that his wealthy friend seemed to be much more interested in the problems then going on in the world than he ever did back in school.[2]

Jack kept a diary on the trip, and his entries highlight his awakening. He wrote: "Would fascism be possible in a country with the economic distribution of wealth as the US? Could there be any permanence in an alliance of Germany and Italy—or are their interests too much in conflict?"[3] He and Lem even got to watch Mussolini deliver a speech. Lem remembered, "He was such an unusual speaker. You know, he'd talk, then he'd jut his chin out."

The next stop was Germany—a nation experiencing a Nazi-driven economic and military revival, one that portended international challenges to come. Jack and Lem drove up through Innsbruck, Austria, and eventually arrived in Munich, where they treated themselves to beer and sausage at the *Hofbrauhaus*. They had conversations with the locals and experienced the strong anti-American sentiment that was taking hold in Germany. Billings saw the Germans as "insufferable, they were so haughty and so sure of themselves," adding, "the German people were going through a very strange period then."[4]

Leaving Germany, they made their way back to the French coast and ferried across the Channel, car in tow, en route to London. After several days there, they were on their way home. It had been a summer to remember, and Jack Kennedy was beginning to take the world and his education more seriously. He would have all kinds of questions for his professors at Harvard that fall.

Around this time, Jack had his first brush with marriage. He had fallen in love with Francis Ann Cannon, a wealthy textile heiress. They dated for nearly a year, and he wanted to marry her. Years later, Francis recalled, "He was the first man who was in love with me. He proposed marriage to me."[5] But her father was against her marriage to a Roman Catholic. They remained close friends and kept in touch during the years that followed.

In fact, there would come a moment when Francis would help Jack become a national hero.

That December, Jack's father received a significant posting from President Roosevelt—U.S. Ambassador to the Court of St. James. This was a plum assignment, one that raised his political profile, as well as his prospects. In early 1938, Joe and Rose and the younger Kennedy children moved to London and took up residence at 15 Princess Gate, a property J. P. Morgan had donated to the embassy in 1920. Jack would travel back and forth between America and England for the next few years, giving him a front-row seat to what Winston Churchill would later masterfully and colorfully describe as "The Gathering Storm."

The summer of 1938, just prior to Jack's junior year at Harvard, turned out to be another crucial time for his intellectual development. He and his brother Joe spent much of it in Paris at the home of U.S. Ambassador William Bullitt. They were there while a new crisis played out between Germany, Czechoslovakia, Britain, and France—one that would put Europe directly on a collision course with war.

Fresh from his success with the annexation of Austria, Adolf Hitler made territorial demands for the Sudetenland, the region of Bohemia and Moravia largely populated with German-speaking citizens. Of course, the dictator's real agenda was to swallow up all of Czechoslovakia, a polyglot nation cobbled together as a successor to the Austro-Hungarian Empire in the aftermath of The Great War.

By the time Jack returned to Harvard that September, a meeting between German, British, Italian, and French leaders bore the fruit of what Churchill would later describe as "the summit of the crisis."[6]

CHAPTER 8

"JFK's Future Ghostwriter"

EIGHT-YEAR-OLD TED SORENSEN SAT ON HIS FATHER'S SHOULDERS trying to catch a glimpse of the President of the United States over the heads of those standing in the large crowd. The date was October 10, 1936. Franklin Roosevelt was in Omaha campaigning for reelection. Speaking from the back of his train, he was flanked by Senator George Norris, who just that year had left the Republican Party and was running for reelection as an independent, FDR smiled and talked about his policies to help the American farmer.[1]

Norris was already Ted's hero, so he was pleased when the President said, "George Norris' candidacy transcends state and party lines. In our national history we have had few elder statesmen who like him have preserved the aspirations of youth as they accumulate the wisdom of years."[2]

Ted also vividly remembered Election Day a few weeks later. Roosevelt won in a landslide, and there was a parade in Lincoln complete with the locals singing "Happy Days are Here Again."

Apparently, Sorensen became a political animal at a very young ago.

Theodore Sorensen grew up on Park Avenue, but not in a pricy New York City apartment; rather it was, as he described it, "a modest two-story stucco house" in Lincoln, Nebraska.[3] Although the Great Depression was hitting some people in a devastating way, the Sorensen household managed to avoid its extremes. They weren't by any means wealthy, just comfortable compared to many Americans. He remembered when they upgraded from an icebox to a refrigerator. Theirs was a pacifist home, with the children getting "Erector sets, a hectograph, and picture puzzles that encouraged creativity," as opposed to the toy soldiers and cap guns enjoyed by other neighborhood kids.

He described his mother as "the lioness" of the household, someone "fiercely protective of her cubs." When he was ten years old, John F. Kennedy's future ghostwriter wrote a poem about her:

> *This poem is about my mother,*
> *When I was sick in bed,*
> *She would bring me up my food,*
> *Which was usually milk and bread.*
> *Against sickness she put up a fight,*

And when I had a large fever
She would stay up late at night
My mother is now 50 years old,
And has lived 10 of those years with me
And I hope I'll support her for the rest of my life
I hope that's the way it will be.[4]

Sorensen recalled, "Whatever capacity I developed as a writer was nurtured in an articulate family."[5] Their house was filled with books and periodicals. Like Jack Kennedy, Ted was a voracious reader. Even as a young boy, he was reading the likes of *Harper's*, *Atlantic Monthly*, and even the *Saturday Review of Literature*. His mother took him and his siblings on a weekly trip to the Lincoln Public Library, "carrying a bushel baskets into which each of us added the books of our choice."

He read everything he could get his hands on, from the works of Dickens, to "stories about the animal kingdom by Thornton Burgess." He also loved to read speeches, something that would serve him well later in life. His own literary flair was influenced by the orations of Thomas Jefferson, Abraham Lincoln, and Franklin Roosevelt. And though he was a hereditary pacifist, Ted, like his future boss, was also a fan of Winston Churchill, at least from a literary perspective. A few years later, he started listening to recordings of important speeches. He was particularly taken with FDR's speaking style, and its "artful combination of humor, eloquence, and political zingers."[6]

The very things for which a future Jack Kennedy speech would be known.

In high school, Ted was the president of the Lincoln High writers' club, as well as editor of the literary magazine, called the *Scribe*. He was also on the school's debate team, an experience that he credited with improving "the clarity, quality, and color" of his writing.[7]

When it came time for him to register with the selective service, Ted Sorensen chose to do so as a noncombatant and a "conscientious objector."[8] Accordingly, he had to file a "Statement of Position" with his local draft board. He wrote: "I am a Unitarian . . . [and I was] taught that every man is my brother, every man has within him the spark of the divine, every man bears this relationship to the totality called God. Thus it is that I could kill no man . . . So it is I am what is called a pacifist—what Jesus called a peace maker. . . ." He also quoted Gandhi and U.S. Supreme Court Justice William O. Douglas, among others.

The statement ran five full typewritten pages.

Holding such views would seem to make Sorensen an unlikely candidate to become a key figure in postwar and Cold War America as an insider on a war hero's team. His profile didn't seem to speak of courage, certainly not the kind needed in a dangerous world where freedom was ever threatened by tyranny. But he viewed the stand he had taken as an act of bravery.[9]

In stark contrast to Jack Kennedy's active combat role, the man who would one day become his virtual alter ego, and the key figure in a drama surrounding a best-selling book about courage, was a determined *pacifist*. Jack and Ted were, at least on paper, an odd couple.

And unlikely soulmates.

CHAPTER 9

"A Big Churchill Fan"

JACK KENNEDY HAD NEVER MADE THE DEAN'S LIST BEFORE, BUT HE DID in his junior year at Harvard.[1] Even with the largest course load he had ever taken, he excelled. He had a new sense of discipline and focus. His political awakening also continued with a course he took early in that academic year. It was taught by Professor Arthur Holcomb, someone who would be one of Jack's "go-to" academicians for the rest of his life.

In fact, nearly two decades later, Holcomb would help with *Profiles in Courage.*

The course, described simply as *Government 7*, was designed to "answer some definitive questions: What would an intelligent citizen expect to learn about the work of his particular representative in Congress from the official publications available to the public in public libraries."[2] From the start, Professor Holcomb was impressed with the way Jack took such a cultivating interest in the project. He recalled Kennedy doing a first-class job as an investigator and called his final report "a masterpiece."[3] Jack was so immersed in the project that he even found time during that year's Christmas break to travel to Washington for the purpose of meeting some of his father's friends and examining congress more closely.

He was becoming a political animal.

Around this time, Kennedy also began to contemplate a subject for his senior honors thesis—even though he had more than a year before he needed to write it. This process, it would turn out, would be Kennedy's first taste of writing success and also the first significant step on his path to an eventual Pulitzer Prize. He wanted to write about how and why Great Britain was woefully unprepared for war. One of his tutors put together a list of books to read on the subject. And when Kennedy took a long-planned academic leave the following February to work with his father in London, he took several of the books with him and began to make notes. That trip would be extended, putting him right in the center of great events as they were unfolding.

Heady stuff for a young man.

The period from February through September in 1939 became Kennedy's greatest educational experience yet. He traveled to Poland, Latvia, Russia, Turkey, Palestine, and the Balkans representing his father. At every stop, he relayed dispatches back to his father. Those dispatches revealed perceptive observations about developments abroad, the kind usually reserved for more seasoned correspondents. Jack witnessed the struggle in Poland as that nation battled Nazi propaganda and braced for war, visited Stalin's Leningrad and Moscow, and was in Palestine to see a flood of Jewish immigrants pouring in. He even returned to Munich, where rocks were thrown at his car.

Eventually, Jack made his way to Prague, which was by then completely under Nazi control. His father had cabled ahead that his son was en route, but the skeleton staff that was left really didn't have time to entertain a guest. One foreign officer, George F. Kennan (later to become a key architect of U.S. Cold War policy), recalled, "We received a telegram from the embassy in London, the sense of which was that our ambassador there had chosen this time to send one of his young sons on a fact-finding tour around Europe, and it was up to us to find means of getting him across the border and through German lines."[4]

Years later, James MacGregor Burns, the *Pulitzer Prize*–winning historian and eventual JFK biographer, examined the letters Jack sent to his father that summer. He was impressed that they were "probably the best source of on-the-spot reporting which [Joseph] Kennedy received at the U.S. Embassy in London."[5]

Jack was seated with his father, mother, brother Joe Jr., and sister Kathleen in the Stranger's Gallery of the British House of Commons on September 3, 1939, to witness the formal declaration of war with Germany. He listened as Prime Minister Chamberlain, whose efforts to avoid war had failed and humiliated him in the face of Hitler's duplicitous treachery—efforts fully supported by Joe Kennedy—called it a sad day. Rose Kennedy remembered it as a "heart-broken, heart-breaking speech."[6] Whatever Jack thought it about, he was more interested in what the man scheduled to speak third that day would have to say.

Winston Churchill.

Jack had been nurturing a growing sense of hero worship for several years. Reading Churchill's 1938 book, *Arms and the Covenant*, which focused on Great Britain's woeful lack of preparedness for the coming conflict, greatly influenced his thinking. Demonstrating great political courage, Churchill took the leaders of his own political party to task.

The book also greatly influenced public opinion in the wake of the ill-fated Munich Conference, which turned the very mention of "Munich" into code for the abject failure of appeasement. Kennedy ultimately used Churchill's book—which was released in the United States bearing the title *While England Slept*—as the "touchstone for his own work."[7]

Even the title.

While Chamberlain's remarks that day in the House were subdued, Churchill seized the moment and seemed determined to inspire a spirit of resolute duty. He said, "We are fighting to save the whole world from the pestilence of Nazi tyranny and in defense of all that is most sacred to man."[8] Jack Kennedy, who was already a big Churchill fan, sat there transfixed. He was deeply moved and certain in that moment that the Englishman he admired most would one day soon lead his nation during times to come.

Churchill thought so, too.

He had just been appointed as First Lord of the Admiralty, the same post he had held when war broke out back in 1914. And just a few hours after Chamberlain announced the declaration of war, a message was telegraphed to the entire British fleet. It contained but three words that were met with applause from ship to ship: "WINSTON IS BACK."

He had been back at the Admiralty post but a few hours when Churchill faced his first crisis. A British passenger liner was making its way out to sea after leaving Glasgow, Scotland, on September 1, with following stops at Liverpool and Belfast en route to Montreal, Canada. The SS *Athenia* was under the direction of Captain James Cook, and he was very conscious of the warning all seagoing vessels had recently received from the Admiralty—a warning to be on war footing. Aboard were 1,103 passengers and 315 crew. The passenger list included 311 Americans. Cook hugged the coast while he could, keeping the lights out, even telling passengers not to smoke on deck. As he turned away from the Irish coast toward open sea, he took the ship in a zig-zag course to make it difficult for German U-boats to target her.

But it was to no avail.

At 7:40 p.m. that evening, a torpedo from the German submarine U-30 hit the ship's stern. Soon she was at the bottom of the sea. Other ships came to rescue the survivors, but 117 lost their lives, including

28 Americans. The sinking of the *Athenia* was a sudden and sobering reminder that the world had changed dramatically.

In a move that likely raised a few eyebrows, Ambassador Kennedy sent Jack to Glasgow to meet with the American survivors, rather than going himself. It was young Kennedy's baptism into public life. Newspaper reports about his meetings with *Athenia* survivors reached all the way back to the United States. There was also newsreel coverage. The *London Times* told the story: "U.S. SURVIVORS IN GLASGOW— MR. JOHN KENNEDY'S VISIT."[9]

Mr. John Kennedy, second son of the American Ambassador in London, visited Glasgow today to look after the interests of American survivors of the Athenia disaster. Mr. Kennedy was met by Mr. Leslie Davies, the American Consul-General in Glasgow, and Lord Provost Dollan, who explained to him the arrangements already made for the comfort of American survivors. Mr. Kennedy expressed the appreciation of the United States Government for the magnificent generosity with which his fellow countrymen had been treated by the citizens of Glasgow.

Jack visited hospitals to meet with the injured, and he had meetings with the rest of the survivors at Glasgow's Beresford Hotel. Some of the encounters were tense, with the survivors understandably on edge. He assured them that the embassy would provide funds for clothing and luggage and that a ship from America was already on the way to take them home. Then he returned to London to brief his father.

Jack's friend Torby MacDonald recalled that "it was a tough situation for a young man to be thrown into . . . what he did was try to reunite families, which he did very successfully, apparently, and also giving people who had lost their money and their possessions in the torpedoing, hurrying up their processing through our embassy."[10]

Kennedy had experienced his first taste of "public crisis," and he got high marks all around.[11]

Jack stayed on in London for a few weeks that September, missing the first few weeks of his senior year at Harvard. He wrote a letter on September 13 to the university registrar on letterhead bearing the header, THE FOREIGN SERVICE OF THE UNITED STATES OF AMERICA. "As I am now working in charge of the Committee for the evacuation of the '*Athenia*' survivors," he wrote, "and due to the lack of transportation, it appears now that I shall not be able to return back to America before the twenty-ninth of September."[12]

When he did make it back to Harvard, it was as a celebrity of sorts. There had been extensive media coverage of his work with the *Athenia* survivors. This attention enhanced his image, and he was determined to leverage his recent experience in ways to become a public figure.[13]

He liked the attention.

CHAPTER 10

"What's That Limey Been Telling You?"

JACK FIDGETED IN HIS CHAIR AND DRUMMED HIS FINGERS ON HIS KNEE as he listened to the speaker deliver a surprisingly engaging talk titled *New Facts in International Relations: Europe*. It dealt with the recent, and already infamous, Munich Conference—a meeting between Adolf Hitler and Britain's Prime Minister, Neville Chamberlain—and the ready-to-explode European crisis. The lecturer's name was John Wheeler-Bennett, a Brit who currently presided over a weekly seminar at the University of Virginia Law School. He had been invited to Harvard by Professor Bruce Hopper to address the seniors in his *Government 18* class.

Dr. Hopper was Jack's senior honors thesis advisor.

Wheeler-Bennett was thirty-six years old, though he dressed in the manner of a much older man. He wore a monocle and always seemed to have a carnation in the buttonhole of his jacket—a near professorial caricature. His good friend, future prime minister Harold MacMillan, said Wheeler-Bennett was "one of the best talkers" he ever met.[1] As he brought his lecture to a close that day, he dramatically displayed the gas-mask he had been issued in London as war loomed. He told the seniors that he carried it everywhere with him.

It was a great prop.

Recently returned from London himself, and thoroughly familiar with the international situation, Kennedy was captivated by Wheeler-Bennett's lecture. He was also determined to talk to him. As his class-mates gave the guest speaker a respectable ovation, Jack swiftly pushed through the crowd and made his way to the front of the room to intro-duce himself. He dropped his father's name, of course. Wheeler-Bennett was impressed by the young man. As they shook hands, Kennedy men-tioned that they had met once before. Wheeler-Bennett indeed recalled that earlier meeting and how the Ambassador had spoken of his sons as if they hadn't been in the room. He launched into an imitation of Jack's father, "I'll tell you about these boys. There's young Joe, he's going to be President of the United States; and there's Jack, he's going to be a univer-sity president; and there's Bobby, he's the lawyer."

Mildly amused, Jack smiled and then asked Wheeler-Bennett if they could have a private chat while he was in town. The lecturer was staying with Professor Hopper and his wife at their place in Cambridge.

They made an appointment to meet the next day.

Kennedy and Wheeler-Bennett, a cane now added to his carefully affected ensemble, met and walked along the Charles River for a couple of hours on a beautiful New England autumn day. Jack told him about his thesis idea and how he wanted to examine the appeasement policy of Prime Minister Neville Chamberlain. He was surprised to learn that the lecturer was thinking about writing a book on the same subject.

The professor judged Jack as worthy of his help. He traveled from Charlottesville to Cambridge several times over the following months. He suggested books for Kennedy, as well as issues to research. And because Kennedy was planning an extended trip back to London in February 1939, Wheeler-Bennett recommended a study of Edmund Burke while there. It is likely that he was using Jack as a stalking horse for some of the spade work for his own envisioned book. He told Jack that Burke's writings about revolutionary France might offer some interesting parallels to the current international situation.[2]

Ambassador Kennedy was less than pleased by his son's relationship with Wheeler-Bennett. He would often ask: "What's that limey been telling you?"

Past the halfway mark of his tenure at Harvard, Jack began to focus on the one career idea that appealed to him—to be a *writer*. The idea of pursuing his own ideas through writing offered him the chance to cultivate his own identity. It was also a way to keep himself out of his older brother's shadow.[3] Another way was to join the *Spee Club*, one of several fraternity-like organizations that competed for elite members.

Kennedy threw himself into work on his senior honors thesis in a way he had never before approached anything education-related. Having witnessed history firsthand in Europe, he decided to leverage his travel observations into a manifest, one he hoped would transcend a mere academic submission. Elements of the research, writing, and subsequent publication of his work yield clues about a future endeavor—*Profiles in Courage*—that would put him on the map as a critically acclaimed man of letters.

Kennedy biographer Robert Dallek saw the story of Jack's honor's thesis as "a microcosm of his privileged world."[4] Through his father,

Kennedy was able to confer with the British Ambassador to the United States, Lord Lothian, both in Palm Beach and in Washington, D.C. In fact, he later wrote to Lothian that their conversations had "started me out on the job." And Jack's father instructed his press secretary in London, James Seymour, to give his son any help required for the project.

James W. D. Seymour had graduated from Harvard a month after John F. Kennedy was born. Ten years later, he was the university's director of publicity. It was in that role that he first encountered Joe Kennedy, who had by that time added movie-mogul to his resume. The elder Kennedy had been recently profiled in *Moving Picture World* as "a new, big figure on the motion picture horizon, a natural leader and organizer."[5] Using those celebrated skills, he was organizing a lecture series for the Harvard's business school. Kennedy also pledged money—$30,000—to underwrite research on the motion picture industry.

Seymour, described as "a courageous, imperturbable, sensitive man,"[6] clearly impressed Kennedy, who soon hired the publicity man as an assistant at his offices in Hollywood. He left Joe's employ after a few years and dabbled in screenwriting for *Warner Brothers*. But when Kennedy was appointed as U.S. Ambassador to the Court of St. James, he needed someone savvy to run his public relations machine, and soon Seymour was on his way to London as Joe's press secretary.[7]

On January 11, 1940, Jack sent a cable to Seymour in London: "SEND IMMEDIATELY PAMPHLETS, ETC, CONSERVATIVE, LABOR, LIBERAL, PACIFIST ORGANIZATIONS FOR APPEASEMENT THESIS DISCUSSING FACTORS INFLUENCING PRO CON 1932 TO 1939 STOP SUGGEST LASKEY [*sic*] AS REFERENCE ALREADY HAVE TIMES, MANCHESTER GUARDIAN, HANSARD THANKS, JACK KENNEDY."[8] Seymour cabled back: "HURRYING MATERIAL WRITING, REGARDS." Seymour then reached out to Professor Laski via cable: "PLEASE TELEPHONE ME EARLIEST CONVENIENCE."

And so, it began.

Seymour found it rather easy to gather materials for young Kennedy, he said, "organizations fell over themselves to comply." In a letter to Jack, Seymour summarized his first efforts, "I am checking with *Chatham House* and *Oxford University Press.* The latter has nothing on the subject among their recent pamphlets or books and Chatham House is to let me know. Likewise London School of Economics has evacuated to Cambridge, but I reached Laski by wire."[9] He also indicated that he had recruited a few booksellers and that he was compiling a list of relevant works at the British Museum Reading Room.

The press secretary worked tirelessly on Jack's project for several weeks compiling materials about Britain's foreign affairs since the end of the Great War. Regular dispatches traveled via the embassy's diplomatic pouch. The materials would arrive at Joe Kennedy's personal office in Manhattan and were then forwarded to Jack at Harvard, who would be notified by letter from Seymour. For example, on February 8, he wrote to Jack, "On receipt of this letter will you please immediately telephone the Mail Room of the State Department in Washington and tell them that six packages of printed matter have arrived in the pouch addressed to the Ambassador in your care."[10]

At one point, the Ambassador, while he was back in America briefly, sent a cable to the embassy in London on Jack's behalf. The cable said, "RUSH PACIFIST LITERATURE."[11] All for Jack's research. But the message was intercepted by British Intelligence and they passed it along to other parties as further confirmation of what was described as Joe Kennedy's "treacherous behavior."

They had no clue the Ambassador was simply helping his son with his homework.

CHAPTER 11

"How's Your Book Coming?"

JACK KENNEDY NEVER HAD DIFFICULTY GETTING OTHERS TO ASSIST him. He had the kind of charisma that drew devotees into his orbit, people who would often go above and beyond the duties of everyday friendship. When the research phase gave way to the actual writing of his thesis, Jack Kennedy recruited a cadre of helpers, as he would years later with *Profiles in Courage*. Because he had the financial means, he was able to pay a personal secretary throughout the process. Pretty good for a college kid. He asked his friend Torbert Macdonald to place an advertisement in the *Harvard Crimson*:

> *WANTED. Stenographer, young, to furnish typewriter, assist on thesis; capable taking shorthand. $20. Apply Wednesday, F-14 Winthrop House Harvard College.*[1]

The ad ran for several days and drew 60 applicants, causing no small stir in the dormitory. Jack settled on an 18-year-old girl named Marie, who worked on the project for several weeks. A few other secretaries were also involved, but Marie was main one.

Just as Professor Bruce Hopper had mentored Jack during the idea and research part of the project, so another professor, Payson Wild, guided him during the actual writing. He helped Jack with the outline. Jack would write chapters which would then be reviewed by Wild. The professor said, "He was pretty thorough on some things, as I recall. Both Bruce Hopper and I would have to say, 'Well, get along with it, Jack. Now you can't be definitive on every point'."[2]

Jack's classmates took note of his newfound focus. One Harvard classmate, James Rousmaniere, remembered Jack in research mode. "There was a library, where portraits hang,"[3] he remembered. "Jack used to study there quite a lot. Jack always had a typist somewhere." He described Kennedy's process: "He would get his typed manuscripts delivered to the *Spee Club*. A steward would pick them up, and he'd be reading the manuscripts in the *Spee*." His friends would tease him, "How's your book coming? Not really thinking it was gonna be a book. We only saw these manuscripts coming in the door from the typist wherever."

Decades later, historian-journalist Garry Wills wrote that Kennedy "assembled the paper in a mad flurry of work with a team of hired secretaries to whom he dictated pointing out passages for copying, working more as a compiler than prose artist."[4]

It was a trial run for *Profiles in Courage*.

The thrust of his argument in the 153-page paper echoed his father's sympathetic attitude toward Neville Chamberlain and his predecessor, Stanley Baldwin. The Ambassador had been outspoken in his support of the Prime Minister's policy of appeasement. Jack argued "that there were deeper institutional reasons for the Munich Pact."[5] He posited that Chamberlain, despite growing unpopularity for his leadership, had actually "successfully prepared his nation for war." But he faulted him as politically vulnerable because of his "failure to bring the country [to] the realization of the great dangers with which it was faced." With Winston Churchill increasingly being seen as an attractive alternative to Chamberlain in Great Britain, an important shift was taking place. Kennedy wasn't making excuses for Baldwin and Chamberlain. He argued that the policy of appeasement was a direct result of Britain failing to rearm in the mid-1930s. Of course, Jack was careful to avoid anything that might be seen as a departure from the views of his high-profile father.

As biographer Robert Dallek has suggested, Jack's primary argument was "one originally made by Alexis de Tocqueville over a hundred years before: Popular rule does not readily lend itself to the making of effective foreign policy . . . Democracies, Jack asserts, have a more difficult time than dictatorships mobilizing resources for their defense." Only "pervasive fear" can bring about the kind of mobilization needed.[6]

Kennedy wrote his thesis with more than a good grade in mind—he thought it might possibly make a good book in keeping with his ambition to be a writer. So he crafted the research paper with an eye on eventual publication. Toward that end, Jack told the story of Britain's failure to prepare for war as a cautionary tale for the United States. He wrote: "We must always keep our armaments equal to our commitments. Munich should teach us that; we must realize that any bluff will be called. We cannot tell anyone to keep out of our hemisphere unless our armaments and the people behind these armaments are prepared to back up the command, even to the ultimate point of going to war."[7]

The first name he thought of for his paper was *England's Foreign Policy Since 1931*, but he eventually settled on, *APPEASEMENT AT MUNICH: The Inevitable Result of the Slowness of Conversion of the British Democracy from a Disarmament to a Rearmament Policy.* It was written while Ambassador Kennedy was seen "as a close associate of the Chamberlain government."[8]

And no fan of Winston Churchill.

Jack, on the other hand, clearly admired him, writing, "In the light of the present day, we are able to wonder at the blindness of Britain's leaders and the country as a whole that could fail to see the correctness of Churchill's arguments."[9] The paper was due on March 15, 1940, but Kennedy missed the deadline by a couple of days. It was read by four members of Harvard's faculty, who formed a committee of review. They were divided in their opinions about the Jack's work. The report card called for the reviewer to "Indicate whether the rank is summa cum laude, magna cum laude, or cum laude, or not of distinction grade (C, D, or E). Use plus or minus, where necessary."[10]

Professor Henry A. Yeomans described *Appeasement at Munich* as "badly written; but a laborious, interesting, and intelligent discussion of a difficult question." He graded it magna cum laude. Professor Carl J. Friedrich was tougher, writing, "Fundamental premise never analyzed. Much too long, word, repetitious. Bibliography showy, but spotty . . . Many typographical errors. English diction defective."[11] He graded it "cum laude plus." He was also overheard suggesting privately that Kennedy's paper might have been better titled "While *Daddy* Slept."[12]

But the professors who functioned as Jack's thesis advisors were more positive about it. Payson Wild recalled, "he was pretty thorough . . . I don't recall any great problems."[13] Hopper noted "Jack's imagination and diligence in preparedness as outstanding as of that time."[14] Both graded it magna cum laude.

Kennedy would graduate from Harvard with that distinction.

Jack's brother Joe read the thesis and wrote to their father that it "seemed to represent a lot of work, but did not prove anything." Of course, this was likely coming from jealousy. Two years earlier, he may have had ambitions for his own senior honors thesis. It was titled *Intervention in Spain*, and he drew, at least in part, from his own firsthand observations of that country's civil war. But no copy of Joe's work can be found. It was likely destroyed, as one historian wrote, "so that the Kennedys would not have to explain Joe Jr.'s enthusiastic support for [Francisco] Franco," the new dictator, who had been supported by Hitler and Mussolini.[15]

No book deal for young Joe there.

For the balance of Jack's academic courses that final semester he may have also been helped along by a service he and his friends had used before, one that would ultimately be banned on campus. It was nicknamed "cram school,"[16] and Jack's good friend, Torbert MacDonald remembered "Jack utilized those services," which were provided by "Wolfe's Tutoring Service," run by a fellow named Harold Wolfe. MacDonald acknowledged using the service, as well. Apparently, Wolfe had helped many students along the way, most famously Franklin Roosevelt Jr., the son of the President of the United States.

Nearly two months later, the very day that he finished his senior year final exams at Harvard—May 10, 1940—Jack read newspaper accounts describing the fall of Neville Chamberlain and ascension of Winston Churchill as Prime Minister of Great Britain. In the immediate wake of that day's initiation of a new German advance on the Netherlands, Belgium, and France, Jack was forced to revisit his thesis if he expected to publish it as a book.

The lull in the Nazi advance, often referred to as "The Phony War" or "Twilight War," had given way to a renewed existential threat on Great Britain. His thesis had been "a well-documented, though not entirely convincing, defense of Neville Chamberlain machinations at Munich."[17] He had described Chamberlain as "having successfully prepared his nation for war,"[18] an argument that was obviously no longer operative. Kennedy's somewhat sympathetic defense of Chamberlain written *before* the new German assault was also no longer marketable. The story was changing dramatically, and any potential book would need to reflect the new reality.

Establishing a pattern that would be reprised years later with *Profiles in Courage*, Jack, with significant help from his father, recruited a team of operatives, one that gave him "the kind of help in preparing his book manuscript that few authors receive."[19] One friend—Blair Clark, an isolationist who had been editor of the *Harvard Crimson*—recalled that "he and Jack worked together rewriting two of the chapters." Kennedy and Clark met for a few afternoons in the Harvard Widner Library. Clark later reflected, "I might have written a few paragraphs that were original, but mostly I rewrote and edited."[20] He was apparently less-than-impressed with Jack's work, adding: "Frankly, I was surprised he found a publisher for it."

Jack Kennedy graduated cum laude from Harvard on June 14, 1940. His mother and a few siblings attended the ceremonies, but his father was still in London. The graduate had to settle for a cable from Joe: "TWO THINGS I ALWAYS KNEW ABOUT YOU THAT YOU ARE SMART AND TWO THAT YOU ARE A SWELL GUY."[21]

CHAPTER 12
"Why England Slept"

ARTHUR KROCK WAS USUALLY THE ALPHA MALE IN ANY GROUP—
certainly with the staff at the *New York Times* where he had served as chief
of the Washington Bureau for almost a decade. It was said that he "had
a way of fixing a man on the spot."[1] The journalist, who had already won
two Pulitzer Prizes by 1940, en route to a total of four, had an intimidating air about him, and only a few close friends dared to call him anything other than *Mister* Krock. One of those familiar friends was Joseph
P. Kennedy—who usurped Krock's alpha role when it came to their personal relationship.

Maybe it was his experience in Hollywood during the 1920s, but the
multimillionaire had developed an instinctive grasp of the importance
of image. It became an obsession of sorts, one that he would pass down
to his sons. Kennedy was determined to be seen as "a hard-working and
successful businessman who adored his strikingly large family."[2] Once
the political bug bit him during FDR's 1932 campaign for the White
House, Joe nursed an ever-growing political ambition. And when he was
appointed as U.S. Ambassador to Britain, he saw the presidency as something within his grasp.

He cultivated relationships with journalists along the way, feeding them tidbits in hopes of fueling articles about him and his family.
Ultimately, he zeroed in on Arthur Krock, paying the *New York Times*
man "$25,000 to keep his name in the newspapers."[3] Decades later, Jack
Kennedy would try to manage news from the White House the way he
learned from his father and Krock.

Krock remembered Joe Kennedy as an amoral man. "I was not
shocked in the least. I expected, and still do, that politicians and big-
business men don't have any morals," he said, adding, "I've often reflected
since those days that he probably never liked me at all, but found me useful and thought he might be able to make use of me."[4]

He certainly did.

Shortly after Jack finished the first draft of his thesis, Joe directed
him to show it to Krock, and the newspaperman encouraged him that it
was "solid enough to be turned into a book."[5] In early April, Krock sent
a note to the Ambassador in London seeking permission to look for a
potential publisher.[6] That permission was readily granted. And of course,

Krock stepped up. "I worked two weeks on it, night and day, delivered it at four o'clock in the morning," the newsman recalled, years later.[7]

The Ambassador's publicist, Harvey Klemmer, was also tasked with helping shape Jack's prose. Working out of his London embassy office, he described the writing as "a mishmash, ungrammatical. He had sentences without subjects and verbs. It was a very sloppy job mostly magazine and newspaper clippings stuck together. I edited it, and put in a little peroration at the end."[8]

The young lady, Marie, who had worked on the thesis with Jack was hired again during the book phase. Working in Bronxville, New York, she was put up at the *Hotel Gramatan*. Years later, Mrs. Marie Baker recalled that "every morning the family chauffeur would call for me and take me to the Kennedy home where I worked on the manuscript."[9]

Krock persuaded his own literary agent, Gertrude Algase, to shop the manuscript for a publisher. She approached Harper & Brothers first. In the cover letter she sent with Jack's manuscript, she dropped Arthur Krock's name and said that the Pulitzer Prize–winning journalist "read it, and praised it. And referred him to me."[10] She added, "I read the script and found that it was really a masterful handling of a subject." Then, she included a teaser as bait: "Jack's brother is going to write a book, too, personal experiences when in Spain which entail some material never before released for publication." But that wasn't the end of her sales pitch. Gertrude brought up the potential for a future book by the Ambassador himself. "I cannot make any promises," she wrote, "but I do hope he will write his book someday!"

On June 18, Edward C. Aswell, an editor at Harper & Brothers, wrote a lengthy rejection letter citing another book that was in the pipeline "that would take the wind from Kennedy's sails."[11] Aswell, a fellow Harvard graduate (class of '29), was currently immersed in his most significant work—editing a pair of novels by Thomas Wolfe, who had died two years earlier, for posthumous publication.[12] Possibly out of respect for Jack's family, Aswell wrote an in-depth explanation for passing on the book:

The disastrous turn of events in France, has, we think, so shocked and shaken people in this country that, in our judgment, it would be

practically impossible to get attention for any historical survey as this,
even though the period covered is a very recent one. Events which
preceded the outbreak of the war now seem to have occurred years
ago, so rapidly has history moved since May 10. Also, the collapse of
France has made only one question seem important in people's minds,
namely, what will England do now? And of course as a corollary
to that, what will we do? In the face of this grave crisis, nothing
else seems important . . . Won't you please be good enough to show
this letter to Mr. Kennedy, because we should like him to understand
our reasons. Under the circumstances, there is nothing we can do
except to cancel the contract. The manuscript is being returned to you
herewith.[13]

Years later, Harper & Brothers would, however, take a chance on another Kennedy book—*Profiles in Courage.*

The agent's next pitch was two days later to *Harcourt Brace*, telling them, "I suggested to young Kennedy that your house would be my first choice," something not quite true. She also dropped the name of Harold Nicholson, an outspoken British politician who was bitterly critical of Chamberlain's dealings with Hitler, suggesting, incorrectly, that the member of the House of Commons was going to write a foreword for Jack's book. Nicholson had been part of the British delegation to the Paris Peace Conference in 1919. But *Harcourt* also turned it down because they had a dim view of the project's success.

Algase's third try, however, was charm—*Wilfred Funk, Inc.*, of New York.[14] The much smaller publisher hit the ground running and worked quickly to prepare the book for publication. Krock volunteered to edit the book. He also suggested the book's ultimate title, in part for its similarity to Winston Churchill's book, which was then making an impact in America—*While England Slept.*

Kennedy's work became, *Why England Slept.*[15]

Toward the end of July 1940, *Wilfred Funk, Inc.*, shipped the first review copies to forty-six individuals and periodicals from a list supplied by the Ambassador, in a campaign to gain his son's book a favorable reception. This effort yielded several "significant notices for his book."[16]

The next month, as the title was rolled out to the general public, it was favorably reviewed in the *New York Times Book Review*, a placement no doubt influenced by Krock. That review described the author's "mature understanding and fair-mindedness," and commended his "careful analysis of the data."[17]

Chapter 13

"Henry Luce"

"You would be surprised how a book that really makes the grade with high class people stands you in good stead for years to come,"[1] Joe Kennedy told his second-born son. As would also be the case years later when *Profiles in Courage* was published years later, Jack's father played a significant role in the transformation of his thesis into a *New York Times* bestseller. He encouraged his son's effort and threw his significant business and political weight around liberally. Joseph P. Kennedy perceived the value a significant literary effort would have on his son's future career—whatever that might be. However, the Ambassador's contributions were not purely limited to marketing and promotion.

He was also a *collaborator*.

Jack's relationship with his father was, as is so often the case with dads and their boys, a complicated one. Joe Kennedy was a tough taskmaster, and he held his children to high standards. In Jack's case, there was one factor that set him apart from his siblings when it came to vying for the attention of their father—his chronic illnesses. The parental dynamic at play in the Kennedy household was far from the traditional model of the times, with mother as caregiver and father as distant and disciplinarian. A clear example of this is seen in the way Joe Kennedy became—early on in Jack's life—the primary caregiver when he was sick. It was "his father, not his mother, who visited him, cared for him, and watched over his recovery," for the most part.[2] And "with each illness, accident, operation, and convalescence, the bond between father and son grew stronger and more resilient."

The lifeline for their relationship, because they were often not sharing the same space, whether it had to do with Joe's travels, Jack's hospitalizations, or being away at school, was letter writing. In a world long before email and other forms of electronic communication were even imagined, personal correspondence was the primary—sometimes only—way to be in touch with loved ones. The letters dealt with everything from the commonplace to the consequential.

On May 20, 1940, less than two weeks after Jack finished his studies at *Harvard*, his father wrote to him in great detail about the thesis. He began:

I have shown your thesis to various people around here. Everyone agrees that it is a swell job. And that you much have put in some long hard hours assembling, digesting, and documenting all of this material. Most people, I believe, will agree with the fundamentals of your thesis. However, one or two of those who have read it complain that you have gone too far in absolving the leaders of the National Government from responsibility for the state in which England found herself at Munich . . . I am having a mimeographed copy edited here and will get it on the next Clipper. You might also be trying to improve the writing. After you are satisfied with it, ask Krock to go over it again . . . Check your references. We have found several misspellings of names and a couple of wrong dates.[3]

The five-page letter included several significant suggestions about changes in the prose. Jack was clearly receptive, maybe even intimidated a bit, because the finished manuscript includes significant language almost verbatim from Joe's letter. Here are a few examples:

LETTER: *"Germany got a head start on the allies before they were able to comprehend what she was about. She probably got this head start not so much through the manufacture of actual implements of war, but through laying a foundation for their manufacture."*

BOOK: "The truth is that Germany got a head start before the Allies grasped what she was a bout. This was accomplished not so much by the manufacture of actual implements of war, as by laying a foundation for their manufacture."

LETTER: *"The German locomotive industry, for example, was turned over to the manufacture of tanks instead of rolling stock for the deteriorating German railways."*

BOOK: "The German locomotive industry, for example, was assigned to the manufacture of tanks instead of rolling stock for the deteriorating German railways."

LETTER: *"Germany was especially smart in getting tooled up for aircraft production."*

BOOK: "Germany was shrewd in getting tooled-up for aircraft production."

LETTER: *"Germany got the jump principally through getting everything set for a large-scale output rather than through the output itself, even though the latter certainly was considerable."*

BOOK: "Germany got the jump principally by getting everything set for a large-scale output rather than actual output itself, though its output was considerable."

There are many other passages in *Why England Slept* that are clearly drawn from Joe's letter.[4] At the end of the book, for example, there is a lengthy passage drawn almost word-for-word from the missive, ending with:

LETTER: *"We should profit by the lessons of England and make our democracy work. We must make it work right now. Any system of government will work when everything is going well. It's the system that functions on the pinches that survives."*

BOOK: "We should profit by the lessons of England and make our democracy work. We must make it work right now. Any system of government will work when everything is going well. It's the system that functions in pinches that survives."

As the book was being edited and readied for publication, Joe Kennedy thought about just whom to get to write a foreword for it. Harold Nicholson, conservative MP in Great Britain, was mentioned early on by the literary agent, but his name would hold little weight with American readers. Arthur Krock had hopes that he would be tasked with the Foreword, but despite all his loyal work for Joe over the years, including significant efforts for *Why England Slept*, the Ambassador came up with what he thought was a much better idea.

Henry Luce.

It's hard today to comprehend just how big Luce was in 1940. He had started *Time* magazine in 1923, launched *Fortune* magazine in 1930, and acquired *Life* in 1936—transforming it into the first manifestation of photo journalism. It quickly became the most popular periodical in the country and "could be found in virtually every middle class home."[5] He has been described as "a seminal figure" in American journalism. And he ruled over a media and business empire.

But he was also a strong and early advocate of American intervention in the growing war, something that was out of step with most Americans, including Joe Kennedy. At Luce's direction, "both *Time* and *Life* mobilized their considerable resources for detailed coverage of the war" in late 1939. Each issue of *Life* featured compelling and often graphic photographs of Nazi aggression.

Luce was no Kennedy fan. He thought how Joe conducted himself as Ambassador was nothing short of disgraceful. "It's outrageous," he said, "because he said that England was bound to get beaten."[6] The media mogul talked about how Joe, during the London blitz, telephoned him "on the open transatlantic phone saying the jig was up for England. You must don't do that kind of thing. The British never forgave him for that."

But if the Ambassador sensed how Luce felt about him, he ignored it. After all, he had been having an affair with Luce's wife for several months.[7] Clare Booth Luce was a playwright and journalist. She also had as much ambition for power and influence as any man around her. They had met in Paris in April 1940 and spent much time together at the Ritz Hotel, just a month before Hitler made his move on Western Europe. Mrs. Luce saw things differently than her husband and was an ardent isolationist, which meshed with Joe Kennedy's view of things.

Their romance, however, did not keep Joe from reaching out to his lover's husband on Jack's behalf. He knew Luce's name and endorsement would greatly enhance the prospects for his son's forthcoming book.

When Joe asked Henry Luce if he would be willing to write a forward for *Why England Slept*, the media mogul was open to the idea saying, "Well, send the manuscript and let me look at it."[8] He later recalled, "When the manuscript, or rather the proofs, arrived, I was very impressed by it. I was impressed by the scholarly work, because this book was based on a comparative review of proceedings in the House of Parliament for several years. At this time, of course, it was after Munich and the hot war was on. England, as they said, stood alone and the popular tendency was to put all the blame on the so-called appeasers, namely, Mr. Chamberlain and the Tory appeasers. This book showed that blame would have to be shared quite generally by nearly all aspects of British opinion, including the Labour Party."

Luce's forward was laudatory. "I cannot recall a single man of my college generation who could have written such an adult book," he wrote.[9] "If John Kennedy is characteristic of the younger generation, many of us would be happy to have the destinies of this republic handed over to his generation at once."

But Joe must have been disturbed by some of what Luce wrote. He pointed out parts of the book where he disagreed with Jack. For example, he wrote, "Some readers of this book will no doubt regret, as I do, that Kennedy has not devoted more attention to the practical possibilities of what was called Collective Security." He also rebuked the young author for dealing "too lightly" with "the almost criminal folly" of key British policy makers. These and other critical comments were carefully sandwiched between positive remarks, but what he wrote reads more like a semi-critical book review than a traditional foreword.

Nonetheless, Luce's endorsement, mixed though it was, effectively served its primary purposes—publicity and legitimacy.

CHAPTER 14

"A Simple Case of Message Meeting Moment"

UNFORTUNATELY FOR JACK, WHEN *WHY ENGLAND SLEPT* WAS RELEASED he was in no condition to savor the moment. He was back at the Mayo Clinic in Minnesota dealing with severe abdominal pain, spastic colon, and significant weight loss. He was no stranger to the famous hospital, having made several visits, the first in 1934, when he spent a month there.

He seemed to be never entirely free from pain and illness. Dr. Paul O'Leary told Joe Kennedy that Jack's "blood pressure was exceedingly low, being in the neighborhood of 85, and for a boy of this age it should be approximately 120. This so-called static hypotension is a comparatively recently recognized entity and might well be that some of Jack's gastrointestinal difficulties are attributable to this finding."[1]

Despite his son's illness and pain, Joe Kennedy wanted to get the maximum exposure possible for *Why England Slept*. He arranged an interview with a local radio station, KROC. Jack prepared for it like he would for an exam, writing out lengthy answers to potential questions.[2]

As the interviewer introduced his young author guest there was no actual mention of the Mayo Clinic. The host began, "At this time, we're indeed pleased to have with us in our studios Mr. John F. Kennedy, son of Ambassador and Mrs. Joseph P. Kennedy, who is in our city visiting Dr. and Mrs. Paul O'Leary. Mr. Kennedy is the author of the recently published book, *Why England Slept*. John F. Kennedy is the son of the American ambassador to the Court of St. James. He spent some time in London and Paris embassies. He is recently out of Harvard and hasn't yet reached his middle 20s. And with that, we want you, too, of the radio audience, to meet Mr. John F. Kennedy, who is known to his friends as Jack Kennedy."[3]

Kennedy gave an eloquent defense of his book. His best exchange coming toward the end of the seven-minute conversation, when the host asked him, "Now, I wonder, is there any particular lesson that carries a lesson to us in this, an election year?"

Jack answered: "Yes. I would say there was. In 1935, England also had its election year, and it was held in November like ours. At that time, the English leaders were becoming extremely concerned about German rearmament, but the British people were strongly pacifistic. None of them wanted arms; they felt that arms would be a step toward war. In order to win the election, not one of Britain's three major parties came out for rearmament. The result was British rearmament was postponed from the end of 1934 to the beginning of 1936, and this was fatal, because this was the great year that Germany got her real start on Britain. In 1936, Baldwin, in trying to explain why he had not started a rearmament sooner, said, I quote, 'I cannot think of anything that would've made the loss of the election, from my point of view, more certain'. No American politician must be able to say that, in 1941, about the people in this country."

Indeed.

The publication of *Why England Slept* turned out to be well timed. As Hitler's war-machine cut through Western Europe like a hot knife through butter, Americans began to awake to the real possibility of war in their future. Though a strong isolationist mood prevailed in much of the country, politicians and policy makers began to make moves toward better equipping the military. On May 16, just a few days after the Germans made their move on Belgium, Holland, and France, President Roosevelt spoke before a joint session of Congress and issued a call for "50,000 new planes a year, as well as creation of a two-ocean navy and a 280,000-man army."[4] His speech received multiple ovations.

And Congress quickly gave him even *more* than he had requested.

Why England Slept was one of the few titles released in mid-1940 that was directly on-point with America's need to get its military house in order as the best potential deterrent for war. But the kind of build-up needed would take years. Raw materials and other key ingredients were in short supply. In so many ways, it was already too late. Chief of Naval Operations, Admiral Harold Stark, said it best: "Dollars cannot buy yesterday."[5]

A couple of weeks later, FDR kicked his rhetoric up a notch. Delivering the commencement address at the University of Virginia in Charlottesville, he said that America was "convinced that military and naval victory for the gods of force and hate would endanger the institutions of democracy in the western world, and that equally therefore, the whole of our sympathies lies with those nations that are giving their life blood in combat against those forces."[6]

Sitting in the audience that day was John Wheeler-Bennett, the British historian who had helped Jack early on during the formative stage of his Harvard thesis. He would later write, "This was what we had been praying for—not only sympathy but pledges of support. If Britain could only hold on until these vast resources could be made available to her, we could yet survive and even win the war. It was our first gleam of hope."[7] Henry Luce's *Time* observed, optimistically and prematurely, that FDR's UVA speech "marked the official end of American neutrality."[8] So, the success of *Why England Slept* was in many ways a simple case of message meeting moment.

And what a moment it was.

Not surprisingly, when *Why England Slept* was published it was a big event in Boston. The *Boston Herald* announced the book's arrival with a banner headline, describing young Kennedy's message as "remarkable for its calm, its grasp of complex problems, its courageous frankness, its good manners, and its sound advice."[9]

Meanwhile, once released from the Mayo Clinic, Jack worked hard promoting the book. One friend, Charles Spalding, recalled visiting the Kennedy home at Hyannis Port at the time. "Jack was downstairs with a whole pile of those books of his, *Why England Slept*," he said. "It was just a wonderful array of papers, letters from Prime Ministers and Congressmen and people you've heard about, some under wet bathing suits and some under the bed."[10] Kennedy seemed to thoroughly enjoy the process and was determined to do everything in his power to make it a bestseller.

Jack even sent an autographed copy to President Roosevelt.

FDR, in fact, read Jack's book and sent a note to the author, calling *Why England Slept* "a great argument for acting and speaking from a position of strength at all times."[11] It was a telling comment as FDR was at the time trying to balance the fact that America's entry into a global war seemed inevitable to him with the political mood of the country. Jack treasured FDR's sentiments "not only because they were praise from a president, but because he saw Roosevelt as someone who had met the challenge he himself constantly faced: surmounting bodily weakness."[12]

Jack admired courage.

CHAPTER 15

"Jack Earned More than $40,000 in Royalties"

AMBASSADOR KENNEDY WAS IN TROUBLE. AS WAS THE CASE A GENERATION earlier with Winston Churchill's father, Randolph—who had been on a track to the pinnacle of power in Great Britain before his ego and erratic political behavior brought him down—so Jack Kennedy's father was about to crash and burn. It is no secret that Joe Kennedy wanted to be the President of the United States and had hoped to succeed FDR in 1940.

But before Christmas, Joe would become a political pariah.

By October 1940, the relationship between Joe Kennedy and Franklin Roosevelt, one that had always been complicated at best, was strained to the breaking point. One historian described them as "two scorpions in a bottle."[1] Each man had been working hard behind the scenes to undermine and manipulate the other. Kennedy knew that FDR, all the President's public protest notwithstanding, secretly wanted America to join the fight with Great Britain. The Ambassador was in a great position to be privy to significant cable traffic between the American president and the new British Prime Minister—Winston Churchill. And because his views about potential American involvement were no deep dark secret in London—or Washington for that matter—Roosevelt kept him in the dark. Kennedy complained to Lord Halifax in London that Roosevelt "had not kept him adequately informed of their policy and doings."[2]

He told one friend, "I'm going back and tell the truth. I'm going home and tell the American people that that son of a bitch in the White House is going to kill their sons."[3] But FDR was reluctant to have Kennedy home during the final weeks of his race for an unprecedented third term in the White House. So, Kennedy poured on the pressure. Joe's friend, Arthur Krock, wrote in his *Memoirs*:

> *On October 16, Kennedy sent a cablegram to the President insisting that he be allowed to come home . . . He had heard that he was not allowed to return until after the election . . . That same day, Kennedy telephoned to Under Secretary Sumner Welles, and said that if he did not get a favorable reply to his cablegram, he was coming home anyhow . . . he had written a full account of the facts to Edward Moore, his secretary in New York, with instructions to release the story to the*

press if Ambassador were not back in New York by a certain date.
A few hours after this conversation, the cabled permission to return
was received.[4]

The very day Kennedy arrived back in Washington, he and Rose were
invited to a dinner with the Roosevelts at the White House. FDR listened to Joe's complaints, then he poured on his legendary charm. By the
end of the evening, Kennedy had been persuaded to make a national radio
speech in support of the President's campaign.

So on the evening of October 29, at nine o'clock, Kennedy spoke for
thirty minutes over the CBS. He had endorsed FDR in 1932 and 1936—
that year even publishing a book, ghost-written by Arthur Krock, titled
I'm for Roosevelt—but in comparison, his 1940 effort was "not nearly as
full-throated or enthusiastic."[5] Still, he ended the speech with the words,
"I believe that Franklin D. Roosevelt should be re-elected President of
the United States."

After the election—which Roosevelt won in a landslide—Kennedy
was back in Boston and met with several journalists for what was described
as an off-the-record briefing. But what Kennedy had to say that day was
too juicy for the reporters to resist. For whatever reason, Kennedy let his
guard down and went into a gloomy rant. "People call me a pessimist,"
Joe vented. "I say, 'What is there to be gay about? Democracy is all done.
Democracy is finished in England. It may be here'."[6]

The Ambassador's comments made the papers the next morning.
And for all practical purposes, any personal political hopes he had were
dead before the year ended. Joe Kennedy would have to settle for living
vicariously through his sons. That became his consuming ambition for the
rest of his life.

Democracy, in fact, would survive.

But Joseph P. Kennedy would not.

Ambassador Kennedy was in London when *Why England Slept* was
released. He wrote to his wife, "I read Jack's book through and I think it
is a swell job. There is no question that regardless of whether he makes
any money out of it or not, he will have built himself a foundation for his
reputation that will be of lasting value to him."[7]

In fact, Jack Kennedy the writer was, in large part, "the creation of Joseph P. Kennedy the promoter."[8] It helped that the Ambassador bought hundreds of copies, sending them to influential people, and did everything in his power to give the impression that *Why England Slept* was a publishing success. Joe Kennedy understood the importance of image and fostered the "idea that his son was an immensely successful young author."[9]

Joe even sent a copy of *Why England Slept* to Winston Churchill on August 14, 1940, with a note that said, "I am sending you herewith Jack's book which I have just finished reading and which I think is a remarkably good job, considering it is the work of a boy of twenty-three. After all, it is a hopeful sign that youngsters in America are thinking this progressively. It is the first real story that's been published in America of this whole picture. Incidentally, it is already a bestseller in the nonfiction group."[10]

The Ambassador also persuaded Harold Nicholson to write an introduction for the British edition.[11] And he made sure copies got into the hands of key people, paying "to send out 250 free copies, over twice the publisher's norm in those days."[12] He was also very interested in having Professor Harold Laski read it. But rather than mail it, or have it delivered by a third party, he wrote to his wife, giving her a message for their son. "Tell him I am taking the book today to Laski and I am going to have Laski give me some suggestions as to what people here might be helpful to get letters for Jack."[13]

But Laski's response to *Why England Slept* was highly critical, much to the Ambassador's chagrin. He mocked the laudatory comments Luce had written in the foreword and told Joe that he regretted "that you let him publish it. For while it is the book of a lad with brains, it is very immature, it has no real structure, and it dwells almost wholly on the surface of things." Laski finished his note to Joe Kennedy with a particularly hurtful observation: "I don't honestly think any publisher would have looked at that book of Jack's if he had not been your son, and if you had not been Ambassador. And those are not the right grounds for publication."[14]

Despite Laski's criticism, *Why England Slept* was a commercial success and made Jack "an instant celebrity."[15] Not yet a month after its release, Gertrude Algase told him that his book "was already in its fourth printing, totaling 8,500 copies." She predicted that it would exceed 10,000, eventually. She was wrong. By the next spring, sales numbered more than 80,000. He skillfully promoted his book, doing interviews, radio shows, and book signings—he found "the limelight to his liking."

It also helped that Joe Kennedy was willing to throw his money around. Reportedly, he had agents moving around the country making strategic purchases of Jack's book, sometimes buying out all its stock in local bookstores. The books were then shipped back to Hyannis Port. One college student at the time, hired part-time to work around the Kennedy compound, recalled an interesting scene. "I spent a week in the attic and basement of Joe Kennedy's house counting copies of *Why England Slept*," he said.[16] The worker's name was Tom Bailey, and he told author C. David Heymann, "They were stacked from floor to ceiling in boxes cartons, and crates. I'd never seen so many books in one place before, all by the same author. I counted maybe thirty to forty thousand copies."

Jack earned more than $40,000 for *Why England Slept*.[17] The royalties he earned from sales in Great Britain were donated to provide assistance to the people of Coventry, a city that was savagely bombed by the German Luftwaffe in November 1940. In one attack that lasted nearly twelve hours, more than 500 tons of bombs rained down on the historic city located a little more than 100 miles northwest of London. So many died that city officials forbade individual funerals, opting for a series of mass burials for those killed in the raids. The destruction of Coventry became the standard of measurement RAF pilots used thereafter to estimate how effective they were in raids over *German* towns. Their bombing results were rated as "1 Coventry, 2 Coventries, and so on."[18]

Jack also used his father's influence in Hollywood to "fund relief organizations aiding civilians who had lost their homes in the bombing."[19] He did, however, keep enough to purchase a new convertible.

This one was a Buick.

At the mid-point of 1940, Europe was ablaze and that fire was about to go global. Kennedy was twenty-three years old and part of a generation destined to fight those flames. He was becoming a minor celebrity. His thesis-turned-best-selling book was the first key element of Kennedy's development as a leader and legend, much of which, one historian suggested, "would turn on his future treatment as a scholar, an historian, a writer."[20] The book became, in effect, "the debut of John F. Kennedy on the American stage."[21]

Yet another historian described *Why England Slept* as "the crucial first text in the product of John F. Kennedy, in terms of both Jack's projection of his own ideal image and his father's and others' collaborative presentation of that image as an idealized representation of its reader."[22]

Joe Kennedy, with his Hollywood background and connections, knew his way around the world of public relations. He was clearly the driving force behind the entire thesis-to-book-to-bestseller process. He was so effective at this that by the latter part of 1940 Jack was becoming as well known as more any actor or actress his old man had groomed in Hollywood.[23]

And he was about to add the role of *hero* to his public image.

CHAPTER 16

"They Thought She Was a Nazi Spy"

ON OCTOBER 16, 1940, NEWSPAPERS ACROSS AMERICA CARRIED A STORY about the millions of young men registering for the draft, as called for by the Selective Training and Service Act of 1940. Along with the story, there was a photo of one of the first draftees—John F. Kennedy. Now a celebrity best-selling author, he was in Palo Alto, California, where he had enrolled late that summer at Stanford University's School of Business.[1]

Though enrolled in the business school, clearly his interests were more focused on writing and international affairs. That December, he participated in a seminar sponsored by the *Institute of World Affairs*, a gathering of political scientists and West Coast academic types.[2] Jack was tasked with drafting a report on the discussions. According to one participant, Charles Martin, the chair of the political science department at the University of Washington in Seattle, Kennedy "kept busy, reporting four round tables in five day sessions . . . He was meticulous in attending the staff meetings and was interested in doing a good technical job . . . young Kennedy was on the alert to get the best he could from anything in the area of his current operations at any given time." A nearly 300-page report—twenty-one of them written by Kennedy—was published after the conference.

Shortly after that, Jack left Stanford and went back east, checking in to the New England Baptist Hospital. More pain. More tests. While there, another writing opportunity presented itself. His literary agency received a request from *King Features*, part of the *Hearst Syndicate*, to write an article for them about Ireland's neutrality in the war between Great Britain and Germany. They offered him $100 for a 1,500-word piece. He wrote it while in the hospital, and it was published on February 2 in the *New York Journal-American* with the headline: *IRISH BASES ARE VITAL TO BRITAIN*.[3]

Any thoughts Jack may have had about a career as a wordsmith, however, had to be put on hold. The growing global conflict would soon draw America into its violent vortex. His brother Joe had signed up with the Naval Aviation program, and Jack tried for Army Officer's Candidate School. But he failed the physical. It was the same with the navy. Eventually, likely because of his father's influence, he was accepted into a navy officers training course and received his commission.[4]

Assigned to the Office of Naval Intelligence (ONI) in Washington, D.C., he prepared daily and weekly bulletins. While there, he met a former Miss Denmark named Inga Arvad, a reporter with Washington *Times Herald*. She was so taken with him that she wrote a profile of him for her paper. Jack, of course, had the writing bug, so he was drawn to her and her work. They soon had a whirlwind romance.

But there was a problem.

Inga "Binga," as Jack called her, was under FBI investigation as a possible Nazi spy. Jack, however, was smitten. Some people close to him were sure she was the love of his life.[5] Arthur Krock even sent Inga a condolence letter shortly after Kennedy's assassination. He wrote: "I think I told you before that every time I saw President Kennedy he would say to me with a twinkle in his eye, 'How's Inga?'"[6]

According to her biographer, Jack wanted to marry her, even though she was a Protestant, even worse, a divorced Protestant. He was so serious about her that he even reached out to someone in the Catholic hierarchy about the possibility of having Inga's marriage annulled. But Jack's father would have none of it. And, when he needed it, he got some help cooling the lovebirds off from one of the most important media stars of the day.

Two of every three Americans either listened to Walter Winchell on the radio or read his columns that ran in more than 2,000 newspapers across the country. On January 12, 1942, this juicy nugget appeared under his by-line: "One of Ex-Ambassador Kennedy's eligible sons is the target of a Washington gal columnist's affections. So much so—she's consulted her barrister about divorcing her explorer-groom . . . Pa Kennedy no like."[7]

The very next day, Jack was transferred to Charleston, South Carolina. He later told a reporter, "They shagged my ass down to South Carolina because I was going around with a Scandinavian blonde and they thought she was a Nazi spy."[8]

Inga, however, found her way to him, and some of their conversations and intimacies were surreptitiously recorded by the FBI as directed by J. Edgar Hoover himself. Ms. Arvad was certainly a subject of interest to many in the intelligence community.[9] A few years earlier, she had interviewed and charmed Adolf Hitler himself—an eyebrow raiser on its own, but when combined with the fact that she was intimately involved with a Navy Intelligencer Officer who was the son of a wealthy former U.S. Ambassador, the story was potentially explosive. With Jack's work as an intelligence officer compromised, he set his sights on the South Pacific, where he would ultimately land a job as the skipper on a patrol torpedo boat—*PT 109.*

He had a rendezvous with a chance to demonstrate the virtue he admired most—courage.

A PT boat became Jack's ticket to military action. The vessels were light and could maneuver well, moving along at more than forty knots. They could "move in on targets silently with muffled engines, launch torpedoes, and then skim away smoothly."[10] Dispatched to Tulagi, in the Solomon Islands, Lieutenant Kennedy was assigned as the "skipper" on *PT 109* on April 23, 1943. The vessel was in rough shape, so his first job was to restore the boat and gather a new crew, shaping them into a fighting unit.

The *PT 109*, along with other similar boats anchored at Tulagi, harassed Japanese ships in the so-called "Tokyo Express," a steady stream of enemy vessels bringing supplies to Japanese-held islands in the archipelago. That August, intelligence reports indicated that the Japanese had several destroyers ready for a run, and several PTs, including number 109, were ordered to respond.

About 2:30 a.m., on August 2, Kennedy's vessel was idling with its lights out in the pitch black, when suddenly a ship was spotted bearing down on them. It was the Japanese destroyer *Amagiri*, moving at a forty-knot clip. And in less than a minute "the steep prow of the *Amagiri* crashed at a sharp angle into the starboard side of *PT 109* beside the cockpit."[11] Kennedy "was hurled against the rear wall of the cockpit, his once-sprained back slamming against a steel reinforcing brace. It was the angle of the collision alone that saved him from being crushed to death." Two other men were killed in the collision.

Eleven survivors, including Lt. Kennedy, were in the fight of their lives.

CHAPTER 17

"The Skipper Hero"

YEARS AFTER KENNEDY'S HARROWING EXPERIENCE IN THE SOUTH Pacific, when asked about becoming a hero, he would sometimes remark, "It was involuntary. They sank my boat."[1] But this laconic comment, and Jack's frequent attempts to downplay the story down through the years, were in contrast to an aggressive public relations campaign designed to ensure that everyone who heard his name would attach the idea of war hero to it.

The story of *PT 109* is about a man in charge, someone who stepped up and did extraordinary things to save the lives of those entrusted to his care. Moments after the collision with the *Amagiri*, Jack was issuing orders and organizing the surviving crew members. Sizing up the situation and weighing his options, he led his men to leave the remnants of their ship and swim nearly four miles in convoy to Plum Pudding, a tiny island no wider than a football field. He had been on the Harvard swim team, so he was comfortable in the water.

He even pulled one of the injured men using a belt through his teeth.

From there, Kennedy swam several times to a nearby strait, hoping to flag down a passing ship, to no avail. After a couple of days, he led his crew on a swim to another island, again pulling that same man using his teeth. He tried to send a message via some natives they encountered, eventually prompting a visit by two men who worked as scouts for the Allies. One man was named Bike Gasa. Gasa showed Jack how to scratch a message onto a coconut: NAURO ISL COMMANDER NATIVE KNOWS POS'IT HE CAN PILOT 11 ALIVE NEED SMALL BOAT KENNEDY.

Ultimately, on the morning of August 8, the men of *PT 109* were found and rescued.

John F. Kennedy was awarded the Navy and Marine Corps Medal, as well as the Purple Heart in the aftermath of the *PT 109* disaster. But the long-term awards were still in the formative stages. Meanwhile, Jack and his crew spent some time in the hospital at Tulagi, healing from their injuries. Kennedy's back had been badly injured, adding to his chronic problems the problems in that area.

In October, Lieutenant Kennedy was given another ship—*PT 59*. But six weeks later, he was relieved of his command due to illness. His back troubles were now compounded by malaria. He was sent stateside and wound up back in Rochester, Minnesota and the Mayo Clinic. He would never return to active duty and retired due to physical disability in March 1945.

But long before he left the navy, he was a celebrity war hero.

Beyond the original notices in the American press shortly after the *PT 109* incident, Jack's story was boosted by two women who had once been romantically involved with him. First, there was Inga Arvad.

By 1944, Inga, the lady Hitler had once described as "the perfect Nordic beauty," had moved to Los Angeles and continued her work as a journalist for a news service.[2] When Jack told her all about his experience in the South Pacific, she wrote a flattering article about "the skipper hero." It was picked up by several newspapers, including the *Boston Globe* and the *Pittsburgh Post-Gazette*.

But it was another "ex" who really helped the *PT 109* story become well known across the country.

Until his courtship and marriage to Jacqueline Bouvier, Francis Ann Cannon had been the closest thing to an actual bride in Jack's life. While Jack went to war, she married another—his name was John Hersey. And like Jack, Hersey wanted to be a writer. The difference between Kennedy and Hersey was that Hersey fulfilled his ambition, becoming a very successful journalist. In February 1944, Jack visited New York City. Francis and her husband invited him to the La Martinique, a popular nightspot located in a basement on West Fifty-Seventh Street, where the latest craze, the singer-comedian Zero Mostel, was in a $4,000 per week engagement.

Hersey was always looking for a great story, and he would one day win his own Pulitzer Prize. When Francis spoke with Jack about his PT boat ordeal, her husband was intrigued and wound up interviewing his wife's former boyfriend during dinner. Hersey later remembered Kennedy sharing "a rapid account of the experience of the sinking of his PT boat," adding, "it was a good story whether he was Kennedy or not. The story itself was so dramatic."[3]

Kennedy and Hersey thought Henry Luce's *Life* Magazine would be the best venue for the account, but the story—titled simply, *SURVIVAL,* was eventually published by *The New Yorker* in its June 10, 1944, issue. It was Hersey's first submission to that magazine, but the next year his account of Hiroshima and the atomic bomb would take up almost an entire issue. Jack's father, however, was disappointed that *Life* had passed on the *PT 109* story, so he worked his persuasive magic and arranged for *Reader's Digest* to publish it, as well.

That version would go on be reprinted and distributed in bulk every time John F. Kennedy ran for office.

As a postscript to the story about Hersey's article, Jack persuaded the writer, *The New Yorker*, and *Reader's Digest* to make donations to the Navy Relief Fund for the benefit of the family of one of the men who had died when the *Amagiri* slammed through *PT 109*'s plywood hull.

Whatever thrill, however, Jack may have experienced with his renewed celebrity status, this time as a war hero, soon vanished. On Sunday, August 13, 1944, he was with his family at Hyannis Port. They played football and had a picnic lunch. Two priests arrived around two o'clock. They were bearing bad news. Young Joe had been on a secret mission, one that involved a great measure of daring. He was flying a PBY 4 that had been gutted and filled with explosives. He was supposed to get it up in the air and on course then bail out once the plane was aimed at its target in France. Joe was to broadcast the code word "Spade Flush" just before leaving the aircraft.

The priests had been briefed by the military and shared details with only the Ambassador. Nearly a half-hour after takeoff and just after the code words were transmitted, there was "a sudden gasp and then a huge fireball and an explosion so great that its concussion damaged aircraft flying support and forced them to land."[4] The next morning, the front page of the *New York Times* bore young Joe's picture and the headline: SON OF J.P. KENNEDY KILLED IN ACTION.

When he learned of his brother's death, Jack left the house and took a walk along on the beach contemplating their relationship and rivalry. He knew what it might mean for him. As for Ambassador Kennedy, the tragic death of his son was more than a loss of a life he loved, his namesake had been his hope for the future. Joe Jr. was supposed to be the one— the chosen one—destined to reach the pinnacle of power and success, in his father's stead. He was supposed to become the first Irish-Catholic President of the United States.

Part of the way Jack processed the death of his older brother was by using his writing skills to put together a memorial book. He functioned as editor and invited others to share their remembrances. In the introductory essay to the volume, Jack wrote: "I think that if the Kennedy children amount to anything now or ever amount to anything, it will be due more to Joe's behavior and constant example than to any other factor."[5] Jack began work on the book in September 1944, and it was titled *As We Remember Joe*. Privately published, only 360 copies were printed, each one packed in a maroon box.[6]

It wasn't long after Joe's death that Jack became, at least in his father's eyes, a stand-in for his older brother. With the oldest child of Joe and Rose gone, Jack was the heir apparent. It was a burden he would bear for the rest of his life.

The Ambassador's grief was ongoing and often manifested itself in anger. As November approached, with Franklin Roosevelt running for an unprecedented fourth term, vice-presidential candidate Harry Truman came to Boston. When Joe Kennedy had a chance to speak privately with the man from Missouri, he angrily said, "Harry, what are you doing campaigning for that crippled son of a bitch that killed my son Joe?"[7]

Arthur Krock recalled that the Ambassador's response to the death of his son was "one of the most severe that I've ever seen registered on a human being," and the newspaperman thought he knew why. His anger was rooted in his years in London, his support for appeasement, and his strong reluctance to see the United States join the war. Years later, Krock said, "Joe Jr., when he volunteered on this final mission which was beyond his duty, beyond everything, he was seeking to prove by its very danger that the Kennedys were not yellow. That's what killed that boy. That's why he died. And his father realized it. He never admitted it, but he realized it."[8]

CHAPTER 18

"I Always Sensed I Had a Larger Purpose"

HARRY HOPKINS, AIDE EXTRAORDINAIRE TO PRESIDENT FRANKLIN Roosevelt, outlived his boss, but only by a few months. The intense and driven man had worked on his memoirs about his time with FDR, but hadn't gotten very far into the project before he succumbed to the stomach cancer he had somehow managed to hold at bay for several years. It fell to the playwright Robert E. Sherwood, who had served FDR as a speechwriter and became Hopkins' friend, to pick up the mantle and finish the project. The book came out in 1948 and won the 1949 Pulitzer Prize for Biography. It was titled *Roosevelt and Hopkins: An Intimate History*.

Hopkins, who had been regarded by some as "a sinister figure, a backstairs intriguer, an Iowan combination of Machiavelli, Svengali, and Rasputin," was the one person on whom Roosevelt totally relied, especially during wartime.[1] He was, as Sherwood put it, "in large measure Roosevelt's own creation. Roosevelt deliberately educated Hopkins in the arts and sciences of politics and of war and then gave him immense powers of decision for no reason other than he liked him, trusted him, and needed him."

Ted Sorensen, a student at the University of Nebraska when it was published, devoured the book.

He found it both interesting and inspiring.

The story of, as Ted wrote in his own memoirs, "a progressive president from the aristocratic East and his trusted, nerdish liberal aide from the Midwest," presaged his own future relationship with John F. Kennedy, though Ted never actually wielded Hopkins-like power.[2]

Sorensen entered the University of Nebraska in the fall of 1945 at the age of seventeen. With the war over and so many GI's returning home, the school modified its program allowing some students, including Ted, to begin law school studies after just two years of undergraduate work, enabling someone to emerge after six years with a bachelor's and a law degree. He served as the editor in chief of the law review, giving him further writing experience. It was a point of pride for him that his father had held the same post a generation earlier. One of his articles even made it to an issue of the *Progressive*, a periodical that was a favorite in the Sorensen home.

The piece was titled *Can't Teachers Be Citizens Too?*

Ted was politically active in college. He was asked to serve as chairman of the Lincoln Social Action Council, recalling it years later as "a stirring experience."[3] He plunged into an effort to see a law passed by the Nebraska State Legislature, one that helped ensure fair employment practices. Sorensen led a frenetic effort, "speaking, lobbying, organizing letter-writing campaigns." He testified in public hearings on behalf of the bill.

So did the leader of Nebraska's Communist Party—a fact that horrified Ted.

The bill died in committee in 1947, but was revived in 1951, just before Sorensen graduated. It failed then, too. It would be 1965 before any such legislation became law in Nebraska.

Though Sorensen had gone to law school to follow in his father's footsteps and presumably work in Nebraska—as his lobbying work already seemed to indicate—he ultimately decided to move to the nation's capital. As he put it in his memoirs, "I loved Lincoln, it's serenity, its greenery, and its friendly people. But I always sensed that I had a larger purpose; I aspired to something I knew I would not find in Lincoln."[4]

His interest in the field of public law was piqued in school via courses on international and constitutional legal matters. But it was two lawyers from Washington, D.C. who visited the school during Ted's senior year that sealed the deal that would take the Nebraska eastward—and upward. He was impressed by a recruiter from a Washington firm that handled a lot of work for the Federal Communications Commission, and the work sounded very interesting to him.

Also, an attorney named Stanley Gewitz, who worked in a Washington, D.C. firm and was chairman of the local chapter of Americans for Democratic Action (ADA), encouraged the bright soon-to-graduate lawyer to apply to his firm. After all, Sorensen was the editor of the school's law review and was tied for first place in his class. He was the plum pick of the litter.

He also had a family to support, having married classmate Camilla Palmer in September of 1949. They had a son named Eric. So, a good job was essential. But no offers were forthcoming, so, as he put it years later,

"With no advance notice to my wife or parents, I decided to go to Washington to pursue my job search in person."[5]

Ted's father was proud that his son had been so successful in school, but that quickly gave way to disappointment. He had hoped his son would join his law own practice, but Ted never really considered it. The young lawyer was hungry for much more than anything Nebraska could offer. So, he left it all behind, even Camilla and baby Eric (they would join him later). On July 1, 1951, the man who would soon give John Fitzgerald Kennedy his voice, boarded an eastbound train to Chicago, once there he transferred to the Capitol Limited to Washington, D.C.'s Union Station.

He recalled, "All I could think about, on that train ride, was the immense gamble I was taking."

CHAPTER 19

"Kennedy Will Not Be Filing Tonight"

As the war approached its end, it was becoming clear to John F. Kennedy that his father's expectations for him had changed in the wake of the death of his older brother. Joe's second son, however, still had his sights set on writing, with two books—one a bestseller and the other a privately published memoir—under his belt, along with a few published newspaper articles. His father, likely because he saw Jack's writing as a good way to keep his son in the spotlight, decided to help him and reached out to a friend from his Hollywood years.

William Randolph Hearst.

Kennedy and Hearst had met in the early 1920s during Joe's days as a Hollywood power broker. He visited Hearst and his mistress, the actress Marion Davies, often at San Simeon. They "were taken with Kennedy's charm, humor, smarts, and lack of pretense."[1] Sometimes Joe would bring his own mistress, Gloria Swanson, along. Hearst saw himself as a Napoleonic figure and he presided over a media empire.

Joe asked Hearst to hire his son.[2]

Jack was back in the Mayo Clinic when he received a telegram from Louis Rupper, the editor of the *Chicago Herald-American*. He wanted Kennedy to head out to San Francisco, where a conference was about to start—the founding of the United Nations in April 1945. The idea was for Kennedy to report about it "from the point of view of the ordinary GI."[3]

The next day, the paper carried an article with the headline, "HERO COVERS PARLEY FOR H-A." It was accompanied by a picture of Jack in his uniform. The article talked about the *PT 109* incident as well as a mention of *Why England Slept*. His war record was chronicled:

> *Rejected for Army enlistment early in 1941 because of a back injury suffered in a football scrimmage of Harvard University's junior varsity team, underwent five months of almost tortuous exercises and manipulation to strengthen his back so that he was fit for acceptance in the Navy.*

The assignment would put Kennedy in the middle of one of the most important meetings in world history and in close proximity to powerful people. To say that it was a plum assignment for a young man whose father was grooming him for a political career would be more than an understatement.

Jack would be paid $250 per article.

When the late English historian John Keegan reviewed Margaret Mac-Millan's book about the 1919 Paris Peace conference, he wrote: "Four times in the modern age men have sat down to reorder the world—at the Peace of Westphalia in 1648 after the Thirty Years War, at the Congress of Vienna in 1915 after the Napoleonic Wars, in Paris 1919 after World War I, and in San Francisco in 1945 after World War II."[4]

It was that big.

By April 25, 1945, fifty nations had sent 850 delegates, accompanied by 3,500 staffers to the City by the Bay. And another 2,500 members of the press and media made the gathering likely "the largest international gathering ever to take place."[5] John F. Kennedy was one of those members of the press covering the story. It was an exclusive and historic political stage, and he had a front-row seat.

From his room at the Palace Hotel, where President Warren G. Harding died in 1923, Jack worked and played. The city's nightlife was irresistible to him, and he wasn't above blowing off a scheduled column. One observer recalled a night when Jack chose pleasure over productivity:

Jack, dressed for a black-tie evening, with the exception of his pumps and dinner coat, was lying on the bed, propped up by three pillows, a highball in one hand and the telephone receiver in the other. To the operator he said, "I want to speak to the Managing Editor of the Chicago Herald-Examiner." (After a long pause) "Not in? Well, put somebody on to take a message." (Another pause) "Good. Will you see that the boss gets this message as soon as you can reach him? Thank you. Here's the message: Kennedy will not be filing tonight."

A few hours later, Jack was on the dance floor, cutting in on Anthony Eden, the British Foreign Secretary, who was dancing with a beautiful lady.[6] Eden was not pleased.

But Jack managed to send sporadic dispatches. The first one appeared in the paper on April 28, 1945. Jack wrote, "There is an impression that this is the conference to end wars and introduce peace on earth and goodwill toward nations—excluding of course, Germany and Japan. Well, it's not going to do that." He ended the piece with, "The average GI in the street, and the streets of San Francisco are crowded with them, doesn't seem to have a very clear-cut conception of what this meeting is all about. But one be-medaled marine sergeant gave the general reaction when he said: 'I don't know much about what's going on—but if they just fix it so that we don't have to fight any more—they can count on me'." Jack added, "Me, too, sarge."[7]

On May 1, his dispatch was published with the headline, "WORLD COURT REAL TEST FOR ENVOYS."[8] He began, "This conference from a distance may have appeared so far like an international football game with Molotov carrying the ball, while Stettinius, Eden and the delegates tried to tackle him all over the field."

Each article averaged about 400 words and was a blend of reportage and opinion. Kennedy had a flair for language and the fact that he was captivated by international affairs came through in his writing. He also used a measure of wit, "The word is out more or less officially that Molotov is about to pick up his marbles and go home."[9] His dispatches were given preferred treatment by the Hearst syndicate, always with Kennedy's photo (in uniform) and a short bio. He was able to rub shoulders with the biggest names in journalism, people such as Eric Sevareid, William Shirer, and the Brit, Alistair Cooke. Kennedy enjoyed meeting Cooke, who was, by far, the most prolific of the bunch, sending more than 400 cables back to the *Manchester Guardian* during the conference.

Jack's time covering the San Francisco Conference had a significant impact on his future career. In fact, biographer Nigel Hamilton suggested, "it would be no exaggeration to say that it was in San Francisco in the spring of 1945 that Jack's political career actively began."[10] While in San Francisco, Kennedy interacted with key players in the field of foreign policy, including three men who would one day play roles in his own presidential administration: Averell Harriman, Adlai Stevenson, and Charles Bohlen.

Kennedy later recorded his opinion of the conference: "The conference at San Francisco suffered from inadequate preparation and lack of fundamental agreement among the Big Three; from an unfortunate Press which praised it beyond all limit at its commencement which paved the way for subsequent disillusionment both in England and in this country."[11] In all, he filed 17 articles from San Francisco between April 28 and May 28. While still reporting from the conference, Jack got word of his next assignment.

He was heading back to London.

Great Britain was in the midst of its first national election since before the war, and Kennedy was there to cover the story for the Hearst newspapers. In the aftermath of the surrender of Germany in early May 1945, Winston Churchill had hoped to continue his coalition government, at least until the eventual surrender of Japan. But Clement Attlee—the Labour Party leader—was opposed by a faction led by the socialist professor Harold Laski and was forced to let Churchill know that their coalition, one they had both served and held together for the duration of the European war, was, in effect, dead.

On May 23, Churchill made his way to Buckingham Palace to resign as Prime Minister. King George asked him to form a caretaker government until elections could be held. Winston agreed and the national election was scheduled for July 5, with the results to be announced roughly three weeks later. The British government had been governed on a nonpartisan basis for half a decade, but all that was changing.

And Churchill thought he was sure to win.

In his final dispatch from San Francisco, Jack Kennedy told his readers that "the British Labour Party is out for blood."[12] "They are going all the way," Kennedy wrote. "Public ownership of the Bank of England, Government control of rents and prices, gradual Government ownership of mines, transportation, planned farming—the works." He also wrote of his concern that Churchill might not be able to "buck the recent strong surge to the left."

Turns out, Jack was a prophet.

On his way from California to England, he stopped off in Massachusetts to visit his father, who was still overwhelmed with grief over the loss of Joe Jr. The Ambassador arranged for Jack to give an address in Boston about his observations on the San Francisco Conference. The *Boston Globe* reported on June 12 that young Kennedy "expressed disappointment" about the conference. His father was delighted and more convinced that his second born son was going places.[13]

CHAPTER 20

"A Diary He Kept for a Brief Time"

BECAUSE HE ADMIRED CHURCHILL SO MUCH, JACK FOUND IT HARD TO watch what was happening in the election campaign. Great Britain seemed poised to move sharply to the left, confounding many. Jack was among the first American journalists to report on the possibility of a Churchill loss. On Sunday, June 24, he told readers:

> *Britishers will go to the polls on July 5 in the first general election in almost ten years and there is a definite possibility that Prime Minister Winston Churchill and his Conservative party may be defeated. This may come as a surprise to most Americans, who feel Churchill indomitable at the polls as he was in war.*[1]

In retrospect, it seems unthinkable that the man who inspired Great Britain during the darkest days of the "blitz" would be politically vulnerable in the immediate aftermath of ultimate victory in Europe. But having spent years making the sacrifices necessary to defeat Hitler, many Britons hungered to see the resources of the nation dedicate to things that would make their previous privation seem more worthwhile. They wanted to "defeat poverty, remove slums, and improve education and services."[2] Though the term "welfare state" carries with it a negative connotation to many in our day, right after World War II it was a popular public policy buzz term in England. Churchill, however, saw the Labour Party as advocating the kind of socialism they had just defeated on the field of battle. And in his first campaign broadcast, he framed his argument.

He also sealed his political doom.

He told his countrymen that "a Socialist policy is abhorrent to the British ideas of freedom." That itself would not have been problematic, but he added, "I declare to you, from the bottom of my heart, that no Socialist system can be established without a political police." He then said that "some sort of Gestapo" would be needed to make things happen, evoking the image of the recently defeated enemy. Churchill warned, "This would nip opinion in the bud; it would stop criticism as it reared its head and it would gather all the power to the supreme party and the party leaders, rising like stately pinnacles above their vast bureaucracies of Civil servants no longer servants and no longer civil."

But the great man who, as Edward R. Murrow would later famously say, had "mobilized the English language and sent it to war," was woefully out of touch with the fast-changing British political mood. Jack Kennedy was positioned to see the story develop firsthand. In a sense, he was not only following one of his heroes around the country, he was walking in Churchill's footsteps. As one biographer noted, Kennedy's reportage "demonstrated something of the same animation that had driven the young Winston Churchill in earlier years as a newspaper correspondent."[3] In fact, it was as a journalist that Churchill had first made a name for himself. He then leveraged that celebrity into a political career, with writing as a sideline all along the way.

Possibly, Jack thought the formula would work for him.

He recorded his own thoughts about the British election results in a diary he kept for a brief time: "My own opinion is that it was about 40 per cent due to dissatisfaction with conditions over which the government had no great control but from which they must bear responsibility— 20 per cent due to a belief in socialism as the only solution to the multifarious problems England must face—and the remaining 40 per cent due to a class feeling—i.e.; that it was time 'the working man' had his chance."[4]

Churchill and his Conservative Party were soundly defeated, giving him what he called "the royal order of the boot."

Following his coverage of the British elections, Jack traveled on the European continent, surveying the damage and carnage inflicted by years of war, and sending dispatches back to the newspaper. Being an eyewitness to such historic happenings in politics and international affairs seemed to further kindle his desire to become more than a mere observer. It was that summer, while watching world leaders, he began to morph into a politician. Writing would be a part of it, but he wanted to be in the arena himself. His diary entries that summer provide clues about Jack's state of mind as he pondered the future.

Published years later as *Prelude to Leadership: The Post-War Diary of John F. Kennedy*, Jack eventually gave the diary to a young staffer, Deirdre

Henderson, in 1960, as she worked on Kennedy's foreign policy positions for the presidential campaign. She kept the journal for thirty years before deciding to publish it along with her editorial comments. The diary suggests that Jack may have entertained writing a book at the time. In her editor's preface, Henderson speculated that "the example of young Churchill may have lurked somewhere in the back of Kennedy's mind . . . He did tell me once that he had been a great admirer of *Fortune* magazine and its writers and had thought he might want to start some kind of writing career on the publication."[5] Henderson added, "Kennedy's mental picture was, to a large degree, that of a writer."

Jack visited Ireland that summer, and he had a personal meeting with the President of the Irish Free State, Eamon De Valera, who had hoped for Nazi win in the war, even going so far as to express condolences to the German government when Hitler died. Jack stayed with the American Minister to Ireland, David Gray. His host took a dim view of De Valera and thought that the Irish leader was "a paranoid and a lunatic."[6]

From Ireland, he flew to France, "where he found President Charles de Gaulle unpopular, food in short supply, and the quality of French perfume in precipitous decline."[7] While in France, he connected with his father's friend James V. Forrestal, the Secretary of the Navy, who offered Jack a ride to Berlin, where Stalin, Prime Minister Clement Attlee, and the new American president, Harry Truman, were gathering for a summit in nearby Potsdam.

In Berlin, Jack saw devastation everywhere. He recorded in his diary, "There is not a single building which is not fitted. On some of the streets the stench—sweet and sickish from dead bodies—is overwhelming. The people all have completely colorless faces."[8] After visiting Hitler's Reich Chancellery, he wrote about Hitler's death: "There is no complete evidence, however, that the body found was Hitler's body. The Russians doubt he was dead."

He accompanied Forrestal to Frankfurt several days later and met General Dwight D. Eisenhower, the hero of D-Day, and the man he would one day succeed as President of the United States. In his diary, he noted, "It was obvious why he is an outstanding figure. He has an easy personality, immense self-assurance, and gave an excellent presentation of the situation in Germany."[9]

Before leaving Germany, Jack visited Berchtesgaden, where Hitler had maintained a palatial home for years. He saw the handiwork of 12,000-pound bombs dropped on it by the RAF. "Leaving the chalet," Kennedy wrote, "we drove to the very top of the mountains (about 7,000 feet) where the famed Eagle's lair was located. The road up was covered with solid rock in many places and was clearly camouflaged. On arrival, we entered a long tunnel carved through the rocks and came to an elevator which took us up through the solid rock for the last 600 feet. The elevator was a double-decker—a space being left on the lower deck for the SS guard . . . The lair itself had been stripped of its rugs, pictures, and tapestries, but the view was beautiful—the living room being round and facing out on every side on the valley below."

Jack then wrote a passage that, quite fortunately for him, never saw the light of day until thirty years after his death:

> *After visiting these two places,* **you can easily understand how that within a few years Hitler will emerge from the hatred that surrounds him now as one of the most significant figures who ever lived** [emphasis added] . . . *He had boundless ambition for his country which rendered him a menace to the peace of the world, but he had a mystery about him in the way that he lived and in the manner of his death that will live and grow after him. He had in him the stuff of which legends are made.*[10]

Yes, he was writing about *Adolf Hitler.*

It is hard to imagine Jack Kennedy getting elected to any political office just after the war, or even years later, if a political opponent had uncovered that statement written in JFK's own hand.

Kennedy was homeward bound and somewhere over the Atlantic on a C-54 with Secretary Forrestal when they received word that an atomic bomb had been dropped on Hiroshima, Japan—the other side of the planet. By the time they were wheels down back in the States, the world had changed.

Having watched the world's movers and shakers in action that year Jack's thoughts about his future began to crystalize. Biographer Robert Dallek suggested that watching "fallible men . . . stirred feelings in Jack that he could do as well."[11] He was increasingly convinced that his own ideas were every bit as effectual as those of the various dignitaries he had recently seen in action.

All he needed was a vehicle for his voice.

CHAPTER 21

"The New Generation Offers a Leader"

A FEW WEEKS AFTER HIS BROTHER DIED, JACK WAS HANGING OUT AT Hyannis Port with his navy pal, Paul "Red" Fay, who had trained for PT boat service under Kennedy. He saw his father walking in the distance and said to Fay, "God! There goes the old man. There he goes figuring out the next step. I'm in it now, you know. It's my turn. I've got to perform."[1] A couple of months later, this time in Palm Beach, he told the same friend, "I can feel Pappy's eyes on the back of my neck. When the war is over and you are out there in sunny California, I'll be back here with Dad trying to parlay a lost PT boat and a bad back into a political advantage. I'll tell you, Dad is ready right now and can't understand why Johnny boy isn't 'all engines full ahead'."

As 1945 entered its final stretch, Jack Kennedy pondered his future. His brother's death had changed things for him, but he still had a couple of paths he wanted to explore before surrendering to his father's will. One passion was, of course, journalism. His enjoyed his work for the Hearst syndicate and he knew that, with his father's help, he could leverage what he had already done into a full-fledged career as a writer. He had a flair for it, and now he had the requisite experience.

In fact, he bought a newspaper—or at least a partner's share of one. He had met James Reed on the troop ship taking them to the South Pacific, and they remained friends. Reed had another navy friend, Fred Wilson, who was interested in buying a small newspaper, *The Narragansett Times* in South County, Rhode Island. The small weekly paper didn't cost an arm and a leg, and Kennedy contributed "$2,000 for 20 shares of stock."[2] Years later, Reed said that Kennedy "was interested in a general way in anything that touched on journalism," adding, "he thought it was a good investment which it turned out to be, by the way, for him."[3]

Jack sold his interest in the paper for a nice profit in 1947

He also thought about attending Harvard Law School, as had his brother Joe, but there was little passion on that front. And Jack knew his father had other plans. But it is not likely that he had a clue his father had doubts about his ability to fill Joe Jr.'s shoes. The old man's firstborn son had been carefully groomed for a political career. His father later said that he "used to talk about being President one day, and a lot of smart people thought he would make it. He was altogether different from Jack—more dynamic and more sociable and easy going."[4] Joe and Rose, in fact, had a hard time seeing Jack as a politician. They were pretty sure he would wind up in journalism or as a university professor. But Jack *was* ready to run for office.

He just didn't know which one.

It seemed to be well known in the family that Joe Jr., whose political ambitions were obvious, had planned to start his own political career with a run for Lieutenant Governor in Massachusetts. That was now one of Jack's options, but he rejected it in favor of a run for Congress, following in the footsteps of his politician-grandfather and namesake, John Francis "Honey Fitz" Fitzgerald. The seat Jack had his eye on was representing the Eleventh district, the same seat held more than 100 years earlier by John Quincy Adams after he had served as the sixth President of the United States.

At that time, the seat was held by the legendary Boston politico James Michael Curley, a man who was loved by some as a benefactor, and loathed by others as politically corrupt. He was also the Mayor of Boston—serving in both roles at the same time. But he was sick with diabetes and facing a federal indictment for mail fraud. Joe Kennedy worked his financial magic in February 1946 and came to an understanding with Curley.[5] The Ambassador agreed to pay all Curley's medical and legal bills and finance his reelection campaign for *mayor*, if he vacated his congressional seat.

Curley took the deal.

Jack made the final decision to enter the Democratic primary for the Eleventh District seat Easter weekend 1946, just before the filing deadline. But his campaign had been organizing behind the scenes for months. The primary was scheduled for June 18, and winning it was tantamount to winning in November, since it was a predominately Democratic district. On Monday, April 22, the *Cape Cod Times* announced his candidacy. And that evening, he delivered the first speech of his political career on a Boston radio station: "Voters of the Eleventh Congressional District, The people of the United States and the world stand at the crossroads. What we do now will shape the history of civilization for many years to come."[6]

The *Boston Herald* ran their political forecast with a banner headline: "KEEP AN EYE ON HIM: Mr. Kennedy will not be twenty-nine years old until next month and in the probable event of his nomination and election in the Eleventh district, he will go to Washington as one of the youngest, if not the youngest member . . . Certainly there is a ring of statesmanship in Mr. Kennedy's statement."[7]

Jack Kennedy was off and running—against ten others who wanted the same office.

The Ambassador persuaded his cousin, Joe Kane, to manage Jack's race for Congress. Kane was sixty-three years old, but he used much younger operatives. He put together a team of "young working-class volunteers from the district."[8] One of them, a fellow named Billy Sutton, became Jack's secretary. Kane came up with a slogan for the campaign: THE NEW GENERATION OFFERS A LEADER.

Money was apparently no object. Joe Kennedy clearly intended to bankroll a take-no-prisoners victory. This was business as usual those days in Bean Town. And the Ambassador was well acquainted with that particular business. Thomas P. "Tip" O'Neill, then in the Massachusetts House of Representatives, recalled, "Every time a Democrat ran for governor, he would go down to see Joe, who would always send him home with a briefcase full of cash. The word was that if Joe Kennedy liked you, he'd give you fifty thousand dollars. If he really liked you, he'd give you a hundred thousand."[9] He remembered the 1946 congressional race vividly. He said, "The Kennedys offered a number of large families fifty dollars in cash to help out at the polls. 'They didn't really care if these people showed up to work. They were simply buying votes, a few at a time, and fifty bucks was a lot of money'."

O'Neill also recalled something Joe Kennedy told him: "Never expect any appreciation from my boys. These kids have had so much done for them by other people they just assume it's coming to them."

Joe also used his influence with William Randolph Hearst to get the *Boston Herald* to refuse advertising from other candidates in the race. Not only that, he spent nearly $500,000 on billboards, newspaper ads, radio, newsreel publicity, and national-magazine ads. Nearly every billboard in the district displayed the campaign's slogan.

But the most effective investment made by Joe Kennedy was when he paid for thousands of reprints of the *Reader's Digest* article from 1944 about *PT 109*. The riveting account of Jack's heroism would become a staple in every one of Jack's campaigns to come. It seemed to seal the deal for the campaign. There was even a story noised about that "after one of the opposing candidate's wife had read the reprint, she said she'd have to vote for Jack."[10]

Jack, however, ran his race as if not a penny was being spent by his wealthy father. He campaigned with a sense of determined desperation. According to Billy Sutton, Kennedy "met city workers, he met letter carriers, cabbies, waitresses, and dock workers. He ate spaghetti with Italians and Chinese food with the Chinese. He was probably the only one of the pols around here to go into the firehouse, police stations post offices and saloons and poolrooms, as well as the homes, and it was the first Jack ever knew that the gas stove and toilet could be in the same room."[11]

Over the course of the two-month campaign, Jack made more than 400 speeches, even though he was not a natural orator. Years later, Kennedy was regarded as almost Churchillian with his eloquence, but he didn't start out that way. His voice in 1946 was described as "somewhat scratchy and tensely high-pitched," and he "projected a quality of grave seriousness that masked his discomfiture."[12]

But he worked hard on his content and delivery, with Joe's help. His sister Eunice bore witness to this effort, recalling how their father worked with Jack. "I can still see the two of them sitting together," she said, "analyzing the entire speech and talking about the pace of delivery to see where it worked and where it had gone wrong."[13]

Whatever Jack may have lacked in oratorical ability, he seemed to have good instincts when it came to reading an audience. One evening, accompanied by his mother, he was scheduled to address a local chapter of the Gold Star Mothers, a group of ladies who grieved the loss of their sons. When Jack rose to speak, they all stared at him and seemed to be whispering to each other, "He reminds me of my son."[14] Sensing the mood of the group, Jack said, "I know how you feel. My mother is a Gold Star Mother, too." In response, "the audience rushed forward to embrace both mother and son."

And then there was the issue of his health. His longtime friend Lem Billings said that Jack "may have been in pain, like he was so much of the time, but if he was, his mind was on other things." Billings added, "He was thin, as pictures will show, but he certainly was working as close to twenty-four hours a day as a man can work. He never let up—many healthy men could not have kept up that pace!"[15]

On primary day, Jack won big, which was hardly a surprise to anyone watching the race. Headlines in the region's newspapers told the story: "YOUNG KENNEDY ASSURED OF SEAT; KENNEDY NOMINATED FOR CURELY'S SEAT; KENNEDY GOING TO CONGRESS; KENNEDY PT BOAT HERO, WINS SEAT IN CONGRESS."[16] The election in November would be a mere formality. For all practical purposes, John F. Kennedy was the congressman-elect representing Massachusetts Eleventh District, though he would not actually take his seat in Washington until January 1946. The *New York Times* had a headline that said, simply: "KENNEDY MAKES A POLITICAL BOW."

Jack's victory was also noticed nationally, not only because of his famous name, but also because he was a Democrat winning election against the backdrop of a significant Republican sweep. The GOP took control of both houses of Congress for the first time since before the Great Depression. Kennedy would enter Congress as part of the minority.

The trend seemed to look on the surface as the polar opposite of what had happened a year before in Great Britain when voters there gave Winston Churchill and his Conservative Party what he described as the royal order of the boot. In that case, there was a clear lurch to the left, as citizen looked for a welfare state. But in the United States, the first postwar election moved the nation to the right and a rejection of New Deal government experimentation and intervention. But the new congressman from Massachusetts was fine with that.

After all, he won his race often referring to himself as "a fighting conservative."[17]

Less than two weeks after his primary victory, Henry Luce's *Time* magazine published a flattering article about Kennedy in its National Affairs section. Titled "PROMISE KEPT," it described him as "boyish-looking" and how "he worked hard to prove he was no snob."[18] The piece high-lighted his military exploits and began, "In his opening campaign speech, young Jack Kennedy recalled a promise he had made when he was a PT boat skipper in the Solomons. Said he: 'When ships were sinking and young Americans were dying . . . I firmly resolved to serve my country in peace as honestly as I tried to serve it in war'. His method of serving was to try for Congress as a Democrat from Massachusetts' Eleventh District."

On November 5, he was elected, again by a landslide—this time over his Republican opponent, Lester W. Bowen. And a few days later his navy pal and newspaper partner, James Reed, joined the family and a few friends for dinner. The Ambassador was there, as was Grandpa "Honey Fitz." At one point, Jack's grandfather proposed a toast to his grandson—"To the future President of the United States."[19] Reed recalled that the old man looked right at Jack and everyone joined in, without "any degree of levity or frivolity." He added, "It was a serious toast, really, that pro-posed to Jack, and I think everyone there the thought that one day Jack would be President of the United States."

But first he had to pay his dues as a back-bencher in the Eightieth Congress.

CHAPTER 22

"John F. Kennedy and Richard M. Nixon"

"I SAW A CRUSHED MAN TODAY. HE NEEDS OUR HELP. I TOLD HIM TO go upstairs and have a drink with his wife and avoid making any decision until the thing brightens up," Richard Nixon said to a friend.[1] He had just been to the Oval Office to see Jack Kennedy. It was April 1961, and the fiasco at a place called Bay of Pigs in Cuba was playing out. Nixon had lost to Kennedy in 1960, but the margin was razor-thin, and Kennedy needed friends and support.

The two rivals, who had once been friends, possibly recalled their first meeting as part of their friendly conversation that day. For at least a moment, the fierce feelings of the presidential campaign were absent, and they spoke as colleagues. Though Kennedy had written *Profiles in Courage*, and it along with the Pulitzer it won were factors in his victory, Kennedy seemed to be, at that moment, devoid of the courage he admired.

Nixon recalled seeing him "pacing around the room cursing, using his down-to-earth Irish vocabulary rather than his Harvard vocabulary, he told me how disappointed he had been in the advice he had received" from his military advisers. Nixon's advice about Cuba to Kennedy was, "I would find a proper legal cover, and I would go in."

Before Nixon left that day, Kennedy had some advice of his own for the former Vice President. He encouraged Nixon to write his memoirs, sharing his father's opinion, "There's something about being an author which really builds the reputation of a politician."

Nixon took the advice and wrote a bestseller of his own with an eye on his next bid for the White House.[2]

On January 3, 1946, several newly sworn-in congressmen made their way from the floor of the House of Representatives, where the official festivities had taken place, to the thirteenth floor of a famous building in Washington, D.C.—located at 529 Fourteenth Street, NW—the home of the National Press Club. They had been invited to a special reception for new members of the Eightieth Congress—particularly those who had served America during the recent world war.

As several men crowded into an elevator, the discussion was about the day in general, their excitement, and the unique presence of television cameras—something that would not happen again in that way for several decades. These were men who had returned from battle and were determined to make a difference in peacetime. They had seen the world at its worst, and they were devoted to the idea of ensuring something like that devastating war never happened again.

Among the handful of new legislators that day at the National Press Club were two men whose lives and careers were destined to interact, overlap, and rival—John F. Kennedy and Richard M. Nixon.[3]

Nixon was elected to Congress after a hard-fought campaign against Jerry Voorhis, a popular Democrat who had represented California's twelfth district for a decade. One of the most liberal members of Congress, Voorhis was a passionate supporter of President Roosevelt's New Deal. He had been thought unbeatable in the race, but the combination of hard work and a campaign that kept Voorhis on the defensive won the day. Some would later look back on the 1946 campaign as an indicator of Nixon's no-holds-barred methods that became his political trademark.

Billy Sutton was at the reception that day with Jack Kennedy. He had arrived in Washington, D.C., a few days earlier to set up Kennedy's office. He was nervous and agitated. Kennedy had waited until that very morning to get to Washington. John McCormack, veteran congressman and leader of delegation from the Bay State, had called Sutton several times asking for Jack.

Kennedy chose to drive to town through a snowstorm in his sister Eunice's Chrysler. When he made it to the Statler Hotel, Sutton wanted to get him over to Capitol Hill immediately. But Jack insisted on having a couple of eggs first, telling Sutton, "Mr. McCormack has been getting along without me here in Washington for twenty-eight years. He can get along without me for another fifteen minutes." That kind of thing was business as usual for Kennedy, but it exasperated Billy Sutton.

Billy was standing near his boss at the *Press Club* when he noticed Richard Nixon standing by himself several feet away. "Jack, follow me. There's a guy here I want you to meet," Sutton said. Kennedy walked with Sutton over to where Nixon was. "Jack Kennedy, this is Richard Nixon from California."

Kennedy, who had seemed to just be going through the motions by following his press secretary, was instantly animated. "You're the guy that beat Voorhis."

"Yeah," Nixon said, looking Kennedy over. He thought the man he was meeting looked as if he was just getting over a long illness. He was thin, almost frail, and his skin seemed yellowish.

"That's like beating John McCormack up in Massachusetts, because Voorhis was a big New Dealer," Kennedy said in a tone indicating he was impressed with Nixon's political victory.

"Well, I guess I feel great," Nixon replied in a sort of deadpan manner.

"Well, you should be thrilled. You must have some talent, we need to get acquainted. Where did they put you? My office is on the third floor of the House Office Building."

"I'm two floors above you. I think it's in the attic, at least that's what the low ceiling makes it feel like."

"I'll come up some time," Kennedy offered.

"That'd be great, Jack—nice to meet you. We're gonna be on the Education and Labor Committee together. But on opposite sides," Nixon said with an awkward laugh.

After a while, the men being honored were invited up to the front of the room. There was a single microphone and Warren B. Francis, the President of the National Press Club who worked at the *Los Angeles Times*, singled out Nixon who seemed to be the star of the class, for a handshake. He had covered Nixon's campaign against Voorhis.

Francis said a few words about heroism, service, and sacrifice, while photographers snapped several shots of the vets who were now congressmen. Kennedy and Nixon were next to each other in the back row. Dick looked serious and focused, while Jack looked around and seemed almost too young to be in that group of men.

Jack moved into a rented town home at 1528 Thirty-First Street NW in Georgetown. He shared it with his sister Eunice, who kept tabs on her brother for their father. The place became known as "the Hollywood Hotel because of frequent parties and occasional visits from movie starlets."[4] He lived a relatively luxurious life, with a full-time housekeeper and valet.

The Eightieth Congress would prove to be a bitterly partisan. Republicans, having been out of power for so long, were determined to seize the moment and reverse as much of FDR's legacy as possible. For his part, President Harry Truman, would prove to be a feisty and formidable adversary. But in his State of the Union address on January 6, he struck a conciliatory tone—noticeably avoiding any mention of Franklin Roosevelt. Biographer David McCullough wrote of this effort, "The speech went far to raise Truman's standing with Congress."[5]

The biggest *international* issue at the moment was the emerging Cold War. Winston Churchill, hosted by President Truman, had traveled more than a year earlier to tiny Westminster College in Missouri to deliver what would become known as his "Iron Curtain" speech (though the speech was actually titled "The Sinews of Peace"). Churchill revisited his pre–World War II role as a voice crying in the wilderness. He warned of Soviet ambitious expansionism. Whatever hope there had been for a world without the threat of war in the aftermath of the defeat of Germany and Japan was gone. Truman addressed Congress in March, articulating what would be known as the Truman Doctrine, a strategy to contain Stalin and the Russians. Jack supported the president completely, when Truman said: "I believe that it must be the policy of the United States to support free peoples who are resisting attempted subjugation by armed minorities or outside pressures." Another Truman biographer, Robert J. Donovan (who would also write the definitive account of Kennedy's *PT 109* story), wrote that the speech "was certainly the most controversial of his presidency and remains probably the most enduringly controversial speech that has been made by a president in the twentieth century."[6]

But on the domestic front, the major issue facing the nation was labor unrest.

CHAPTER 23

"They Stayed Up Talking throughout the Night"

AMERICANS WERE HAPPY TO HAVE THE BOYS HOME FROM WAR, BUT those boys needed jobs. World War II had accomplished what the New Deal could not—it pulled America finally out of economic depression. And those who knew their history understood that when the American warriors "over there" in Europe came home after the First World War in 1918, the economy had devolved into panic mode.

President Truman wanted to get ahead of the problem, convening national labor-management conference in Washington, but it had no effect on the mood of labor leaders. Strikes became chronic throughout the country. In 1946, there had been nearly 5,000 of them, involving 4.6 million workers. A national steel walkout alone in 1946 "took 400,000 workers off the job, at the time the largest coordinated work stoppage in American history."[1] When 300,000 railroad workers voted down a settlement that had been orchestrated, in part, by the government, Truman threatened "to have the government run railroads and to deploy soldiers to defend replacement workers."[2]

The Republicans, now in charge of Congress, came up with several proposals to modify the National Labor Relations Act of 1935, known as the Wagner Act. Sponsored by New Jersey House member Fred Hartley, and Robert Taft, senator from Ohio, their efforts became known as the Taft-Hartley Bill. The legislation gave workers the right not to join unions, thus ending the closed shop.

Jack, while concerned about some of the excesses of American labor, spoke out against the legislation, considering it too restrictive of unions. As part of the House Labor Committee, he warned it would "bring not peace but labor war—a war bitter and dangerous. This bill in its present form plays into the hands of the radicals in our unions, who preach the doctrine of class struggle."[3]

As Taft-Hartley was making its way through the legislative pipeline, the proposed bill brought to pass an interesting, but now largely forgotten, moment in political history. It involved another freshman member of the Labor Committee—Dick Nixon. The two low men on the committee's totem pole were asked by Pennsylvania Congressman Frank Buchanan to debate the bill's merits before a civic group in his home town.

McKeesport, Pennsylvania.

Located about twelve miles southwest of Pittsburgh, McKeesport was known as "tube city" because it was the world's largest producer of, well, steel tubing. Back then, 50,000 people called it home and its National Tube Works employed 5,000 workers around the clock to keep up with demand. Kennedy and Nixon were to have their first debate in the ballroom at the city's quaint but elegant Penn McKee Hotel. The group sponsoring the event was called the Junto Group, but because two young congressmen were to be there, many others showed up—about 200 people in all. Nixon was an experienced debater—in fact a college champion—and he spoke in favor of the bill, while Jack, still unsteady as a public speaker, argued against it. After the debate, they went to a nearby eatery, The Star Diner, near the rail station, and had hamburgers and pie, while chatting with a few locals.

As fate would have it, these two future presidents were booked on the same overnight train back to Washington. In fact, the same Pullman compartment on The Capitol Limited. They flipped a coin to see who would get the top bunk. Nixon won. But they didn't sleep that night. Instead, they stayed up talking throughout the night. Nixon wrote about it in his 1962 book, Six Crises: "I remember that our discussions during the long, rocky ride related primarily to foreign affairs and the handling of the Communist threat at home and abroad rather than the Taft-Hartley Act. I do not recall the details of our talk but of one thing I am absolutely sure: neither he nor I had even the vaguest notion at that time that either of us would be a candidate for President thirteen years later."[4]

They formed a friendship of sorts. One Nixon biographer wrote, "Soon Dick and Pat were attending parties at Kennedy's town house in Georgetown. When John Kennedy married Jacqueline Bouvier, the Nixons were invited to the wedding."[5]

More than fifteen years later, shortly after Nixon's book came out, and just a week before then President John F. Kennedy saw the first photographs of Soviet Missile bases being built in Cuba, Jack returned to McKeesport to campaign for local candidates in the upcoming midterm elections. Addressing a crowd of 25,000 in a large parking lot just a few blocks from the Penn McKee on October 13, 1962, he said: "Ladies and Gentlemen, the first time I came to this city was in 1947, when Mr. Richard Nixon and I engaged in our first debate. He won that one, and we went on to other things. We came here on that occasion to debate the Taft-Hartley Law, which he was for and which I was against."[6]

Ultimately, Taft-Hartley was passed by both Houses of Congress and vetoed by Truman. Congress then successfully overrode the President's veto, and Taft-Hartley became the law of land in June 1947.

A few years later, when Kennedy was in the Senate and Nixon was Vice President, their offices were right across the hall from each other. Kennedy's secretary, Evelyn Lincoln, said the two men had a relationship that "was very nice."[7] She said, "The Vice President, at first, would stop in evenings and put up his feet on the desk there with Senator Kennedy and discuss things." But she remembered that the meetings took place "less and less as the time went on."

Indeed.

Jack spent six years in the House of Representatives. They were years of growth—and pain. His health challenges and back troubles led to a lot of time off and away from Washington. There are, however, several things worth noting. He was a loyal party member, though he had the capacity to display his independence. He voted as a middle-of-the-road liberal on domestic matters. But he could be hard-nosed on international matters. He was also a strong Cold Warrior.

There is no doubt that his chronic health issues hindered his effectiveness as a congressman. His Addison's disease was diagnosed in 1947, but he likely knew about it much earlier, and he denied it ever after. He also dealt with colon issues, stomach issues, and problems with his back. His colleagues in the House describe him as a "frail, sick, hollow man."[8]

In May 1948, his sister, Kathleen, was killed in a plane crash in France. Jack took this very hard and spent months grieving. The death of his two closest siblings, and his diagnosis with a potentially life-threatening illness, marked what historian Doris Kearns Goodwin described as "the beginning of a terrible period of confusion for Jack."[9] He seemed to be preoccupied with death and mortality—particularly his own. He told newspaper columnist Joseph Alsop that he had a disease, describing it as "a sort of slow motion leukemia."

Jack said he had doubts he would live to see the age of forty-five.

He was also restless and bored. He wanted more. Years later, he reflected that being in the House, "You are one of 435 members. You have to be there many, many years before you get to the hub of influence, or have an opportunity to play any role in substantive matters."[10]

CHAPTER 24

"He Had a Knack for Alienating"

THE WASHINGTON TED SORENSEN FOUND WHEN HE STEPPED OFF his train at Union Station in July 1951 was a city in the grip of a new "red scare," as well as a "police action" in a faraway place called Korea. It was also tough place for a young *liberal* longing to make his mark. Conservatism was ascendant, and the town's mood was laden with fear and suspicion. But it was where Ted wanted to be. As one biographer put it, Sorensen "was not interested in the parochialism of state politics," but rather, "the heart of national government was the only suitable destination."[1]

Much of the political talk of the town had to do with whether or not President Harry Truman was going to run for reelection in 1952. A new poll conducted by George Gallup's American Institute of Public Opinion was out reflecting a surprising resurgence for the Man from Missouri. A few months earlier, only 40 per cent of those polled thought Harry would run again, but the most recent numbers showed 61 per cent thought he would make the run.[2] The Twenty-second Amendment to the Constitution was the new law of the land, limiting Presidents to just two terms, but it didn't apply to Truman, who was grandfathered. Ever the man to tease, the President announced months earlier that he had, in fact, made his decision about 1952, but wasn't divulging his secret.

Ted appreciated what he called "President Truman's Midwestern Liberalism," but he was put off by the President's loyalty policies for federal employees.[3] At any rate, Sorensen had been hearing and reading good things about Adlai Stevenson, the liberal Governor of Illinois. Of course, presidential issues were more than a year away. Sorensen's main purpose when he hit town was to find a job.

Unfortunately for him, his first day in DC was the Fourth of July and all government offices were closed.

Ted's first few days in the city were discouraging. He literally walked several miles, going door to door in the summer heat trying to find work. He recalled years later, "Almost all the lawyers to whom I was introduced, whether in government or private practice, gave me encouragement and hope, but no job, each promising to call another office on my behalf, as they sent me off on another weary journey."[4] Finally, he was hired by the Federal Security Administration (FSA). He wrote about it to his father back in Nebraska: "The FSA building is new and beautiful and air conditioned, with its own lunchroom and cafeteria, and as an agency is generally very progressive and alert. Physical facilities, office, desk, telephone, steno services, all better than elsewhere."

Camilla and young Eric soon joined Ted.

Ted's salary that first year on the federal payroll was $3,285, but it didn't stretch all that far in the expensive city. He liked the work, but he had his eyes on bigger things and better pay. Often during his lunch hour, he would skip the FSA cafeteria, opting to take a sandwich and walk over to Capitol Hill, where he would watch the Senate in session, or maybe drop in on a public hearing. This continued his political education. He said, "In time I came to see politics as the arena in which both an ambitious young idealist can realize his highest ambitions and a greedy demagogue can exercise his worst traits."

The FSA was a good fit for Ted. He was particularly impressed with the agency's work on behalf of Black Americans.[5] Also while there, the director of the agency introduced legislation designed to provide health insurance for people over the age of sixty-five—the first such bill of its kind.

But Ted didn't stay at the FSA long, opting to take a job on Capitol Hill working with the Railroad Retirement System, an important entity in the days before air travel began to surpass trains in the hearts and plans of most Americans. While there, he met Robert Wallace, who was also a legislative assistant to Senator Paul Douglas of Illinois. It would prove to be a very beneficial connection.

The Railroad Retirement Act of 1934 restructured the Railroad Retirement System to provide annuities to retirees based on rail earnings and length of service. It was modified by Congress several times in the ensuing years. But in 1946, benefits were extended to survivors, based on combined railroad and Social Security–covered employment. This extension demonstrated congressional concern for the social goal of providing income security in old age, or social insurance, rather than simply rewarding career performance.

Wallace recalled, "This committee was set up in 1952. It was a short term kind of a thing, eight months or so, so it was not feasible to pull in a special staff for this when it was likely to fold up very quickly.[6]

Senator Douglas was named chairman of the committee and he made me staff director." He needed a junior lawyer. Someone told him about Ted Sorensen, so he set up a meeting. He was impressed. "He was only about 23 years old at the time. But he was obviously very intelligent, very bright," Wallace recalled. He told Ted that the job was temporary. But the salary was nearly double what he had made at FSA, so he jumped at the offer.

Sorensen's job was to gather information about existing benefits, organize committee meetings, and even, on occasion, to interrogate witnesses. He used his research and writing skills to put together thorough study of the program.

Wallace said Sorensen's "work was truly outstanding."

But he also noted that Ted "had a knack for alienating anybody who was at his level or below him." He was particularly hard on the office secretaries, who all "disliked him intensely." Ted was ambitious, likely this came through and was off-putting to many. One day Ted hosted a party at his house, one that Wallace attended. They played a game called twenty-five squares. The next day when Wallace got to the office he talked to a secretary who had refused to attend because of her dislike for Sorensen. She asked him, "How was the party?"

"Oh, it was alright," he replied. "We played a game called twenty-five squares."[7]

"Oh," she said sarcastically, "where there that many of you there?"

CHAPTER 25

"The Political Equivalent of Perfect Pitch in a Crooner"

JACK KENNEDY WAS A RESTLESS MAN. ALWAYS IN A HURRY. SO, IT SHOULD come as no surprise that he saw the House of Representatives as a stepping stone to something more. Tip O'Neill wrote years later that Kennedy was "a fish out of water" in the House.[1] "He didn't get along with the leadership, and they resented his frequent absences and his political independence," O' Neill added. Almost from the moment he entered the House in 1947, he pondered his next political steps. He was ambitious.

So was his father.

Jack's goal was to eventually run for statewide office in Massachusetts. There were two options to match his ambition: governor or senator. He would not make the final decision on which one until early 1952, but he was running toward them in 1947. In fact, one of his aides, David Powers, put a map of the state on the bedroom wall of Jack's Boston apartment, so that when he was in town he faced it each morning. Colored pins were placed on each town Kennedy visited, with the goal to "blanket the map."[2]

Kennedy spent the next four years visiting more than 350 cities and towns in the Bay State. His pattern was to fly from Washington most Thursday nights when Congress was in session. He would spend the weekend at political events, then take an overnight train back to Washington Sunday night. Though his attendance record on the floor of the House was sometimes lacking, his regular visits back to his home state were more frequent than those of most of his colleagues.

The visits and speaking engagements were designed to create a following and build a political organization statewide. Jack would write down the names of people who impressed him as potentially helpful and gave them to a secretary who "typed the information onto index cards and filed them for future reference."[3]

By 1951, the time had come to decide whether to run for governor or senator. A lot depended on the incumbent Democratic governor, who had not yet decided about running for reelection. On the Senate side of the equation was the possibility of running against the Republican Henry Cabot Lodge, a popular figure from a prominent Boston political family. But Jack told one friend that the idea of being governor didn't interest him the way the senate did. "I don't look forward," he said, "to sitting there in the governor's office and dealing with sewer contracts."[4]

Two of his congressional colleagues from the "freshman class" of 1947 had already moved up to the Senate—George Smathers of Florida and Richard Nixon from California, feeding Jack's competitive bent. Also, Kennedy's interest in foreign affairs made the Senate a better fit for him than the Massachusetts State House.

He announced his candidacy for the Senate April 7, 1952, and set his sights on defeating Henry Cabot Lodge in what was already shaping up to be a strong year for the Republicans. Unlike his first race in 1946, this one would be an uphill battle. Many observers didn't give Kennedy much of a chance.

Henry Cabot Lodge, Jr., was the grandson of Henry Cabot Lodge, the U.S. Senator who led the opposition to Woodrow Wilson's policies after World War I and kept America from joining the League of Nations. In an interesting rhyme of history, Jack's grandfather, "Honey Fitz," had challenged that Henry Cabot Lodge for the Senate in 1916, but was defeated.

Now it would be grandson vs. grandson for the same seat.

The Lodge family had been politically prominent in Massachusetts since the Revolutionary War. He was first elected to the Senate in 1936 and was a very popular figure.

To make Jack's job running against him even tougher, Lodge was also a war hero. In fact, he resigned his office in 1944 to serve with distinction as Lieutenant Colonel in the Army, once single-handedly capturing a German patrol group. So, the *PT 109* story would be neutralized for all practical purposes. Lodge was also one of the key Republicans behind the effort to draft Dwight D. Eisenhower to run in 1952, which would presumably benefit him in a year when Ike put the GOP back in the White House after a twenty-year absence.

The Kennedy campaign waged a no-holds-barred attack on Lodge from the beginning. They compiled a 162-page report called "Lodge's Dodges," detailing the Republican's many policy shifts during his time in office.[5] They attacked Lodge "from the left" on domestic issues, and "from the right" on foreign policy.

And they attacked his character.

Kennedy said, "A lack of integrity is a serious thing," and he accused his opponent of "hypocrisy." Ironically, "he audaciously blasted Lodge for being more interested in global affairs than matters that directly affected his state."[6] Jack even criticized Lodge for traveling so much while in the Senate, though he himself had probably traveled even more while in the House.

In retrospect, Kennedy's campaign against Lodge was every bit as aggressive as was that of his former House colleague Richard Nixon against Helen Gahagan Douglas two years earlier in California. But the stigma of being a negative campaigner never attached itself to Kennedy the way it did to Nixon.

As had been the case in 1946, and, presumably in 1948 and 1950, when Jack was reelected to the House, Joe Kennedy was hard at work behind the scenes in 1952. His invisible hand was felt in two primary ways—his network of rich and powerful people, and his willingness to use his money with almost reckless abandon. And sometimes the two overlapped, as in the case of John Fox, the editor of the *Boston Post*. It would not become public knowledge for several years, but Joe Kennedy loaned Fox $500,000 for a personal matter. Then, just a few weeks before election day, Fox's newspaper, long a supporter of Republicans in general and Lodge in particular, endorsed Kennedy.[7]

Some estimates put Joe's spending in 1952 to elect his son to the Senate "ran into the millions." One labor leader remarked, "You could live the rest of your life on the billboard budget alone."

One other key way Joe Kennedy helped with the election was by keeping Joe McCarthy from campaigning for Lodge. McCarthy was popular in the Bay State, and "his appearance on behalf of the Republicans would have sunk Kennedy."[8] To run interference, Joe Kennedy made "a large donation" to the McCarthy's own campaign that year, and he also arranged for Richard Cardinal Cushing to quietly urge the Wisconsin Senator to stay away from Massachusetts.

The main way, however, that Joe Kennedy's influence was felt in 1952 was the installation of Jack's younger brother, Bobby, as the campaign manager. Robert Kennedy was then just twenty-six years old and fresh

out of the University of Virginia Law School. He was woefully inexperienced and not at all acquainted with key political people in Boston and
the rest of the state. Described as "brash, tough, hard-working, well organized,"[9] what he lacked in experience he made up for by the most important factor—the full support and trust of both his father and brother. The
Kennedy brothers both understood their father's primitive philosophy:
"family came before anything, and that in a crunch, it was only your siblings and parents you could count on."[10]

Bobby organized and ran a brilliant campaign, recruiting nearly
30,000 volunteers who went door-to-door throughout the state delivering nearly a million copies of a specially created campaign newspaper
bearing the headline, "JOHN FULFILLS DREAM OF BROTHER
JOE WHO MET DEATH IN THE SKY OVER THE ENGLISH
CHANNEL." The focus was on the family's supreme sacrifice rather than
solely Jack's heroism.

He also organized house parties—sometimes called "teas"—as part
of a campaign for the female vote. Jack was among the first American politicians to truly tap into that demographic effectively. In all,
more than 70,000 women participated in these events, with many then
becoming volunteers. Bobby even had his sisters and mother wearing
skirts with the words "VOTE FOR JACK KENNEDY" embroidered
on them.

It all worked. On election day, though Eisenhower carried Massachusetts by 200,000 votes, Jack beat Lodge by more than 70,000. Henry
Cabot Lodge was shocked. He told a friend, "I felt rather like a man who
has just been hit by a truck."[11]

Bobby Kennedy had proven himself as a tough, sometimes ruthless,
political practitioner. And he had only just begun managing the nuts and
bolts of campaigning with his older brother. The 1952 race for the Senate
has been described as "a blooding and a bonding" for Bobby.[12] And both
would dynamics continue for the rest of Jack's life.

Writing in the *Manchester Guardian*, British journalist Alistair
Cooke, who had first met Jack in San Francisco during the U.N. Conference in 1945, said, "Kennedy was the Frank Sinatra of the Democratic
party, bringing to the platforms of bigger men who don't forget a boyish

pompadour crowning a handsome grin, a gift of appropriate sweet-talk, which is the political equivalent of perfect pitch in a crooner."[13]

John F. Kennedy was now a national figure. Biographer Robert Dallek described his election to the United States Senate in 1952 as the beginning of "a romance between Jack Kennedy and millions of Americans." He added, "It would be one of the great American love affairs, and in his election day grin, it was just possible to imagine that Jack himself knew the match had been made."[14]

And he was about to connect with someone who would help him develop the political voice that would eventually take him to the White House.

CHAPTER 26

"I Would Rather Win a Pulitzer than Be President"

In the spring of 1953, Margaret Coit, like most girls in the country, found newly elected Senator John Fitzgerald Kennedy from Massachusetts very attractive. She recalled years later, "He was the golden boy . . . every girl in Massachusetts wanted to date him, and I wasn't any exception." Jack was settling into a job he already found to be rather boring.[1]

Miss Coit was a writer—a very good one. Her first book, a critically acclaimed biography of the famous South Carolina statesman John C. Calhoun, had been published a couple of years earlier. It won the 1951 *Pulitzer Prize* for biography. Not bad for a first effort. Sticking with the genre, she chose the powerful financier and political mover and shaker Bernard Baruch as her next literary subject.

Baruch had made a fortune as a savvy Wall Street speculator early in the twentieth century. He was also a man of considerable political influence, particularly when Franklin Roosevelt resided at 1600 Pennsylvania Avenue. Toward the end of his life he defended the idea of being a speculator. "Modern usage," he wrote in his autobiography, "has made the term 'speculator' a synonym for gambler," he said. "Actually the word comes from the Latin *speculari*, which means to spy out and observe. I have defined a speculator as a man who observes the future and acts before it occurs."[2] It was this quality that drew young and ambitious Joseph P. Kennedy to Baruch. Theirs became an informal mentor-protege relationship, and the two men had become wealthy power brokers by the time each had managed to hedge bets and avoid the widespread financial calamity known as the Great Depression.

Margaret sought a way for her research on Baruch to lead to a face-to-face meeting with the young and handsome senator from Massachusetts. First, she tried going through Jack's father. Before contacting the Ambassador, she read *Why England Slept*. When she finally got up the nerve to call the Ambassador on the telephone, he "barked" and "roared" at her in an intimidating way and the call went nowhere. So, she decided on the direct approach and called for an appointment with the senator himself.

She was surprised when he agreed to meet with her.

She had come to town as a delegate with a group of Republican women. Margaret Coit was remarkably similar in appearance—from height and weight, to hair color and style—to a certain Jacqueline, whom Kennedy had met a little less than two years earlier, and with whom he had an ongoing relationship. In fact, Jackie Bouvier had recently been Jack's date for President Eisenhower's inaugural ball on January 20. But at age thirty-four, Margaret was much closer to Jack's age—just two years his junior.

It was an unseasonably hot afternoon and Margaret had dressed up so as to make a good impression—"a little gray suit," complimented by "pink lace gloves" and "a little gray bonnet with a pink lace veil, and a pink rose." The heat was amplified by the fact that Kennedy's lack of seniority did not afford him an actual air-conditioned space in the Senate Office Building, something she noticed the moment she arrived.

Six staff girls were busy in the outer office. Margaret looked them over for a moment, noting that none of them were particularly pretty, "or chic, or young," which eased her mind a bit. She also saw a young-looking fellow with horn-rimmed glasses befitting a much older man. But he never looked up from his work. He was writing furiously on a yellow legal pad.

After a few moments, Jack Kennedy came into the room. Now, Margaret Coit was no novice at senatorial interviews. She had discussed politics and world affairs with the likes of Senators Stuart Symington, Harry Byrd, and even "Mr. Republican," Robert Taft. But she wasn't ready for Jack. He had "piercing eyes" that looked at her "searchingly." He wore a gray suit. In fact, everything about him seemed to be gray, from his skin, to a bit of his hair.

She managed to pull herself together quickly enough to begin the interview, asking about his time in England with his father just before the war. As he talked, she made copious notes and sensed that Jack was taking her in, later saying that he was "looking me right over and through me." After a few minutes, Kennedy interrupted her questions. "I am going to be giving a party at my house in Georgetown in a couple of days. Do you want to come?"

Did she ever.

A couple of days later, Margaret took a taxi from her esthetically challenged rooming house on Sixteenth Street SE to the elegant Georgetown townhouse Jack shared with his sister, Eunice—and would one day share with his wife. The small home had a hallway that led to two reception rooms that were filled with people.

Jack welcomed her. He then ignored her for the better part of the next three hours, spending most of his time across the room deep in conversation about foreign policy with Missouri Senator Stuart Symington. Feeling alone in the crowd, she wandered about looking for a familiar face. Finally, she saw one. The man said, "I won't tell on you if you don't tell on me."

It was Vice President Richard Nixon.

Margaret had first met Nixon just the night before at a Republican gathering. After a bit of awkward small talk with a man not known for it, Margaret comforted herself with a bowl of shrimp and sour cream hoping to get Jack's—or anyone's—attention. Finally, Jack's brother, Bobby—who was there with his wife Ethel—came over to talk, as did Jack's sisters. One of them said, "Oh, I know your Calhoun. It is a marvelous book." Margaret noted that Jack's sisters had "frosted" hair—something she had never seen before.

Bobby invited Margaret into another room where they talked about her book. She noted a contrast between the brothers, with Bobby being "ruddy and warm, and full of fun and jokes." Finally, Jack noticed Margaret again and tried to make up for his lack of attention by putting his arm around her and saying to no one in particular, "Isn't she the prettiest little thing you have ever seen?" Then he dropped a bit of a bomb. "I can't take you home. I have to fly to Chicago. So I'm going to send you home with the Mayor of San Diego. I'll call you in two or three days and we will have a date."

Disappointed and feeling more than a little bit dismissed, she rode in Mayor John D. Butler's car back to her rooming house.

A few days later, Margaret was working at the Manuscript Division at the Library of Congress, continuing her research into the life and work of Bernard Baruch, when someone came up to her and said, "Someone is calling you. A very New England accent." Of course, she knew who it was.

"Would you come over to the office and meet me there about three or four o'clock in the afternoon?" Kennedy asked.

When she entered his office, Kennedy was busy with paperwork. She looked around and saw some of the wall space adorned with framed letters written by people such as Andrew Jackson and Daniel Webster, all mingled with photographs of the senator with various luminaries. The other walls were covered with messily packed bookshelves. Kennedy noticed that Margaret was examining some of the titles and said, "Try me on them; I've read them all."

Jack worked diligently to present himself as a thinking-man's kind of politician, someone one who not only read books, rare enough for an office holder, but penned them, as well. Winston Churchill, whose many works adorned Kennedy's bookshelves, was his "literary model."[3] And Jack was already a successful author.

Jack loved all of Churchill's books, but returned most often to a book called *Great Contemporaries*, published in 1937. It was a collection of profiles about world leaders at the beginning of the twentieth century. And just as *While England Slept* surely influenced Kennedy's 1940 book, so *Great Contemporaries* would soon inspire yet another. In *Great Contemporaries*, Churchill wrote: "Courage is rightly esteemed the first of human qualities because it is the quality which guarantees all others."

Jack loved that quote.

He would soon write his own volume dedicated to that very quality—*Profiles in Courage*. It would be his own catalogue of essays about political greatness. He would begin his bestseller, one that would go on to win a Pulitzer Prize, with these words: "This is a book about the most admirable of human virtues—courage."[4] One JFK biographer would later suggest that *Profiles in Courage* was, in effect, "a version of Great Contemporaries."[5]

Margaret and Jack chatted as he continued to sign letters—what seemed like hundreds of them. "Don't you see how hard a senator works?" he asked with a flirty smile. She assured him that she did. He popped a few questions about Bernard Baruch and told her a slightly malicious story about Clare Booth Luce, the wife of *Time-Life* publisher Henry Luce. Clare had only a month earlier been appointed as U.S. Ambassador to Italy by President Eisenhower, the first woman to ever serve at that diplomatic level.

She had also had an affair with Jack's old man.

Finally, he put down his pen. By that time, everyone else in the office had gone home. He came over and sat with her on the couch, where he almost immediately dozed off for a few minutes. When he revived, Margaret said, "I think you are too tired to take me out tonight. Why don't you take me home?"

"You are very kind," he replied. "I am tired. I will take you home." He grabbed some crutches and they walked down the hall of the empty building. At one point, Kennedy pulled out a stick of *Juicy Fruit* gum. "You want some?" She nodded, and he tore the piece in half. They got into his convertible and took off.

His driving did not impress her. It was on the aggressive side. He even drove on the streetcar tracks to get ahead of traffic. A streetcar driver yelled at him to get off the tracks, but Kennedy cursed at him like the sailor he was.

When they arrived at her place, she invited him in. He went to the sofa and then tried to pull her down to him. "Don't be so grabby," she said. "This is our first date, we have plenty of time."

Kennedy said, "But I can't wait, you see, I'm going to grab everything I want. You see, I haven't any time."

Margaret was taken back. "We had been talking about books and ideas," she said, and then "he was like a 14-year-old high school football player." She added, that Jack "scared her" a bit.

After a little while, they got back into Jack's car for another ride. As they passed the White House, "he looked at it without a smile" and said, "I am going to go *there*."

Later, as they returned to her rooming house, he abruptly said, "My brother Bobby told me you had won the Pulitzer Prize. You never told me that. You are very, very modest." Then he added: "You know, I would rather win a Pulitzer Prize than be President of the United States."

CHAPTER 27

"Enter Ted Sorensen"

BEING FRANKLIN DELANO ROOSEVELT'S GODSON WAS A FACT THAT
Langdon Marvin—"Lang," as his friends called him—found a way to
work into the conversation almost immediately after meeting someone.
He and Jack Kennedy had roomed together briefly at Harvard, though
Jack (Class of '40) was a year ahead of Lang. They would remain friends
for life, but Kennedy would find ways to distance himself when necessary.

You see, Lang was a bit of an operator.

Langdon P. Marvin, Jr. had a lifelong passion for aviation, and he was
among the first to recognize how it could help the military in noncombat-
related ways. During the war, he had carved out a niche for himself as
a voice in the wilderness, believing that using aircraft to transport war
supplies as an alternative to using ships—many of which were being ban-
ished to the bottom of the sea by German U-Boats—was an idea whose
time had come. As a young officer in the navy, he worked his way into
a role with the War Production Board (WPB), becoming the chairman
of its Shipping Priorities Committee. From this perch, he orchestrated
significant shifts of cargo crossing the Atlantic, from ships to aircraft.
He then leveraged this into the creation of a new WPB entity called
the Interdepartmental Air Cargo Priorities Committee, with him as its
chairman.[1]

After the war, he transferred his passion for the potential of air cargo
into advocacy for similar *civilian* service in peacetime. He became an
unofficial advisor to Congressman, then later Senator, John F. Kennedy in
the 1940s and 1950s. He would continue to provide counsel on aviation
matters in the Kennedy White House, working as an "unofficial" advisor
[Read: not on his official paid staff] out of several rooms at the Library
of Congress—a courtesy reserved at the time for those helping members
of Congress.

In 1951, as Jack Kennedy was contemplating his run for the U.S.
Senate, Lang facilitated a meeting between Kennedy and Robert Wallace,
an aide to Illinois Senator Paul Douglas. Jack was a fan of a Presidential
Commission led by former POTUS Herbert Hoover—one that was created to find ways to make government more efficient. The Hoover Commission had made suggestions about separating air mail subsidies from
postal rates, and Lang was studying this on Jack's behalf. According to

Wallace, Kennedy "admired Douglas because Douglas was a liberal who was hard-headed about money matters."[2] He had been considered a long shot when he sought to unseat a popular Republican senator in 1948, and his campaign became a model for Kennedy's race against Lodge in 1952.

Bob Wallace and his wife joined Jack Kennedy and Langdon Marvin for dinner one night at the University Club in Washington. Lang brought Nancy Hanschman (later television commentator Nancy Dickinson), while Jack's date was Mary McGrory, a journalist then working for the *Washington Star*. Kennedy was on crutches and in some pain because of his ever-present back problems. They talked about the kind of campaign Senator Douglas ran in 1948—one that involved frenetic statewide travel—and Wallace later recalled wondering Kennedy was going be able to campaign statewide on crutches.[3]

Wallace and Kennedy hit it off and stayed in touch as the congressman ran a campaign for Lodge's seat modeled, at least in part, on Douglas's in 1948, per that dinner conversation. Meanwhile, Wallace became staff director with the railroad committee. In that role, he had the chance to build a small staff, and he looked for someone who would work for the modest salary available. Someone mentioned the name of a young man to him—a twenty-three-year-old attorney from Nebraska who was then working for the FSA. Wallace met with the young lawyer and was impressed with his intelligence, a quality that would be needed because there was a great amount of material that had to be organized and put in report form.

Enter Ted Sorensen.

Late in 1952, and as a result of the Eisenhower-led Republican sweep, Ted was looking for a new job. Bob Wallace wrote a glowing letter of recommendation for him, sending it to several of his contacts, including the senator-elect from Massachusetts. He described Sorensen's "ability to write in clear understandable language, to master any legislative problem . . . pleasant to work with, self-confident, but modest . . . a sincere liberal, but not the kind that always carries a chip on his shoulder."[4]

Wallace recalled that Sorensen "had a way of going through masses and masses of material and pulling out the salient parts."[5] Also, Ted had "a code of some sort so that he could dictate something and put it in a code so that this would show him where to find his material in his files." When he recommended Sorensen to Kennedy, he mentioned his writing skills.

Having written many articles himself for publications such as *The New Republic* and *Atlantic Monthly*, Wallace asked Sorensen one day to take a look at something he was writing. Ted said to him, "I'll take it home tonight and look at it." He brought the piece back the next day and Wallace said, "I'll tell you, it just transformed the piece. It was amazing." He added, "Sorensen had this flair for elegance in phraseology."[6] In fact, Wallace recruited Ted—this was before he went to work for Kennedy— to write the first draft of an article for Senator Douglas, one that would appear in *The New Republic*. "Douglas always paid me half of the fee when I did such drafts," he said.[7]

Senator Douglas also wrote a letter of recommendation for Ted, recalling, "Our committee was closing down and Sorensen was more or less without permanent work and Kennedy was looking for staff. I recommended Sorensen to him and the two, of course, hit it off perfectly from the beginning."[8] Douglas added, "I personally felt very gratified at having put the two in touch with each other."

An interview was set up, but Jack Kennedy had not yet moved into his Senate office and, because his House office was in transition, he and Sorensen had to sit in two chairs that had been moved out into the hallway. They looked each other over. Ted noted Jack's "tailor made suit"[9] and that a "thatch of chestnut hair was not as bushy as cartoonists had portrayed it." For his part, Ted was impressed by the fact that Kennedy did not try to impress *him*. He also noticed that Jack had a nervous habit, the "tapping of his fingers on his teeth and knee."

Kennedy's questions had to do with Sorensen's legal skills, since he needed someone to help him draft legislation. That first meeting lasted just five minutes. They agreed to meet again a few days later for more detailed conversation. Assuming the role of interviewer for a few minutes, Sorensen quizzed Kennedy about his father and their Catholicism.

He also had some blunt questions about the senator from Wisconsin, Joseph R. McCarthy.

CHAPTER 28

"Ted Became His Intellectual
Blood Bank"

JOE MCCARTHY, ELECTED TO THE SENATE FROM WISCONSIN IN 1946, had effectively exploited the concern many, if not most, Americans had during the first decade of the Cold War—a concern about Soviet expansionism through possible infiltration of the centers of American power. He had leveraged the impact of one speech in 1950, in which he claimed to have proof of 205 Communist agents or sympathizers in the U.S. State Department, into a wide-scale hunt for subversives. He was well on his way to becoming one of the most famous demagogues in American history.

McCarthy was elected to a second Senate term in 1952, and with the Republicans taking control of that body on the coattails of the Eisenhower landslide, he became the chairman of a powerful Senate committee. With that committee as his platform, he launched new investigations into purported Communist activity in and out of the government. The fact that there had been, in deed, high-profile cases of Americans spying for the Soviets made it open season for McCarthy. His efforts polarized the country, but early in 1953, he was viewed as too powerful to fight.

So, when Jack made his run for the Senate he avoided anything even remotely connected to McCarthy, who was very popular in Massachusetts, especially with Irish Catholic voters. But the issue was complicated because McCarthy was a friend of the family. In fact, Joe had dated two of Jack's sisters: Eunice and Pat. He had even spent time with the family at Hyannis Port. Jack recalled years later, "He went out on my boat one day and he almost drowned swimming behind it, but he never complained. If somebody was against him, he never tried to cut his heart out . . . He was a pleasant fellow."[1]

Joe Kennedy also enjoyed McCarthy's company. "He admired him for his big mouth, his outspoken confrontations with the government establishment (especially the State Department), his take-no-prisoners attacks on the Truman administration, and his contempt for diplomacy and decorum."[2] It's not hard to see this as part of Joe's contempt for how he perceived he had been treated both at home and abroad during his time as Ambassador to Great Britain.

So, Sorensen, who had done his homework before interviewing with Senator-elect Kennedy, thought his concern was valid. During their second interview, Sorensen recalled voicing his concern that Jack might be "soft on Senator Joe McCarthy and his witch-hunting tactics."[3] But Jack didn't seem bothered by what other interviewers might have thought was impertinence. Kennedy calmly explained that "McCarthy was a friend of his father and family," adding that he didn't agree with his "tactics or find merit in all his accusations."

The answer assuaged Ted's concerns. After a second interview with Senator Henry "Scoop" Jackson, Sorensen decided to take the job in Kennedy's office. He was among Jack's first hires in 1953. It would also prove to be the most important hire of his entire political career. No one would help John F. Kennedy become a household name and eventual president of the United States more than Theodore Sorensen.

Though Sorensen was more than a decade younger than his boss, he and Jack formed an effective partnership. Sorensen became a key policy adviser, the primary speechwriter, and a valued political sounding board for the senator. Kennedy would later reflect that Ted became his "intellectual blood bank."[4] Even though Sorensen looked nothing like Jack Kennedy, he was observed to be "oddly, even disturbingly, similar to his employer."[5] There were times when Ted would imitate his boss on the telephone, and "it was almost as if an alien spore had taken over Sorensen's body."

Jack's sister Eunice Shriver once told Sorensen, "I heard a compliment about you a couple of weeks ago. Jack said you are the smartest man he has ever met."[6]

Sorensen was destined to become a star in the Kennedy cosmos, the closest thing to an alter ego the future president would ever have, a fact that created the potential for great difficulty a few years later when *Profiles in Courage* was being written.

Jack Kennedy had modeled his 1952 race for the Senate, at least in part, on the one that Paul Douglas ran in Illinois in 1948. He admired Douglas, who was, as already noted, partly responsible connecting him with Sorensen. And there was another significant way Douglas influenced Kennedy.

Senator Douglas used various members of his staff to write articles, something Kennedy planned to do with Sorensen. Douglas had established the practice of compensating a staff member who wrote for him with a sum separate from the Senate salary—"at least one-half of any fees or royalties he received for such publications."[7]

Kennedy made the same deal with Sorensen, though Ted may have received more than 50% on occasion.

Years later, Bob Wallace recalled, "I think Kennedy gave him all the money and profits from any articles they did together. He went to work for Kennedy for about $8,500 a year, but then Kennedy gave him fees for articles."[8] This newfound prosperity enabled Sorensen to purchase a stunning house in McLean, Virginia, as well as the means to make other profitable investments.

During his first Senate years, Sorensen wrote several articles at Kennedy's direction. The pieces appeared in periodicals such as *Vogue, Life, Look*, the *New York Times Sunday Magazine*, the *Kiwanis Magazine*, the *General Electric Defense Quarterly*, and the *Bulletin of Atomic Scientists*. Such writing was, as Sorensen recalled, "a new approach to climbing the national political ladder." Kennedy wanted "articles on serious subjects" to counter the "flood of superficial articles about his good looks and his romance with Jackie." These articles were written with a larger purpose in mind than the mere sharing of information. They were designed to establish the senator as an erudite articulator of important national and international issues.

Jack Kennedy wanted America to know that he was more than just a pretty face.

CHAPTER 29

"A Kennedy Speech Has to Have Class"

THE SENATE WAS WHERE JOHN F. KENNEDY PREPARED TO BECOME THE President of the United States. The presidency was his endgame and had been for a long time. Robert Dallek suggested that "the possibility of becoming the first Catholic president intrigued Jack from the start of his political career."[1] The Senate would be a place for him to live in the national spotlight, creating a name for himself, and carefully cultivating his personal and political image. While his eventual election to the presidency was far from a foregone conclusion as he took his seat in 1953, and the journey from there to the White House would be, at times, a tortured path, several things would happen in the years 1953 and following that became vital pieces of a compelling political puzzle.

His marriage to Jackie in September 1953 was certainly crucial to his political future. Almost becoming the Democratic Vice-Presidential nominee on the ticket with Adlai Stevenson in 1956 was another. However, the most important factor that helped propel Jack Kennedy from the Senate toward serious contention for the highest office in the land was the publication of *Profiles in Courage*, and its subsequent receipt of the Pulitzer Prize for biography.

Without that, Kennedy might have been just another also-ran overshadowed by older men with more experience.

Kennedy and Sorensen quickly developed a working rhythm, both influencing the other. Kennedy's influence was personal, while Sorensen's was purely professional.

Ted was smitten with Jack. He even adopted some of Jack's mannerisms, assuming the "broad Massachusetts inflections and chopping gestures."[2] He took up drinking, abandoning his abstinence in favor of Kennedy favorites—daiquiris and Heineken beer. And he developed that convincing imitation of Kennedy's voice that at times could fool even the closest of the Senator's confidants.

As the youngest member of Kennedy's inner circle during the Senate years, Sorensen was described as having a "square, wintry, bespectacled face that seemed carved from ice,"[3] and a "smile as spontaneous as a bank vault swinging open." Both men were known for their "retentive memories, mental and physical energy, intolerance for small talk, and directness of manner."

He would become Jack's alter ego.

As for Sorensen's influence on the Senator, there were two primary manifestations. First, and most obvious, he helped Kennedy find his *voice* via the written and spoken word. The prodigious output of erudite articles, coupled with the dramatic improvement in the style of his speeches, soon began to put Kennedy on the map in the Senate in ways he had not achieved in the House of Representatives. It was all part of a determined effort to enhance Kennedy's image and transform him into a statesman worthy of the nation's highest office. As presidential historian Michael Beschloss described it, "The hackneyed speeches of Kennedy's congressional years gave way to the staccato phrases, contrapuntal sentences, soaring rhetoric, and quotations from the great for which Kennedy would always be remembered."[4]

Sorensen put it simply: "A Kennedy speech has to have class."

Jack once told Tip O'Neil, his successor in the House of Representatives, "I never had anyone who could write for me before Ted came along."[5] Sorensen helped make Kennedy an oratorical star. Once Ted began to put words in Jack's mouth, "There was a noticeable increase in their range, eloquence, rhetorical power, and concision." It helped that both men were big fans of the kind of "brevity of precision" emphasized in William Strunk Junior's book *The Elements of Style*.

The other way Sorensen influenced Kennedy was in steering him *leftward* whenever possible. He was, by far, "the most serious liberal in Kennedy's inner circle."[6] Early in their working relationship, they had conversations about what Sorensen described as "the senator's willingness to fight the good fight."[7] To Ted that meant the gospel of liberalism. Kennedy defended himself as more liberal than his record suggested, telling his young aide, "You've got to remember that I entered Congress just out of my father's house." Yet, he knew that any advance in his political career in the Democrat Party would require authentic liberal bona fides. And Ted was the sort of brainy, but practical liberal he felt comfortable with.

Jack Kennedy had wanted to write another book since his journalism days after the war. The diary he kept in 1945 bears this out. He considered doing a book titled *Al Smith: Public Servant*, a biography of the first Roman Catholic to be nominated for the presidency by a major party. But the idea never went anywhere. In fact, it wasn't until Ted Sorensen came into his world that he got serious about another effort. By 1953, it had been well more than a decade since *Why England Slept* became a minor literary sensation.

But with Sorensen on board and producing a steady stream of articles, a new book seemed almost inevitable. On Jack's behalf, Ted queried Harvard University Press about a book that dealt with the economy in New England, the focus of much of the senator's attention early in his term, as well as the subject of many of the senator's speeches at the time. It was just an idea—an idea without even a tentative title.

In early September 1953, Thomas J. Wilson, the Director of Harvard University Press, asked Sorensen for an outline. Wilson said, "After consideration of such an outline, it would probably be helpful if you and I got together and talked things over." But Sorensen wanted Kennedy to be clear that he "would not begin work on the book until the outline has been approved by you [Kennedy]." The process seemed to be: Ted outlined the book, then after Jack approved the outline, Ted would write the first draft. He insisted, "with all due modesty," in being part of discussions with the publisher "if I am to write the first draft of such a manuscript, regardless of the position I play in the final publication of the book." He also raised the issue of "recognition of my participation," seeming to want a measure of credit. But he added, "because of our agreement concerning the work and pay for such publications (which agreement has at least temporarily been extremely helpful to me), I am certainly unwilling to push this point."[8]

This was a reference to the agreement pledging 50% of all writing fees and royalties for anything under Kennedy's byline by Sorensen to Sorensen.

Sorensen surmised that the book being proposed would likely come in at around 150,000 words, about 70,000 of which were already extant in speeches he had written for the Senator. Thinking ahead, he also suggested they consider Senator Paul Douglas to write a foreword for the book, but added that it was "premature."

The idea was eventually abandoned, but not before Ted made a significant, and apparently frustrating, effort. That November, he had "a most satisfactory" meeting in Boston with the would-be publisher, where he promised three sample chapters before the end of the year (1953) and negotiated on the senator's behalf. He told Kennedy that "arrangements with respect to publication, circulation, pricing, and royalties all sounded very good to me indeed."[9]

The abortive book project gives us a window into the developing dynamics of the Kennedy-Sorensen process of collaboration. Apparently, Ted was struggling with the development of the writing sample. When he reached out to the Senator, Kennedy did not offer his own help, but rather he encouraged Ted to contact James Landis for assistance.

Kennedy was clearly comfortable delegating the project's details to Sorensen.

Sorensen reached out to Landis, a former dean of Harvard Law School and New Deal official who would go on to contribute to *Profiles*, a few days before Christmas. "When I indicated to the Senator that I felt my own concentration upon this subject matter had left me somewhat stale and dull in its treatment," Sorensen wrote, "He requested that I send it to you, to see if you could not add some sparkle and punch to it. I believe he has called you on this matter from Palm Beach."[10]

Sorensen then instructed Landis, "When you complete your revision of these three drafts, they may be sent air mail special delivery to Cambridge in the enclosed envelope." He also enclosed an already-written cover letter from the Senator, the carbon copy of which bore the handwritten words: "To be dated and forwarded by Dean Landis." Sorensen mentioned to Landis that Kennedy "has not seen the final version of these chapters," so he asked that copies be sent to "this office."

All this occurred while Jack Kennedy was still several months away from being nearly incapacitated by back surgery. Which begs the question: If he utilized Sorensen so much while relatively healthy and active, how much more might he rely on his gifted wordsmith while extremely ill and in painful recovery for several months?

CHAPTER 30

"A Rather Helter-Skelter Relationship"

"GOOD EVENING, I'M ED MURROW. AND THE NAME OF THE PROGRAM IS 'Person to Person'. It's all live—there's no film." The date was October 30, 1953, and the audience was America—from coast to coast.

It is hard to overstate the stature of Edward R. Murrow as a journalist and broadcaster during television's golden era. He was, by far, the very first celebrity newsman, even before the term anchorman had been invented, catapulting into the American consciousness during the dark days of the Blitz in Great Britain with his radio dispatches always beginning with his signature sign on, *This Is London*. Moving from radio to television was seamless for Murrow, first with a program called *See It Now*, then in the fall of 1953, with an interview show called *Person to Person*.

For years, Murrow was a staple in living rooms across the country with two highly popular weekly shows. He saved the hard-hitting investigative journalism for *See It Now*, but *Person to Person* featured his kinder-gentler side. It was friendly, informal—and got better ratings than the other one.[1] Murrow usually spoke with his guests as they sat in the comfortable confines of their own living rooms. The fifth episode of the new Saturday night broadcast on CBS featured two war heroes, one recently back from Korea and the other a U.S. senator who had shown his courage ten years earlier in the South Pacific.

Crews had been working throughout the day on Friday, October 30, 1953, disrupting traffic on Boston's Bowdoin Street in Boston. One camera was set for an exterior shot of an apartment building over a barbershop not far from Beacon Hill.[2] Other cameras were placed in a third-floor apartment in the building. Long a bachelor pad for Jack Kennedy when he was in town, it became for that brief moment a television stage where John F. Kennedy and his movie-star-beautiful bride of just a month were to be interviewed for fifteen minutes, enhancing their already notable celebrity.

As viewers tuned in at 10:30 p.m. Eastern Time that evening, they saw the image of Murrow, the ever-present Camel cigarette in his hand, as he introduced his first guests. He said that Kennedy had accomplished "what most American boys merely dreamed about doing." With more than a touch of hyperbole, the host described Kennedy as "a football star." He also noted that Kennedy had been a newspaper man himself. Then he mentioned Jack's "attractive bride." The couple sat on a couch, he in a conservative business suit, she in a "simple looking print dress."

The interview was largely small talk. Jack seemed comfortable, but Jackie not so much. Her few contributions to the interview were soft-spoken and brief. Murrow fed them softballs, but then, that was the purpose of the show. The broadcaster reserved his tough stuff for his other program, where he would go on to demolish Senator Joe McCarthy a few months later, live on-air, and raise awareness about poverty a few years later in a famous, and award-winning, expose called "Harvest of Shame."

Kennedy showed off a model of a PT boat, as well as the coconut bearing the carved-out message that led to the rescue of him and his crew in the South Pacific in 1943. Then, toward the end of the interview, Murrow asked Kennedy about his reading. "I used to read much," Jack replied. He then reached for a book and read aloud a favorite passage. It was a letter from the poet Alan Seeger. The passage was titled "I Have a Rendezvous with Death":

Whether I am on the winning or losing side is not the point with me; it is being on the side where my sympathies lie that matters, and I am ready to see it through to the end. Success in life means doing that thing that which nothing else conceivable seems more noble or satisfying or remunerative, and this enviable state I can truly say that I enjoy, for had I the choice I would be nowhere else in the world than where I am.

It was all very intimate, erudite—and effective.

One of his close friends expressed doubt "that Jack would have married if he had lost the senate race in 1952."[3] But Kennedy knew that having a wife was essential for higher office. So, he "reluctantly" decided to marry, "political necessities dictated that he end his career as the 'Senate's Confirmed Bachelor'." The fact was, as Herbert Parmet noted, "having a wife was a necessary prerequisite for anyone bold enough to aim for the White House."[4]

But this is not to say that there was no genuine love between Jack Kennedy and Jacqueline Bouvier. They first met in 1951 at a dinner party hosted by a mutual friend, Charlie Bartlett, the Washington correspondent for *The Chattanooga Times*.

He and Jack, both proud navy veterans, had formed a fast friendship after the war. He was also acquainted with Jackie Bouvier from summers in the Long Island Hamptons. So, when Bartlett's brother got married in 1948, he recalled trying to connect her with Jack at the wedding. In fact, he was leading her across the floor to him and got distracted by introducing her to Gene Tunney, the former heavyweight boxing champ who had dethroned the great Jack Dempsey a couple of decades earlier.

By the time they got to where Jack had been, he was gone.

It took two more years for Bartlett to put them together in the same room, this time at his home in Georgetown. Jack asked Jackie, "Shall we go someplace and have a drink?" She turned him down.[5]

But eventually they got together.

Jacqueline Lee Bouvier was twenty-nine years old when she met John F. Kennedy. She grew up on Long Island's prestigious North Shore and Washington, D.C. She was schooled at Vassar and the Sorbonne. Historian James MacGregor Burns wrote about her "exquisite features and lovely hair, her soft, shy charm, and beautifully modulated voice,"[6] as the things that attracted Jack to her.

But he took his time.

In July 1953, the cover of *LIFE Magazine* featured a photo of Jack Kennedy sailing off Cape Cod in the company of a very attractive young lady named Jacqueline Bouvier. They were smiling and looked windblown as they lounged on the sloping deck of the boat. The headline read, "Senator Kennedy Goes A-Courting."[7]

Jackie recalled, "It was a very spasmodic courtship." They went months at a time without seeing each other. "He'd call me," she said, "from some oyster bar," to catch up. Of course, he was busy running for the Senate. Meanwhile, Jackie took a job as a photographer for the Washington *Times-Herald*.

He rarely sent flowers or candy.

Books were their love language of exchange.

After two years of what was described as "a rather helter-skelter" relationship, Jack took Jackie to dinner at *Martin's Tavern* on Wisconsin

Avenue in Georgetown and asked her to marry him. Even before their society-wedding-of-the-year on September 12, 1953, they were already media superstars. Their wedding ceremony took place in Newport, Rhode Island, and was attended by a "who's who" list of more than 600 politicians, diplomats, and other movers and shakers. When she arrived at St. Mary's Roman Catholic Church in Newport, Rhode Island, for the wedding, "a crowd of 3,000 broke through the police lines and nearly crushed the bride."[8] The Archbishop of Boston, Richard Cardinal Cushing, presided, reading a blessing from Pope Pius XII. A crowd of 2,000 cheered the couple as they left St. Mary's. The reception was held at the estate of Jackie's stepfather, Hugh Auchincloss, called Hammersmith Farm, with more than 1,200 guests attending. It took the happy couple more than two hours to shake all the hands.

Some said the wedding was like a coronation.

The next day, the *New York Times* featured a large picture of the bride and groom on the top of page one, with the headline, "NOTABLES ATTEND SENATOR'S WEDDING." It was the fairy-tale wedding of the year. But the writer Gore Vidal described it in cynical terms, as "an eighteenth-century affair: a practical union on both sides."[9]

The newlyweds had barely started their Acapulco honeymoon, when Jack decided they should drive up the coast to Monterey to visit some of his friends. She "found herself subjected to a visit with people she did not know and with whom she was not very comfortable."[10] He even left her to attend a football game. Then after returning back east, they spent much of their time with his family on Cape Cod. Not a smooth start to a what was supposed to be a story-book marriage. But she was determined to make it work and play the part that seemed to be assigned to her, that of the dutiful wife of a statesman-like Senator.

It was all about image.

From the beginning, there was a growing dichotomy between the public image and the private reality in the Kennedy marriage. The first couple of years of married life for Jack and Jackie Kennedy were marked by recurring cycles of pain, surgeries, and recuperation. During this period, they forged a complicated private relationship and continued to cultivate their public image as a couple. They were described as being "like characters out of Fitzgerald, two people with old-world aspirations, but, like most Americans, self-inventing."[11] Arthur Krock had known Jackie ever since she was a young girl. He described her as a "Victorian wife, not the chic Long Island Piping Rock variety, a Beaux Arts type of girl, merry, arch, satirical terribly democratic and, yes, brilliant."[12]

The newlyweds leased a small townhouse at 3321 Dent Place, NW, in Washington within walking distance of Georgetown University. Jack encouraged Jackie to consider taking a course or two at the school—specifically to enhance her grasp of American history, something that would help both of them as his star rose. At that time, there was only one option available to a woman wanting to study at Georgetown—their School of Foreign Service.

She enrolled for the spring semester in 1954.

"Pretty Mrs. Jack Kennedy, married to a rich and handsome young Senator, is determined to help her husband politically, even if it means long hours of hard study."[13] So, read the nearly five million faithful readers of *McCall's* magazine in October 1954. The article bore the title "The Senator's Wife Goes Back to School." A two-page spread, complete with six carefully staged photos (out of nearly a thousand negatives), described the young married couple. "Shortly after the Kennedy's moved into their Georgetown house Jackie, who is a George Washington University graduate, decided to go back to school. At Georgetown University's Foreign Service School she's studying political history. According to one of her professors, she's a remarkably good student. No nonsense, he says, about cutting classes because such a diplomatic reception kept her out late at night."

The story had been pitched to Kennedy's Senate office months earlier, with a five-day photo shoot scheduled for the first week of May. It was an exercise in image building, but as one of Jackie's biographers suggests a "disillusioning knowledge on her part that makes her complicit in fashioning public image so at odds with the facts."[14]

Though Jack was almost tied to his crutches at the time of his shoot, he threw a football around with his brother Bobby. The couple is pictured walking arm in arm along the cobblestoned streets. One picture shows Kennedy helping his wife with her homework, while the reality was that

Jackie knew her husband not all that interested in her studies—or her for that matter.

Though the feature was supposed to be about her, it was quickly obvious that Jack saw it as more about him than her. But the photos flattered her, with captions like "Jackie asks questions her teachers describe as brainteasers," and "Jackie's no cook, but she sets a fine table."[15] Most likely, there was a copy of that October *McCall's* issue in the waiting room of Manhattan's Hospital for Special Surgery when Jack checked in that month for surgery.

And where he almost died.

CHAPTER 31

"A Quality Book"

IT IS DIFFICULT TO PINPOINT THE EXACT MOMENT THE IDEA FOR A BOOK called *Profiles in Courage* was conceived. It may very well have been on John F. Kennedy's mind—at least in a vague conceptual sense—for many years. It is also likely that, just as Churchill's *While England Slept* had influenced the choice of title for Kennedy's 1940 senior-thesis-turned-book, *Why England Slept*, so the Briton's *Great Contemporaries*, one of Jack's favorite books, sparked the notion to write a series of essays about great men. It is also clear that Jack Kennedy wanted to be seen as an intellectual man of letters to enhance his political persona. But clearly, conversations Jack and Jackie had during their first months of married life were also a catalyst.

Because he was in so much pain and relegated to extended bed rest, she would read biographies to him, particularly passages about politicians "who had risked their careers over principle."[1] She read to Jack about men such as Daniel Webster, the great orator; and Charles Sumner, "the vehement foe of slavery who had been bludgeoned nearly to death by an incensed Congressman." The senator was enthralled with examples of senators who were more interested in doing "the right thing that was hard instead of the wrong thing that was easy." Whatever the origin of the idea for a book, sometime in the early spring of 1954, Jack Kennedy began to make notes—mental and written—about the nature and practice of political courage.

As Jackie tried to adjust to the challenges of married life as a Kennedy in the public spotlight, she also had to face the fact that the man she had married was not well. His first years in the Senate were filled with health problems. He had been officially diagnosed with Addison's disease back in 1947, and that complicated every other physical challenge he had—especially his chronic back problems.

By 1954, Jack was having significant difficulty moving around. He had to walk sideways to go up or down stairs and experienced unbearable pain as a result of the collapse of his fifth lumbar vertebra. That summer, doctors from the Lahey Clinic in Boston met with him at Hyannis Port to recommend a surgery, with the warning that "so difficult a surgery on someone with Addison's disease posed a grave risk of a fatal infection."[2]

Jack's mother recalled that he "was determined to have the operation." He told his father that, despite the risks, "he would rather be dead than spend the rest of his life hobbling on crutches and paralyzed by pain." His father tried to persuade him against it—reminding his son that FDR had achieved great things from a wheelchair. But Jack told him, "Don't worry, Dad, I'll make it through." After several postponements, Jack finally had the surgery at Manhattan's Hospital for Special Surgery on October 21, 1954. Surgeons "performed a double fusion of spinal discs in a long operation."[3]

And they implanted a silver plate in his back.

Three days later, complications set in. Jack took a turn for the worse and went into a coma because of a serious infection. It got so bad that he was put on the critical list. Arthur Krock saw Joe Kennedy "weeping in a chair," and heard him say that "he thought Jack was dying."[4] The family was gathered, and the last rites of the Catholic church were pronounced.

Jack's recovery would take many months. He remained at the hospital in New York for several weeks in a dark room, with only his immediate family allowed to see him. But he was not getting better. In fact, he was still there in late December, when the doctors decided that he might do better in Florida. So, "attended by his wife and nurse, he was bundled in blankets on a stretcher" and driven out to LaGuardia airport where he was put on a plane to Palm Beach.

Jackie stayed by his side. She had learned how to care for Jack's wounds while in New York and helped with the nursing duties, fed him, and dressed him. She also tried to pull him out of depression, bringing him "tidbits of gossip about his family and friends, read to him, recited poetry, played checkers with him and told him about the new movies that had just been released."[5]

Jack's friend, Florida senator George Smathers, visited and recalled being troubled by his appearance. "Jack had dropped maybe 40 pounds," he said later, adding that Jack's sister joked, "It's nothing serious, just Jackie's cooking."[6] Jackie was absent for a bit during that visit, so it was up to Smathers to change the dressing. "I removed the gauze and found this huge, open, oozing, very sickly-looking hole in the middle of his back." That experience caused him to have great respect for Jackie. He said, "Anybody who could look at that festering wound day after day and go through all that agony with her husband had to have backbone."

Several weeks later, Jack was back in New York for yet another operation. The silver plate that had been implanted in his back the previous October was removed. This time he fully recovered. He walked out of the hospital on his own and headed back to Florida. Joseph Alsop, a prominent newspaper columnist of the day, reflected on Jack's ordeal, including his brush with death, "Something very important happened inside him, I think," he wrote, "when he had that illness, because he came out of it a very much more serious fellow than he was prior to it. He had gone through the valley of the shadow of death, and he displayed immense courage, which he'd always had."[7]

Kennedy returned to the Senate at the end of May 1955, having made great progress with his physical therapy. He received a hero's welcome, both at National Airport and when he arrived on Capitol Hill. Newsreel and television cameras were on hand as he made his way up the Capitol steps. Tourists shook his hand, "and a delegation of textile workers from the South that was passing by stopped to cheer him roundly."[8] When he arrived at his office, it was full of reporters. Telegrams and letters covered his desk, as did "an enormous basket of fruit bearing the tag, 'Welcome home', and signed 'Dick Nixon'."

He installed a rocking chair in his office.

Jack's brother Bobby had worked for Joe McCarthy for much of 1953. That, as well as the fact that the Wisconsin Republican was a family friend, made repudiating him difficult—even if there were policy differences. As historian James MacGregor Burns wrote, "On almost every policy issue involving McCarthy*ism*, Kennedy voted against McCarthy. Yet on the issue of McCarthy himself, Kennedy took no stand."[9]

As the time for a vote on a motion to censure McCarthy drew near, Joe Kennedy lobbied hard for his son to vote no, writing him a letter saying the whole issue was "a lot of bunk."[10] At any rate, when the issue of censure came up for a vote, Jack was still in the hospital in New York following his near-death experience. But there was a way he could have gone on the record.

Pairing.

Basically, it meant that if a senator expected to be absent for a vote, he could "pair off" with another Senator who would be present and who would vote on the other side of the question, but who would agree not to vote. The member in attendance would state that he or she had a live pair and would then announce how each of the paired members would have voted, and then would vote "present." In this way, the other member could be absent without affecting the outcome of the vote.

It is clear that Kennedy considered this, because Ted Sorensen was "at the other end of a telephone, ready and eager to fulfill such instructions on behalf of his boss."[11] But the call never came. Sorensen said, "I think he deliberately did not contact me."

Thus, Jack Kennedy became the only Democrat who did not vote against McCarthy. That singular omission would cause him much embarrassment in years to come, when critics would suggest Kennedy needed "less profile, and more courage."

There can be little doubt that Kennedy's decision to write about courage came about, at least in part, because he wanted to deflect attention from his failure to demonstrate that virtue when it came to Joe McCarthy. Of course, this would be regularly denied down through the years, even by many biographers. But the timing of Kennedy's book was surely more than coincidence.

He needed to work on his image as a politician with a backbone.

Kennedy focused on writing articles and giving policy speeches in an effort to be seen as a serious political leader—one with a promising future. And he began to rely more and more on Ted Sorensen. He cultivated relationships with Democratic leaders—including Adlai Stevenson, the 1952 presidential nominee, and Lyndon Johnson, the Texas Senator who had become the Senate Majority Leader. But it was a hard road for him. Jack's colleagues did not take him all that seriously.[12] He was young, inexperienced, prone to sickness, and despite his marriage, a compulsive playboy. And being a mere bystander the very moment the Senate finally muscled up and gave McCarthy his due, seemed to be a demonstration of excessive caution—some thought, cowardice—at a crucial time.

His thoughts were drawn to courage—the kind he admired but had recently failed to demonstrate.

Just prior to Christmas 1954, Sorensen made a passing reference to his writing work in a letter to the Senator. He told his boss, "I also hope to have ready for your perusal whenever you feel up to it after the New Year, one and possibly two articles to be submitted for publication (on Isolationism for *The New York Times* and on Examples of Political Courage)."[13]

CHAPTER 32

"The House of Harper"

ONE DAY IN DECEMBER 1954, JACKIE TOOK A BREAK FROM JACK'S HOSPITAL beside in Manhattan and took a walk. The city was in full holiday mode. She stopped at Lord & Taylor on Fifth Avenue and, by chance, ran into a friend she had worked with during her time as a photographer at the *Washington Times-Herald*. Angele Gingras was beginning her career as a humor writer, and her name would one day be attached to an award presented annually by the National Press Club. They were in the store's section where fabric to make clothes could be ordered. Pulling up a couple of chairs, they caught up for the better part of an hour. Gingras recalled Jackie talking about her husband's surgery.

Jackie also mentioned that Jack was thinking about writing another book.

Angele knew her way around the publishing business, and Jackie asked her for advice about things like literary agents, recommendations, and making multiple submissions. Gingras advised Jackie not to send the book to "more than one publisher at a time."[1] And Jackie knew just the man she would approach first.

Cass Canfield.

Canfield, a giant in the publishing world, was named after his famous grandfather, the nineteenth-century statesman Lewis Cass, who had served as Governor of Michigan, Secretary of War (under Andrew Jackson), and was the Democratic nominee for President in 1848, losing to Zachary Taylor. Following his education at Harvard, then Oxford, Canfield spent some time in his early twenties traveling on foot along Marco Polo's routes (later called the Burma Road), before moving to New York to work as an advertising representative for a newspaper. Evan Thomas III recalled his father, who worked with Canfield, once saying, "Cass was born with a silver spoon in his mouth and enjoyed the taste of it."[2]

In 1924, Canfield went to work for *Harper and Brothers* and was sent to Great Britain to run the publisher's London office, where he was described as "a refreshing presence among the leading British book publishers."[3]

Canfield was said to have a sixth sense when it came to potential authors. In fact, he liked to carry a blank contract in his pocket just in case. He would go on to run what was dubbed "The House of Harper" for thirty-six years and became "the most demanding editorial figure in the modern history of book publishing."[4] William Targ, an editor who would one day publish Mario Puzo's *The Godfather*, said: "Canfield was a working stiff with style; he was shrewd, nimble-footed, and nervy, able to make a quick decision or a deal. He worked with duchesses as well as longshoremen, not too worried about ethics or fine points of negotiation. A bookman. A collector of William Blake. A cool man, gifted with humor, taste, and especially a zest for good living."[5]

A bald man with a sparse mustache, Canfield stood a little over six feet tall and was seen by many to be as "imposing as Moses." By 1954, he was fifty-eight years old and had been with *Harper and Brothers* (later known as *Harper & Row*) for thirty years. He was chairman of the board and always on the lookout for the next bestseller. "A quality book," he once said, "is the safest thing a publisher can take on."[6] He believed that a good book would find its own market and pay for itself. He loved his work and believed it was a calling, of sorts. His philosophy was that a publisher "should always be on the receiving end. He should take an interest in almost any subject and remain anonymous, letting the author take the center stage." And it just so happened that his adopted son, Michael, was married to Jackie Kennedy's sister, Lee.

On Jackie's recommendation, a proposal was put together for Canfield, one that described an idea for a lengthy article (presumably for *Harper's Magazine*), no doubt drafted and refined by Ted Sorensen, because at the time, Jack was still hospitalized in New York and only slowly recovering from his life-threatening first surgery. Canfield was in Europe when Kennedy's query arrived, so it landed on the desk of one of his editors, Evan Thomas, which turned out to be a very good thing. Thomas immediately saw the potential for more than an article. But when his boss returned and looked the proposal over, he didn't think much of the idea, writing to Kennedy that he "got rather bogged down" when reading it and decided to pass.[7]

Cass did, however—at the urging of Thomas—extend the courtesy of sharing some suggestions that might make for a feasible and publishable *book*. Kennedy was grateful for the encouragement and wrote to Canfield from Palm Beach: "Many thanks for your kind wire and letter concerning my proposal for a small book on '*Patterns of Political Courage*'. I certainly appreciate your willing interest and helpful suggestions."[8]

The idea originally proposed was too small for Canfield's taste. He told Kennedy that "the dramatic interest" could be strengthened by going more in-depth into the "historical context" of each case history. He also suggested that each profile Jack developed should run 5,000 to 8,000 words, and that the book should be at least 60,000 words. Jack took the advice to heart and offered one significant change in his approach to the material. He told Canfield that he was going to "restrict the major examples to acts of political courage performed by United States Senators." Originally, he had thought to include political leaders who had not served in the Senate.

Kennedy remained positive and determined in spite of the publisher's initial rejection, closing his letter to Canfield with the statement, "I intend to begin work on a complete book-length manuscript immediately, and I will be most appreciative for your further suggestions and assistance." Canfield gave Jack's reply and the whole file over to Thomas.

It was good for Kennedy that he did.

CHAPTER 33

"It Was All Very Collaborative"

BACK IN THE 1920S, ADDISON MIZNER, AN ENGINEER WHO WAS passionate about Spanish-style design, structures with barrel-tile roofs and stucco walls, was all the rage in South Florida. In fact, he was the primary driving force for the much of the architectural transformation of South Florida during that decade's real estate boom. Among the many homes he designed in Palm Beach was an eleven-bedroom mansion located at 1095 North Ocean Boulevard. The house was built for Rodman Wanamaker, a department store magnate who owned massive stores in Philadelphia, Manhattan, and Paris.

A few years after Wanamaker's death and as the Great Depression dramatically deflated property values, Joseph P. Kennedy purchased the Florida home, complete with its two outbuildings and 200 feet of ocean beachfront for the bargain basement price of $120,000. The compound became a stomping ground, second only to Hyannis Port, for all things Kennedy for generations to come. In the early 1960s, it would be popularly known as the Winter White House. But in late February 1955, it was, at least in part, a convalescent hospital for Senator John F. Kennedy as he recuperated from the pair of surgeries that had taken him to the brink of death.

Jack spent almost all of his time during the three-month stay in Palm Beach in a specially outfitted two-room suite on the first floor of the mansion, "only a step or two above the level of the lawn."[1] The rooms had been converted into "a bedroom-study." Books were scattered everywhere in suite, "piled high on cabinets, bookcases, and the mantelpiece." Though, Jack had always been a voracious reader, the presence of so many volumes in that small space was indicative of his current preoccupation. There was also a hospital bed surrounded by "work tables, filing cabinets, a dictating machine, and, at a handy distance, a telephone."

As his health improved, Kennedy fell into a daily routine, of sorts. He would start his day around eight o'clock with breakfast in bed, which typically consisted of a couple of poached eggs, toast, marmalade, crisp broiled bacon, orange juice, milk, and coffee. Then he would read several newspapers, usually including the *New York Times*, the *Miami Herald*, the *Boston Globe*, and one of his favorites: *The Christian Science Monitor*. He also read the *Congressional Record* from the previous day.

Then there was the mail.

Jack told one reporter, Minna Littmann from the New Bedford (MA) *Standard-Times*, "Most of my mail has gone directly to my office in Washington, but there is always some to handle here. I have dictated my replies, and send the tape recordings and the originals by air-mail to Washington, every night, for my office staff to take care of." He also spoke by telephone to staff members most afternoons.

Then he found time to write.

He wrote down his thoughts "on heavy white paper in a red stiff-covered 'minute' book of the type used in law offices."[2] Constantly, he found his thoughts "would race ahead of his power to get the words out as he wished them to appear; he paused often to cross out sentences and paragraphs and make additions in the margins." Then, he dictated drafts to a secretary.

Because of his severe back pain, Kennedy would frequently have to work while lying flat on his bed, "writing almost upside down on a board over his head."[3] But there is the possibility that some of this was staged for visitors as Jack wanted to convey the image of a busy senator hard at work even from his sickbed.

Visitors who came by would often be treated to a look at the eight-inch wound on his back, complete with its regular oozing discharge. With his weight down to 115 pounds, his guests were regularly horrified by how he looked.

But whatever the controversy to come about his actual full authorship of *Profiles*, one thing is clear—John F. Kennedy, in fact, demonstrated a great deal of courage and the kind of "grace under pressure" he would describe, by trying to do anything at all under such circumstances.

Sorensen's work on so many articles published in Kennedy's name led seamlessly to his involvement with *Profiles in Courage*. Kennedy called him into his office one day in the autumn of 1954, and they had a conversation about a potential magazine article—this one about "the history of senatorial courage."[4] Jack had been reading *The Price of Union*, by Herbert Agar, and he showed Ted a passage that dealt with John Quincy Adams.

Agar's book was a Kennedy favorite. He always kept it handy. In fact, there was a copy of it on the Resolute desk in the Oval Office on

November 22, 1963. The book discussed the unique kind of democracy in American history—particularly the party system. Kennedy told Sorensen that he wanted to develop a piece "exploring the willingness of elected officials to defy the pressure of powerful interest groups, or the protests of concerned constituents."

Sorensen speculated that because Kennedy's health problems made him face the prospect of an early death, "he decided to make more of his life, to become more serious about his career." He placed the time line of Kennedy's decision to turn the project into a full-length book to when he was convalescing in Florida in December 1954. He had just finished a 1,200-word article for Kennedy that would run in the *New York Times Magazine*, and he told his boss, during a phone call between Washington and Palm Beach, that writing a full-length book "would require the equivalent of fifty such articles."

Sorensen kicked into full research mode and reached out to Dr. George B. Galloway in the Legislative Reference Service at the Library of Congress for help. In a letter written on January 21, 1955, and as his boss languished in pain in Florida, Ted dropped his boss's name: "Senator Kennedy is in the midst of some writing on the subject of historical examples of political courage—men who risked their careers in order to stand up for a principle as their conscience directed. The Senator was hopeful that you would have some additional examples to suggest . . . Inasmuch as Senator Kennedy has rather urgently requested materials on these further examples, I hope to hear from you at your earliest convenience."

In February 1955, as he immersed himself in the project, Ted wrote to Kennedy describing the task at hand, calling it a "monumental work"[5] and "the most gigantic undertaking we have ever gigantically taken." He even, with words bordering on hysteria, compared the project to Gibbon's *Rise and Fall of the Roman Empire*. Soon Sorensen was facilitating the shipment of books and research material to his boss who remained confined to bed. There was a joke around Kennedy's Senate office that the regular shipments were being sent to "the Library of Congress Palm Beach Annex."[6]

By all accounts, Kennedy and Sorensen kept each other very busy during their long-distance period that winter and spring. Daily dispatches from Florida would include material to be typed, tapes to be transcribed, and instructions about additional research that was needed. Sorensen and his secretary flew to Palm Beach twice during Jack's time there, both trips lasting nearly two weeks.

It was all very collaborative.

Many years later, in a candid moment toward the end of his life, Sorensen wrote: "Like JFK's speeches, *Profiles in Courage* was a collaboration, and not a particularly unusual one, inasmuch as our method of collaboration on the book was similar to the method we used on his speeches."[7] Television personality and Kennedy biographer Chris Matthews affirmed this, writing: "Though Kennedy dug up the stories and sketched out his intentions, Ted Sorensen did most of the actual writing. So, it's fair to call the project a collaboration."[8]

More than fifty years after *Profiles in Courage* was published, Sorensen reflected on his involvement: "Is the author the person who did much of the research and helped choose the words in many of its sentences, or is the author the person who decided the substance, structure, and theme of the book; read and revised each draft; inspired, constructed, and improved the work?"

Good question.

CHAPTER 34

"Our Monumental Work"

"The article on 'Political Courage' should be on its way to you shortly, so don't despair," Ted wrote to Kennedy on January 14, 1955.[1] The future bestseller was as yet just an embryonic article. But that was about to change as the Senator tasked him with developing a comprehensive outline for a small book-length treatment of the subject.

Sorensen went to work, spending twelve hours a day on the project over the next few months. He preferred to write by hand. "I literally thought through my pen," he said.[2] He also described his style as "painstaking," choosing each word carefully. And he required a completely quiet environment when working.

Even a surface examination of the correspondence and memoranda going back and forth between Sorensen and Kennedy makes it clear that Sorensen was doing most, if not all, of the actual writing, with Kennedy functioning as more of an editor. And the ongoing collaborative conversation was strongly tilted to one side—with Sorensen initiating contact and asking all the questions.

Jack's sister Eunice Shriver lived in Chicago, where her husband, Sargent Shriver, ran The Merchandise Mart for his father-in-law, Joe Kennedy. She wrote to Ted Sorensen in January 1955: "I talked with Jack last night and he tells me that his article on 'Political Courage' is about to expand into a book." She added, "I heard a compliment about you a couple of weeks ago. Jack said you are the smartest man he has ever met." She later told him, "You may leave your eyes at the blood bank when you die, but please, bequeath your brains to me."[3]

By late January, Sorensen was fully immersed in the new book. He was balancing family and career, with the latter seeming to win much of the time. His wife, Camilla, was due with their third child in March, and Ted was anxious about getting significant writing done before then. The birth of Phillip Sorensen made them a family of five, including Eric and Steve. It was good that his extra income had enabled them to buy the house in McLean "with a built-in football field in the rear and a regular guest room."

He wrote to his boss, "My present suggestion is that I might submit to you a manuscript of the appropriate length desired well in advance of the publisher's deadline, and we could then complete the editing on a joint basis."[4] He was clearly the driving force in creating the book's initial content, bearing in mind that Kennedy was in Florida with a gaping and oozing hole in his back and not able to do much of anything in the interim between his first, unsuccessful, surgery, and the next one that would turn out much better.

On the last day of January 1955, Sorensen sent Kennedy an outline and synopsis of the book, "in order to give me some perspective of the entire work, the references I would need, approximate space requirements, etc."[5] He estimated that the book would not likely exceed 39,000 words. His idea was that it would be a "small book" modeled on one that had been recently written by Senator Paul Douglas called *Ethics in Government*. He did have one task for his boss: "You might want to give some thought as to what well-known figure would write a foreword for you." He suggested a few names: Learned Hand, Walter Lippmann, Bernard Baruch, Adlai Stevenson, and Paul Douglas.

Unlike how he felt about their earlier attempt at a book—the one about the economy in New England—Sorensen found this new project anything but dull and uninteresting. In early February, he sent Kennedy two chapters in, what he described as "our monumental work."[6]

A few days later, Ted sent Kennedy drafted chapters on Edmund G. Ross, John Quincy Adams, Daniel Webster, and George Norris, a fellow-Nebraskan.[7] Sorensen lobbied hard for the inclusion of Norris, but Kennedy had doubts about him, as well as Daniel Webster, as subjects for the book. Sorensen pressed: "I know you have had some doubt about both the Webster and Norris cases," but he had done some research and was convinced that Webster's "Seventh of March Speech was an act of statesmanship; and the abuse Norris received, the critical resolutions of the legislature and his own suggested resignation make his case the best example of twentieth century courage I have been able to find." He also appealed to Kennedy's sympathy regarding all of his effort, hoping to someday "immodestly tell you of our trials and tribulations in turning this out." Sorensen certainly saw himself as the book's workhorse.

With that same letter, Sorensen sent Kennedy six complete chapters, "for a total of 21,000 words (or the equivalent of about nine *New York Times* articles)." That standard of measurement seemed important to him.

He also included a writing schedule that "brings up-to-date my concept of the finished book."

In early February, Ted sent his boss more drafted chapters, this time dealing with John Tyler and Sam Houston, along with a revised outline. He told Kennedy, "Drafts sent to you thus far total 36,500 words (or, as I like to keep reminding myself, about 15 *New York Times* articles)."[8] His progress in that first month was impressive, and it is clear that Sorensen wrote the first draft of the book. He longed for his boss's input, writing "If you can let me know what you feel the gaps to be." He also hoped to meet his boss in person (as Kennedy remained in Florida). "Perhaps if and when we get together, I could bring with me a suitcase full of practically all the major reference texts used, plus all my original research notes."

As already noted, early on in the process, Sorensen lobbied hard to include one of his heroes in the book—Senator George Norris of Nebraska. Senator Norris had ruffled the feathers of his fellow Republicans that election year, by taking a pass on endorsing his own party's nominee for President—Herbert Hoover—in favor of the more liberal Democrat Al Smith, the Governor of New York. As a Progressive Republican, he felt Hoover was heavily influenced by what we would these days call big business. So, Norris came out for Smith, even though that would mean he, as a nondrinker and supporter of Prohibition, would be supporting an anti-Prohibition candidate, who was also Roman Catholic.

Sorensen wrote to his father back in Nebraska asking for anything that might help: "We have decided to expand the Norris chapter to include his support of Al Smith in 1928. As I recall, you headed the Norris for President organization that year (taking time out only to preside over the birth of your favorite son). I wonder if your files might contain some materials relating to Norris's support of Smith . . . as usual, we're in a terrible rush for this."[9] C. A. Sorensen sent his son files with correspondence for the years 1924–1930, along with a selection of newspaper articles he had kept through the years, all of which helped Ted with his research.

Many others gave Kennedy recommendations for his growing list of intrepid statesmen. Arthur Krock, who had been so vital to the success of Kennedy's first book, *Why England Slept*, suggested the inclusion of Robert Taft. Taft would not be the only member of the GOP to be considered for the inclusion in the book—George Norris was also a Republican. But Norris had died more than a decade earlier and had been more in line with what diehards today might call a RINO—Republican in name only. In fact, during his final years in the Senate, Norris switched his party affiliation to "Independent."

Taft, however, was another story.

Though the senator from Ohio had died in 1953, he was not only affiliated with the GOP, he was referred to by most of his colleagues as "Mr. Republican." Taft had spent his career as a vocal opponent of prototypical Democratic policies, such as FDR's New Deal. And he had nearly become the first Republican president in a generation, before losing his party's nomination to a late comer named Eisenhower in 1952.

For his part, Kennedy was initially reluctant to include Taft in the book, fearing that it might imply "endorsement of a contemporary and only recently deceased conservative Republican."[10] But Krock believed Taft's unpopular stand against the Nuremberg Trials in the aftermath of World War II made the Ohioan a perfect fit for the book. Kennedy eventually agreed and Taft made the final cut. The rest of the list was in place by mid-March.

Kennedy's book would shine a light on the political courage of eight U.S. senators at pivotal moments in their careers: *John Quincy Adams, Daniel Webster, Thomas Hart Benton, Sam Houston, Edmund G. Ross, Lucius Quintus Cincinnatus Lamar, George Norris,* and *Robert Taft.*

CHAPTER 35

"The Professor"

GEORGETOWN UNIVERSITY PROFESSOR JULES DAVIDS LOOKED THE PART, like someone direct from Central Casting—with his horn-rimmed glasses, and a pipe usually close at hand—though at thirty-four years of age he was among the younger members of Georgetown University's prestigious faculty. Scholarship was his forte, and he loved helping students realize their goals. One of his colleagues described Davids as "one of our great teachers. And always available for students."[1] To his students, "he exemplified the very meaning of the word, 'mentor'." Brooklyn born and educated at Brooklyn College and Georgetown, Davids went on to become a highly regarded and well-published professor during a forty-year career at Georgetown.

One day in early 1954, Professor Davids was gathering his papers to put them in his satchel as he prepared to leave the classroom following a particularly animated lecture about John Adams' conflict with Alexander Hamilton and the XYZ affair, which led to Adams' political downfall. It was part of the curriculum for a course called *History of the United States II*. He was approached by one of his students who asked if she could speak with him for a moment.

Davids had been embarrassed when he first noticed this young lady in his class a few weeks earlier, because everyone else knew who she was. But he had acted like the classic absent-minded professor undistracted by popular culture. On the first day of class, the small group of about fifteen students applauded when Jacqueline Kennedy entered the room. Davids thought it was because she was a rare female student in the nearly all-male student body at the time. Now, he knew— she was the movie-star-attractive young wife of U.S. senator John F. Kennedy. As they talked, Davids learned that Jackie Kennedy had been captivated by his lectures and had discussed them with her husband at length. She asked Dr. Davids that day if he might be able to help her husband with a writing project he was contemplating by suggesting some historical figures from American politics who had manifested unique courage.[2]

Next to Ted Sorensen, Jules Davids was the most significant contributor to Kennedy's book. Through the years, Davids was insistent that he and Sorensen "did much of the work on *Profiles in Courage*."[3] He was adamant that they "shaped the thing and wrote most of it. You could almost call it a government paper, a position paper, with sundry drafts and revisions prepared by editors, aides, research assistants, secretaries, and advisors."

A quarter of a century after his front-of-the-classroom conversation with Jackie, Professor Davids wrote a letter to Kennedy biographer Herbert Parmet in response to a query about his early involvement in the development of *Profiles*. That letter, dated November 30, 1978, indicated that Davids clearly felt his role had been understated and overlooked. He wrote, "Since the book was to be on political courage, I have always felt that my lecture and Jacqueline's presence in my class were connected directly with triggering John Kennedy's interest in the subject of political courage in American history. It is conceivable that this was coincidental; but I believe not likely."[4] Professor Davids believed that Jackie's studies under him were a real factor helping Jack "to trigger his own contemplation of the American past."[5]

Nearly a year after that initial conversation with Jackie, Davids received a call from Ted Sorensen, who told him that Senator Kennedy was planning to write a book. He asked if the professor would be willing to help. Davids was sure that Jacqueline recommended him to her husband, triggering Sorensen's call. Kennedy's assistant told Davids that the project had a small budget and was not likely to be a commercial success, but he mentioned that the professor would be paid for his assistance.[6]

More than forty years later, a letter was found in a collection of Dr. Davids' materials at the Georgetown University Library. Dated August 5, 1957, it was written in answer to a query from Father Brian McGrath, the Dean of Georgetown's College of Arts and Sciences at the time. He had asked Davids about his role in the research and writing of Kennedy's book.

Davids replied: "In January 1955, Mr. Sorensen in Senator Kennedy's office called me and asked me if I would be willing to help the Senator write a book. He told me that the Senator had requested him to get in touch with me."[7] Sorensen told the professor that the book idea had already been rejected by a publisher, "and the Senator was very anxious to work up four or five chapters in published form to be resubmitted."[8] Davids agreed to help and Sorensen sent him the draft of several chapters.

They were in a "black, loose-leaf notebook." The professor studied the material thoroughly and prepared a memo for Kennedy and Sorensen.

By the time Kennedy saw Davids' memo, he was recovering in Florida from his second surgery. He contacted the professor and told him that his suggestions were "excellent," and then directed the professor to start reworking the chapters. Davids did this and noted later that all of his "recommendations were later used in the final drafting of the book."

Despite a critique that some authors might have found discouraging, Jack Kennedy, without a hint of defensiveness, sent a handwritten reply to the professor. He wrote: "Dear Dr. Davids, I was delighted to learn from Ted Sorensen that it would be possible for you to arrange your schedule to assist us in the preparation of the book. I thought your memorandum was excellent and should prove most beneficial. I will be in touch with you and I will look forward to seeing you in April."

CHAPTER 36

"Davids Was Paid a Mere $700"

Dated February 24, 1955, the Dr. Jules Davids' memo was written on letterhead bearing the words, SCHOOL OF FOREIGN SERVICE GEORGETOWN UNIVERSITY, and was titled "Evaluation of Draft of Patterns of Political Courage."[1]

Davids began, "The basic thesis of *Patterns of Political Courage* is excellent, and a good deal could be done with the material. There are, however, a number of weaknesses in the draft, and before proceeding with additional research, I should like to offer some overall constructive criticism that may be useful."

The professor wrote that the purpose of the book was "generally lost for three reasons, which I wish to explain." Those three reasons, he said, were: The Structure . . . The Method . . . Total Effect."

On the first issue, that of structure, he told Kennedy that he included too many examples of political courage and they "varied in quality and value." He felt that the material emphasized the same points "over and over again." He added, "The result is that many of the chapters tend to become repetitious without any transition from one individual to another." Davids was ultimately responsible for getting Kennedy and Sorensen to focus completely on men who had served in the U.S. Senate.

Regarding the "method," Davids criticized the fact that none of the subjects "become sufficiently alive so that we know them as a person . . . it does not give us insight into the character of the individual, nor the sufficient, historical perspective." He insisted that, "where the Senators are vital and alive, and the issues crucial, the material is excellent, e.g., the chapters on Senators Thomas Hart Benton, Sam Houston, and Edmund Ross; but in most of the other cases, the material becomes dull and uninteresting."

As to the "total effect," Davids made an astute observation: "The examples of political courage are good. But very often, in order to heighten the drama and strength of the political courage, there is a tendency to emphasize the calamity which followed (political defeat or complete ruin), e.g., Edmund Ross and the other Senators who voted 'not guilty' on the impeachment of Johnson, the pathetic disavowal of Sam Houston, the crushing political defeat of Benton, and the like. The effect of this approach is to weaken substantially the inspirational purpose of the book and to produce a result entirely opposite from the one intended, namely, compassion and sympathy for those who boldly expressed their political courage, rather than admiration."

All in all, it was a pretty tough critique. He said, "The beginning is weak, the middle is strong, and it falls to pieces in a hodgepodge at the end." But he offered some constructive suggestions, as well: "The examples might follow a historical chronological order (which appears to be the intention of the book). Each Senator could then be used as a springboard to develop a historical period; the issue pointedly worked out, and great emphasis might be placed on the personality and character of the individual. Some care would have to be taken to make sure that there is some balance in the structure."

He added a few other suggestions. "Chapter 10 should be integrated with chapter 7 on Edmund Ross, or omitted completely," he wrote. He also suggested a "catchy title" for each chapter. He summed it all up in the final paragraph: "I believe that with a more clearly defined approach, and a better handling of the organization, the book would be able to stand on its own two feet. Before I get very far advanced in my own research, I think it is most important to clarify the method of approach, since this would have a direct relation to the type of material I would be interested in extracting."

Professor Davids then went to work on a draft of the chapter about Daniel Webster. Sorensen had indicated a certain urgency, so Davids worked tirelessly for several days, crafting a 22-page chapter on the Massachusetts Senator. He turned the project around quickly, getting it to Kennedy on March 5.

In the cover letter sent with the Webster draft, Davids wrote: "Because of the limitation of time, I have not made any attempt at original research—although this might be possible, since the Library of Congress's Manuscript Division has a huge collection of documents, but it would take a considerable amount of effort to sift through the material."

Sorensen forwarded the professor's Webster material, without his knowledge, to historian Arthur Schlesinger for his review, but Davids never saw any of the notes.

Ultimately, the Georgetown professor sent in a 26-page chapter about Sam Houston, a 24-page section about Lucius Q. C. Lamar, and yet another 26-page chapter on George W. Norris. All this in less than two months. Finally, on April 27, he sent over thirteen pages on "The Meaning of Political Courage."[2]

Kennedy wrote this simple acknowledgment in the Preface to *Profiles*: "Professor Jules Davids of Georgetown University assisted materially in the preparation of several chapters." But it was clearly an understatement. In his 1957 letter to Father McGrath, Davids made a mild complaint. "In view of the subsequent success of '*Profiles in Courage*'," he wrote, I have, of course, felt that the remuneration was pitifully small."

In fact, Professor Jules Davids was paid a mere $700 for all his significant efforts.

Though Davids' involvement in *Profiles* was well known to those closest to him, the public, by and large, knew nothing about it but for the single line in Kennedy's preface, until 1978, when Herbert Parmet highlighted his role in his book, *Jack: The Struggles of John F. Kennedy*. It begs the question:

Why didn't the professor insist on credit?

The answer seems to lie in Dr. Jules Davids' personality. Those who knew him best focused on the man's modesty, describing him as gentle and "not a man interested in fame."[3] He was, in fact, known to "take less than full credit" on many occasions throughout his career.

This begs yet another question: What might have been different if the historian Sorensen and Kennedy relied on for so much of the work on *Profiles* had been someone much more interested in making a name for himself? Or money? A credible claim against Kennedy's sole authorship during the early rollout of Kennedy's book would have certainly threatened his eventual campaign to be president of the United States.

Davids kept his head down and his mouth shut. Likely, he had a sense that he should have insisted on something more for his involvement at the beginning, but that he was stuck with the deal he had struck. He was certainly grateful for the opportunity to help Kennedy, and he was proud of his work. He was also glad to see the book succeed.

He sent Kennedy a congratulatory note shortly after *Profiles* was published. Writing on February 15, 1956, from his home in Kensington, Maryland, he said, "I have been following the reviews and write-ups of *Profiles in Courage* during the past few weeks. It has been a genuine thrill to me to feel that in a small way I was a part of the great book that was written. I want to express my appreciation and thanks for the opportunity you gave me. I feel from the beginning that the theme was excellent. But more than that, you have succeeded in revitalizing our philosophy of American democracy. It has been wonderful to see the effect which the book has had throughout the United States."

Bearing in mind that Davids later described the book as "a government paper, a position paper, with sundry drafts and revisions prepared by editors, aides, research assistants, secretaries, and advisors," it is interesting to note that in his letter to Kennedy, he refers to "the" book and "the great book," seemingly careful not to speak of it as Kennedy's book.

Kennedy possibly picked up on that nuance, as well. In his reply to the professor on February 27, 1956, he wrote: "Many thanks for your letter of recent date and your very kind remarks concerning *my* book [*emphasis added*]. I certainly appreciate your writing me and I want to thank you for your assistance in the writing of the book. It was very helpful."

But the professor's soft complaint to Father McGrath about the size of his "fee" seems to be his final statement on the issue, at the time. Of course, he had already expressed himself in his essay on "The Meaning of Political Courage." He said then:

The strength of character of a person is of tremendous importance. Ambition is a strong motivating force within the individual. And in politics, ambition can frequently be furthered by political opportunism. To rise above personal ambition, and to divest one's self from political opportunism by stubbornly insisting that the matter of principle comes first is not easy. It calls for integrity and an innate sense of intellectual honesty.

Indeed.

CHAPTER 37

"Some Political Scientists and Historians"

JAMES LANDIS SEEMED TO HAVE A PERPETUAL SCOWL ON HIS FACE, ONE that was featured on the cover of *Business Week* magazine in 1934 when he was appointed by President Franklin Roosevelt as one of the directors of the new Securities and Exchange Commission, a New Deal entity created in the wake of the Securities and Exchange Act. Landis was one of the authors of that Great Depression legislation, and he was on loan to the government from Harvard, where he was a law professor.

It was around this time that the lawyer-professor met Joseph P. Kennedy, the SEC's first Chairman. Landis "grew to admire Kennedy."[1] Kennedy quickly discerned Landis to be a talent man and leaned hard on him as his number one assistant. When Kennedy left the agency after less than a year at the helm, Landis took his place as chairman.

Over the next decade, he bounced back and forth between Harvard, where he eventually became Dean of the Law School, and government work. Following the war, he resigned his position at Harvard to become President Harry Truman's Chairman of the Civil Aeronautics Board. But Truman fired him in 1947, leaving Landis unemployed and low on prospects.

Then Joe Kennedy came to the rescue.

Landis got a call from Kennedy, who was at his Palm Beach Estate, with a job offer to be his personal lawyer for, "Kennedy Enterprises." When Landis asked Kennedy what that was, the multimillionaire replied, "Oh, we'll figure that out after you're down here."

While working for Kennedy, Landis formed his own highly successful law firm with offices in Washington, D.C. and New York. Later he helped with Jack's presidential campaign in 1960 and wrote a detailed pre-inaugural report for President-elect Kennedy analyzing the federal government's administrative agencies. He was then appointed to the White House as a special assistant in charge of regulatory reform.

Landis was one of a cast of characters Kennedy enlisted to help with *Profiles*, a group that also included Arthur Schlesinger, Jr., Walter Johnson, James MacGregor Burns, Allen Nevins, and Arthur Holcombe.

On May 3, Landis sent Sorensen a lengthy memo about *Profiles*. He suggested an outline for the book's prologue. "It should be as personal as it can be made," he wrote. "The material on the history and development of the Senate should not be the substance of this prologue, but should be utilized as introductions to groups of sketches, e.g., Adams, then the 1850 group, then Ross, then Norris and Taft."[2]

Landis encouraged "a soul-searching analysis of the role of a Senator," noting, "That role has changed over the years." In the early days, he wrote, "it was an easy role. Today, it is otherwise, and also today, it is frequently forgotten amid the press of business that now absorbed the energies of a Senator." The lawyer told Kennedy and Sorensen that "it will not be easy writing. It requires thought rather than research. But well done, it will hit with the power of a hydrogen bomb."

Jack was likely "amused by the metaphor."[3]

The second professor Jack reached out to was James MacGregor Burns. He really didn't know Burns all that well, and their back and forth early in 1955 was really an introduction of sorts for both men. Burns recalled, "It was my first real contact with Kennedy. He wrote me and I assume other academic people in Massachusetts and perhaps outside. First, as I recall, asking for suggestions for the pantheon of courageous people. Probably spelling out a bit what his criteria were, and I responded to that letter."[4]

Writing from his Williams College office in the Berkshires on March 16, Burns told Kennedy that the list he was developing for the book was "an impressive compilation."[5] He bemoaned the fact that there were only two of the politicians to be profiled who were from the twentieth century. He suggested, "Two or three Senators who opposed the court-packing bill in 1937 at a time when opposition to FDR was not too popular with the people," adding in parenthesis, "I take it that the test here is courage and not necessarily wisdom." He also questioned Jack's decision to limit his case studies to Senators, suggesting, "Some of our Presidents have shown great courage."

Interestingly, it appears that Professor Burns was the first to suggest something that would eventually become part of the very first sentence of

Profiles. He told Kennedy to "include Hemingway's famous remark about courage as 'grace under pressure'." Burns told Kennedy he had discussed the project "with some political scientists and historians," and President Truman's name kept coming up, "his recall of MacArthur, his action in the face of Korean aggression, his fight for reelection, and so on."

Arthur Krock, "the dean of the Washington newsmen," was the Washington Bureau Chief for the *New York Times*, a three-time winner of the Pulitzer, and was on Joseph Kennedy's payroll for many years. He rewrote Jack Kennedy's Harvard thesis to make it publishable as *Why England Slept* and worked tirelessly behind the scenes lobbying the Pulitzer Prize committee in 1957 for *Profiles in Courage*. *Source*: Wikimedia Commons.

HARPER & BROTHERS

PUBLISHERS SINCE 1817

REC'D MAY 10 1957

49 East 33rd Street, New York 16, N.Y.

May 8, 1957

Dear Jack,

Just to put in writing what I told Ted this morning on the phone:

The Book-of-the-Month Club wants to offer their members a special alternate to their August selection; this alternate to consist of PROFILES IN COURAGE, and Kenneth Roberts' BOON ISLAND, for $4.95. This offer is conditional upon both Roberts and Kennedy agreeing, hence my call to Ted. We are reasonably certain that Roberts will agree. So if the deal works out as we expect it to, we will be paid $6,000 against a royalty of 24.-something cents a copy, to be divided evenly between author and publisher. Publisher will bear the cost of any plates which may have to be made, and we will put a part of our share into advertising. The BOM will begin their mailing to 500,000 names. This is obviously good medicine.

I will be in Washington Monday and Tuesday, and will call or drop by. Again, my congratulations on the Pulitzer Prize. Our total sales are now 96,000, and this should bring us over the 100,000 mark within the near future. We have sent books out all over the country on consignment, plus Pulitzer Prize bands to go around the jackets. You have doubtless seen the daily _Times_ ad, and there will be a big two-color ad on Sunday the 19th.

Regards,

Evan (y.y.)

Evan Thomas

P.S. I can't get our friend Chuck Spaulding to answer his mail or his phone. I made a lunch date with him months ago, but he never appeared. Now some new fellow is writing us from the Kraft Television Theatre. Is Chuck alive or dead?

The Honorable John Kennedy
Senate Office Building
Washington, D. C.

EWT:jbp

CABLE ADDRESS : HARPSAM · TELEPHONE : MURRAY HILL 3-1900

Hard-copy sales of _Profiles_ were brisk throughout 1956, reaching the 80,000 mark by the end of the year. _Source_: John F. Kennedy Presidential Library and Museum.

In many ways, there would have been no *Profiles*, no Pulitzer, and maybe no presidency for John F. Kennedy without the support of his editor, Evan Thomas. *Source*: Courtesy of Evan Thomas III.

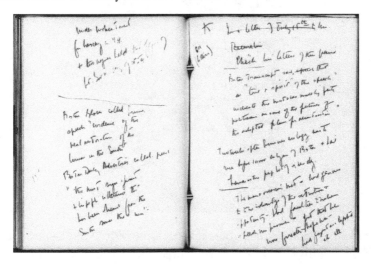

Reading Kennedy's handwriting was a challenge to staff members and editors. *Source*: John F. Kennedy Presidential Library and Museum.

The Ambassador, Joseph P. Kennedy, was the driving force behind his son's Pulitzer Prize award in 1957. *Source*: Library of Congress.

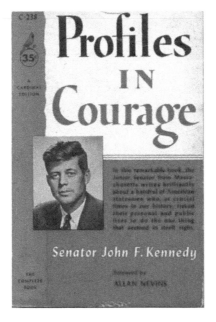

Pocket Books published the paperback version of *Profiles* as a Cardinal Edition. *Source*: John F. Kennedy Presidential Library and Museum.

Jack Kennedy called Ted Sorensen his "alter ego," but Jackie Kennedy thought her husband's relationship with Ted was "creepy." *Source*: National Archives.

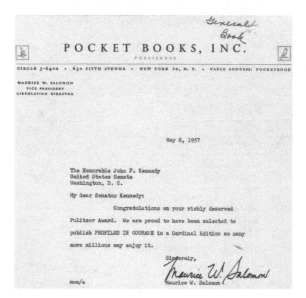

Congratulatory letter to Kennedy for winning the Pulitzer Prize. *Source*: John F. Kennedy Presidential Library and Museum.

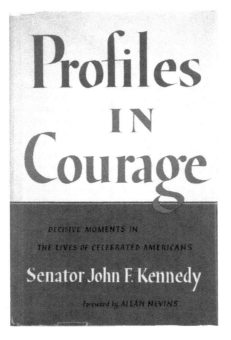

The first edition of *Profiles*, January 1956; the retail price was $3.50. *Source*: John F. Kennedy Presidential Library and Museum.

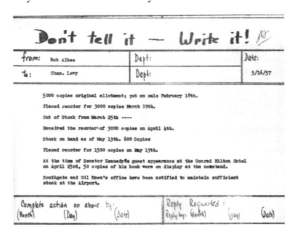

Several paperback editions of *Profiles* were released beginning in late 1956, eventually selling millions of copies. *Source*: John F. Kennedy Presidential Library and Museum.

Check sent do New York for deposit
TO: 1/6/60

— Senator John F. Kennedy   —
  Senate Office Building
— Washington, D.C.   —

/ —   —

WE ARE PLEASED TO ENCLOSE OUR REMITTANCE IN FULL SETTLEMENT OF
THE FOLLOWING:

	AMOUNT
Additional royalty from Book of the Month Club 500 Profile in Courage @ .12375	61.88
Pocket Books 22642 Profile in Courage @.0105 1531 " " " @.007	237.74 10.72
Best in Books 437½½ Profile in Courage @ .0025	1.09
Your share of cash received for Arabic language	25.00
	$ 336.43

NO RECEIPT IS REQUIRED

The hardcover edition of *Profiles* was still in print and selling nearly three years after its release. *Source*: John F. Kennedy Presidential Library and Museum

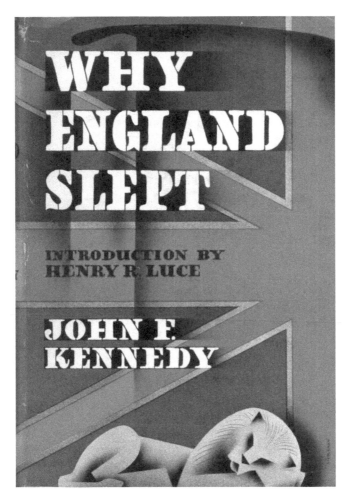

Jack Kennedy turned his Harvard graduate thesis into an international bestseller—*Why England Slept*—in 1940 with a little help from his father and New York Times editor, Arthur Krock. How that book came to be is a window into the writing of *Profiles*. *Source*: Wikimedia Commons.

CHAPTER 38

"I Should Be Glad to Take a Look at Your Book"

ALMOST THE PROTOTYPICAL CARICATURE OF AN ACADEMIC, WITH his professorial glasses and ever-present bowtie, Arthur Schlesinger Jr. had been a boy-wonder in the world of professional historians. At the age of twenty-eight, he won a Pulitzer Prize for his book *The Age of Jackson*. And it was only the beginning of his literary success.

But looks can be deceiving, because the historian was just as comfortable in "the gossipy salon circuits of Washington, New York, and Boston."[1] He was chummy with writers such as Truman Capote, and newspaper publishers like Phil and Katherine Graham.

And, of course, the Kennedys.

He and Jack were the same age, although Arthur finished his Harvard studies two years before Kennedy. They were acquainted but didn't really develop a personal relationship until Jack was elected to Congress. Even before the project had transitioned from article to full-length book, Jack reached out to Schlesinger in 1954. Arthur replied, "Your proposed article on political courage sounds both interesting and timely."[2] He made several suggestions, including the story of Illinois Governor John Peter Altgeld's "pardoning of the men convicted after the Haymarket riot," and Andrew Jackson's "veto of the bill re-chartering the Bank of the United States."

It wasn't until the middle of the next year that Kennedy reached out to him again, this time sending him a draft of the book on June 11, 1955. "Dear Arthur," he wrote, "Would you be so good as to review the manuscript within the next few weeks, and give me your frank criticisms, comments, and suggestions. I would certainly be appreciative for whatever you could do to improve its historical accuracy, style and interest, and general contribution; and if you feel that any or all of these chapters are inadequate, I would be most grateful if you would frankly tell me so."[3]

A few days later Kennedy received a positive response, "I should be glad to take a look at your book," Arthur, who was ready for his summer vacation on Cape Cod, wrote, "I am leaving for Wellfleet on Friday, June 17; so you had better send it to me there."[4]

Schlesinger received and reviewed the manuscript and sent his comments back on July 4. He said, "It seems to me, in the main, historically sound, skilfully [sic] written and a genuine contribution to political discussion," adding, "I very much hope the results of your inquiry rub off on some of your colleagues."[5]

Schlesinger then plunged into his critique. Regarding the prologue as it stood in the draft, he wrote, "I think you should mention the Mexican War here. The acquisition of territory as a result of this war was a major factor in accelerating the pace of the slavery controversy and in bursting the seams of compromise."

As for the chapter on Daniel Webster, Arthur said, "It is not particularly persuasive to me." He took issue with the idea that Webster was right to join with Henry Clay on the Great Compromise." The Compromise of 1850 was a series of laws proposed by Clay designed to defuse tensions between slave states and free states, to avoid military conflict. It was particularly distasteful to Northern Abolitionists (bearing in mind that Webster represented Massachusetts in the Senate), due in part to its bolstering of The Fugitive Slave Act, which said that any official who did not arrest an alleged runaway slave was liable to a fine of $1000." Though profiled as an act of political courage in Kennedy's manuscript, it was, to Schlesinger, quite the *opposite*.

Then he added a particularly pointed barb: "If this was an act of political courage, so was Munich; indeed, you justify the Compromise by identically the arguments which Chamberlain fans invoke to justify Munich . . . I think you are nearer right in the next chapter when you seem to approve Benton's opposition to the Compromise."

The comment could not have pleased Kennedy, whose father had famously supported the British Prime Minister Neville Chamberlain's prewar policy of appeasement back in the day.

When Schlesinger got to the later chapter about Robert Taft and his opposition to the Nuremberg War Crimes Trials, he again pronounced himself "not persuaded." He regarded it as "less defensible than the chapter on Webster." Later he added, "All your other examples of senatorial courage have been based on incidents which took place in the Senate. The Taft incident took place elsewhere. For another, I find it hard to recollect Taft's doing anything else which required political courage." Arthur was, of course, a diehard New Deal Democrat, so his partisanship was showing. But he continued, "His opposition to Truman's strike legislation in 1946 was a popular act . . . He showed no courage in the face of McCarthy."

Of course, nor had Jack Kennedy.

Later, in his comments about the Taft section of the manuscript, Schlesinger brought up the Ohio Senator's vehement opposition to Arthur's beloved New Deal, saying of Taft, "He thought the New Dealers had ridden high too long, and that they had a lot coming to them." It is worth noting that Dr. Schlesinger was at that time writing the first book of what would become a trilogy about "The Age of Roosevelt."

Schlesinger wrapped up his analysis with a recommendation that Kennedy should exclude the chapter about "Other Men of Courage," with a particularly vivid opinion of another Taft, this one Robert's father, former President William Howard Taft. He called that part "terribly farfetched." He derided the man who later was Chief Justice of the Supreme Court as, "a notably timid President. He had less courage in his 315 pounds than T.R., Wilson, F.D.R, or Truman had in their respective little fingers."

After receiving Arthur's critique, Jack wrote back to him. "Many, many thanks for your very helpful comments and corrections," he said. "I have, to the extent possible, followed every one of your suggestions and they were of considerable help in sharpening the manuscript."[6]

But Jack pushed back, at least a bit, "Although I am retaining the chapter on Senator Taft, I have attempted to eliminate some of the overstatement concerning his character and this particular issue." He also told Schlesinger, "I share some of your concerns about the final 'grab-bag' chapter. I have rewritten it somewhat, eliminated some of the examples (including President Taft) . . . I hope you will be pleased with the final product."

CHAPTER 39

"With Something Close to Fascination"

ARTHUR HOLCOMB WAS HARVARD'S EATON PROFESSOR OF THE SCIENCES of Government in 1955 and was preparing to retire at the end of the academic year to take a post at the United Nations. He had been one of Jack's professors and would later go on to mentor Henry Kissinger. So, it was natural that Kennedy would seek the counsel of his former instructor when it came to *Profiles*.

Writing on June 11, Kennedy described his book to his former professor and asked him if he could "review the manuscript within the next few weeks." He asked Holcomb for help with the material's "historical accuracy," and for frank advice "if you feel that any or all of these chapters are accurate."[1]

A few days later, Jack had his answer. Holcomb told him he would be glad to review the book, adding, "It is the kind of book we would like to have our Government concentrators read."[2] Kennedy sent the book to him and Holcomb clearly made it a priority, finishing his analysis in less than a week.

Jack had to be pleased when he read Holcomb's words at the beginning of his treatment: "Years ago, *Plutarch's Lives* was a great favorite among intelligent young Americans and the author's teaching was a solid contribution to the building of character among our people. In recent years, there has been nothing like it on the reading lists of developing citizens and the void has ached for filling. I believe that this new book of yours is going to supply a lot of excellent fill for that void."[3]

High praise, indeed.

But Holcomb noted a few errors, like "that of placing the Boston Massacre on the Common instead of on State Street." Interestingly, that was the kind of mistake that would more likely be made by someone *not* from Boston.

Allan Nevins was a prolific historian who won two Pulitzer Prizes and produced a body of work that was highly regarded by scholars and widely read by the public at large. Jack Kennedy had read several of his books, notably *The Emergence of Lincoln*, which became one of his favorites.

Nevins became aware of Jack's book "at the request of" Cass Canfield at Harper & Brothers, who reached out to his friend and asked if he would consider writing a Foreword for it.[4] Nevins indicated that he would indeed be willing. Canfield relayed the message to Kennedy via Evan Thomas.

As publishing deadlines loomed in the summer of 1955, Kennedy sent nine chapters of *Profiles* to Nevins at Columbia University in New York. Along with the chapters for review, he also asked the famous professor if he would consider writing the book's Foreword. Jack expressed "regret that I have not been able to put this draft into your hands earlier," adding, "*Harper & Brothers* has now requested completion of all editing within the next few weeks."[5]

Nevins replied, "Of course, I feel honored by your invitation to write an Introduction to your book, which covers a subject in which I am deeply interested."[6] He continued, "I have followed your public career with increasing appreciation of the part which you are playing; and I think I can speak for the historians of the country when I say that we are all happy that you find time for research and writing in our field."

Nevins said that he had started his review of Kennedy's material "with something close to fascination." The historian then mentioned he was leaving on an extensive trip for the university, one that would take him to Detroit, Boise, Idaho, and Palo Alto, California. But he told Jack that he would coordinate his Foreword with Cass Canfield, Kennedy's publisher. An old pro in the book business, Nevins tried to ease Kennedy's mind: "Publishers are invariably extremely urgent in their deadlines, but also invariably ready to make concessions." He promised to be "quite frank" in his critique, but added, "from what I have read of the book I feel my general verdict will be enthusiastic."

It was.

The historian completed his review the first week of August and sent his comments directly to Canfield. He told the publisher that *Profiles* "will attract wide attention and have a large sale," adding, "The Senator, for whom I have always had a warm admiration, has added to his stature by this volume."[7]

By this time, Jack was vacationing in Europe, but Nevins wanted to make sure that Canfield would tell him "how much I like his book." He also begged for a bit more time before submitting his Foreword, telling

Canfield, "I am taking great pains with this essay, but you will get it within a few days, not later than next Monday."

When he sent the draft of his Foreword to Canfield, Nevins wrote that he believed the book "will be extremely influential and well received, and that it adds still further to the stature of a Senator he has long admired."[8]

Evan Thomas was impressed with the historian's Foreword. "We have no intention of revising it; it seems not only a marvelous commentary on, and adornment to the book, but also a thing of substance itself."[9] He told Sorensen that Nevins was "turning over *Harper's* honorarium to the support of a paralyzed graduate student."

In June, Jack also reached out to Walter Johnson, a professor of history and political science chair of the history department at the University of Chicago, for his input. Conveniently, Johnson was teaching a course at Harvard that summer and also spending time on Cape Cod.

Kennedy had first met Johnson back in the fall of 1953 at a meeting with Adlai Stevenson at the defeated Democratic candidate's home in Mettawa, Illinois. Johnson had been actively involved in Stevenson's losing race in 1952. Kennedy, as was his custom when meeting academics, "suggested that Johnson send him a copy of a reading list to enhance his own background."[10]

The professor was glad to oblige.

Now, two years later, Johnson obliged once more, sending Kennedy several handwritten pages of critique for *Profiles*, calling the book "valuable and important," adding the advice, "by all means publish it." He also referred to Jack as "unreliable as a party man," which was fine by him.[11] Commenting about chapter nine, he wrote, "Real good on Taft. I'm pleased, but expect to be abused by your A.D.A. (*Americans for Democratic Action*) friends."

Kennedy replied with the same boilerplate language he had used with several of the other professors.

CHAPTER 40

"Evan Welling Thomas II"

IT MIGHT STRIKE SOME AS HYPERBOLE TO SUGGEST THAT THERE MIGHT have been no *Profiles in Courage*, therefore no Pulitzer Prize, and maybe even no John F. Kennedy presidency without Evan Thomas. But a strong case can be made. He is one of those interesting characters, a hero unsung, who comes along in history, a man whose connection with Jack Kennedy at a crucial moment in the formation of the young Senator's brand was worthy of much more than a few footnotes long buried in archival collections and dusty old books.

Kennedy himself acknowledged the editor's work with a mention in the Preface to *Profiles*: "The editorial suggestions, understanding cooperation, and initial encouragement which I received from Evan Thomas of Harper & Brothers made this book possible."[1] But this was more than a perfunctory affirmation, the kind that so often appears in a "thank you" list. Thomas really did make Kennedy's book possible.

He was, in fact, the book's first and foremost *champion*.

Evan Welling Thomas II grew up in picturesque Cold Spring Harbor, a hamlet on Long Island's quaint North Shore. And he continued to live there at 77 Huntington Road in the 1950s. His father was Norman Thomas, the famous leader of the American Socialist Party who ran for President in six consecutive national elections beginning in 1928. Evan remembered his Dad not being around a lot and as a tireless worker. As a young boy, he didn't really know what it meant to be a Socialist, but he knew that when it came to his Dad, "there was something to be proud about," remembering his father as being "very much a crusader."[2]

Thomas withdrew from Princeton University before the end of his senior year to join the American Field Service, working as an ambulance driver with the British Eighth Army in a war that America had not quite yet joined in the summer of 1941. He would eventually join the navy after his service in the AFS in North Africa. On D-Day, he was a Lieutenant JG on a Landing Ship Tank (LST) at Omaha Beach. And he was en route to Japan in August 1945 when the atomic bomb was dropped on Hiroshima.

He actually wrote a book about his some of his wartime experiences, titled *Ambulance in Africa*, which was published by Appleton Century. Written during a short period of time while he was recovering from malaria, it was reviewed favorably by *Kirkus*, as having an "alert quality which makes it good reading."[3] The review further commended Thomas's book as "straight thinking about the war, its casualties and implications, and the personal angle."

This publishing experience gave him an idea about what to do after the war. He thought, "Well, why don't I look into the publishing business? It looks pretty easy."[4] His famous father pulled a few strings and arranged an interview with one of the editors at Harper & Brothers. Evan was hired to work in the trade department, quickly learning that the work was anything but easy.

Cass Canfield was the chairman of the board at Harper & Brothers and soon took the young war veteran under his wing. Thomas said, "Canfield proved to be sort of a second father to me."[5] Eventually, Thomas, who was described as "tall, slim, aristocratic," became the chief editor in the trade department. He was diagnosed with multiple sclerosis in 1950, but the illness was in remission for extended periods of time, and he was able to work without interruption.[6]

Editorial colleague John Appleton called Thomas "the best nonfiction editor in the business."[7] He added, "People, no matter how high their station in the outside world, would be delighted to be turned over to Evan." In 1953, Thomas edited and published Jacques Cousteau's ground-breaking book, *The Silent World: A Story of Undersea Discovery and Adventure*. The explorer-author gave Thomas a two-thousand-year-old Greek vase, which the editor cherished and kept next to his desk for decades.[8] At the time Kennedy's book proposal arrived at Evan's desk, he was finishing his work on a book by Jim Bishop, one that would go to become a national bestseller.

It was titled *The Day Lincoln Was Shot*.

Thomas was the driving force in the decision to expand the two sparse chapters Kennedy first proposed from a single article, presumably for *Harpers' Magazine*, to something more substantial. "JFK didn't know what to do," Thomas remembered. "He wanted Canfield to tell him. So, I suggested that he turn them into a book."[9] Thomas recalled thinking, "I wasn't interested in the magazine making money, I was interested in the trade department making money."

As the project moved forward, Thomas bemoaned the fact "that nobody at *Harpers* thought *Profiles in Courage* was going to sell, including our sales manager and members of the sales force, and Cass." But Evan didn't share the contagious corporate pessimism. He was confident the book would do quite well and fervently lobbied for its publication and promotion. He was a believer in Cass Canfield's commandments about the publishing business, particularly the fourth one: "The publisher, if he thinks someone can produce a first-rate book, should continue to press for it, just short of making himself a nuisance."[10]

Thomas's son, Evan Thomas III, himself a highly regarded best-selling author, and a former top editor of *Newsweek* magazine, remembers his father as the epitome of "a gentleman publisher."

Thomas admired Jack Kennedy, in part because of their common service in the navy. In May 1955, he and Cass Canfield visited Kennedy and his wife at Merrywood, the Potomac River estate in McLean, Virginia owned by Jackie's stepfather, Hugh Auchincloss. Thomas watched as his boss and their author bantered back and forth about the good old days at Harvard. They'd each dabbled in campus politics, though at different times, Canfield having graduated more than two decades before Kennedy. Thomas said Jack was "a very charming guy and we were charmed by him."[11]

Aside from that meeting, Thomas communicated with Kennedy and Sorensen—mostly Sorensen—by telephone or letter—on issues related to the book's editing, publication, and promotion. He later referred to his editorial work on the book as involving minor things like moving more interesting material toward the front of a chapter. But he understated his role. Evan Thomas's help was crucial to making the book noteworthy and prize worthy. For one thing, he chose the catchy title: *Profiles in Courage.*[12]

Evan Thomas really did make Kennedy's book possible.

As *Profiles* was being written the process followed a pattern—a first draft of chapters by Sorensen, then Kennedy's edits, followed by more tweaks by Sorensen. Then the chapters were sent by Sorensen, with a Kennedy cover letter, to Evan Thomas at Harper & Brothers. Thomas would then make comments and send them back to Kennedy and therefore Sorensen.

Writing to Kennedy in April, Thomas said, "I think you have done just what the doctor ordered in the way of making these people vivid, and also, in many cases, their surroundings."[13] He added, "I won't stop to do any detailed editing until I have the complete manuscript." He told Kennedy that he wanted to publish the book the day Congress convened in January 1956, asking that all the "finishing touches" be done by early summer. He had just that morning spent some time selling the project's merits at a general meeting of the publisher's staff. He called it a success.

Thomas then asked, "May I send you a draft contract?"

Kennedy replied a few days later, "I would appreciate your sending a draft to me this time."[14] He also brought up the fact that a friend of his at *Reader's Digest* was interested in doing a condensed version of the book. "Do I assume that any question of this nature, or the question of other magazine articles based on book chapters, would be covered in the contract?" He also pushed for an earlier publishing date, possibly "in the fall, when the peak of legislative activity arouses as much, if not more, interest than the convening of Congress in January." It is possible, however, that he had another reason for wanting it published in 1955—to qualify as a candidate for a Pulitzer Prize in 1956, when he hoped he might be a potential vice-presidential candidate with Adlai Stevenson.

Thomas pushed back on the publication date, telling Kennedy, "we think you are wrong about fall."[15] He was sure they could do a better job of publishing and promotion in January, adding, "there is a minimum interest in this subject during the pre-Christmas book season."

Kennedy's publishing contract with Harper & Brothers was dated April 25, 1955, more than three months after the senator submitted Sorensen's outline and first writing samples.[16] The book's title at the time was *These Great Men*. It was a standard author contract, with a few minor changes here and there. For whatever reason, the copyright section originally read, "The Publisher agrees to take out the original copyright in his own name," but the "in his own name" has a line drawn through it and goes on to read "in the name of the author." The royalty structure was 10 percent of retail cover price for the first 5,000 copies, 12.5 percent for 5001–10,000 copies, and 15 percent "on all copies sold over and above ten thousand (10,000) copies." Kennedy retained the film rights in the contract, which also provided a modest advance to the author of $500 (about $4,500 in today's dollars). Kennedy was to receive ten copies of the book and the right to purchase author copies for "40% from the retail price." The copy of the contract in the Sorensen papers at the Kennedy library in Boston bears the signature of Evan W. Thomas II for Harper & Brothers, but the author signature is blank.

CHAPTER 41

"Your Father Is a Controversial Man"

By mid-June, Thomas was ready to start pushing the still untitled book to others in the company, to, as he put it, "stir some advance enthusiasm."[1] He wrote what he described as "a very preliminary description." He told Kennedy that the description reflected his "personal feeling for the book—and my hopes for it." He added, "I mean what I say."

THE PATRIOTS

by John F. Kennedy

> *In 1954–55, for the better part of a year, Senator Kennedy was deprived of his active role in the affairs of the nation by an unhealed wound incurred as skipper of a World War II torpedo boat. The Senator used his "idle" hours to great advantage; he researched and rediscovered the courage and patriotism of a handful of Americans who at crucial moments in history had revealed a special sort of greatness; men who disregarded dreadful consequences to their public and private lives to do that one thing which seemed right in itself—come what may. These men ranged from the extraordinarily colorful to the near drab, from the natural born aristocrats to the self-made. They were men of various political and regional allegiance—their one over-riding loyalty was to the United States and to the right as God gave them to see it.*
>
> *There was John Quincy Adams who almost lost his Massachusetts citizenship for his support of the Louisiana Purchase; Sam Houston who performed a political act of courage as dramatic as his heroism on the field of battle; Thomas Hart Benton who immortalized the phrase "I despise the bubble popularity" and said, "Whenever I fight, sire, a funeral follows, sir!"; and Daniel Webster; and Edward [sic] Ross who "looked down into his open grave" as he saved President Johnson from impeachment; and Norris of Nebraska; and Taft of Ohio; and Lamar of Mississippi (who did as much as any one man to heal the wounds of civil war). For the most part Kennedy's patriots are United States Senators, but he also pays tribute to such men as Governors Altgeldt of Illinois and Smith of New York, to President Grover Cleveland and Charles E. Hughes.*

Senator Kennedy has used wonderful skill in transferring the cold facts of history into dramatic personal stories. There is suspense, color and inspiration here, but first of all there is an extraordinary understanding of that intangible thing called courage. There is the fact that courage such as these men shared is the basis of all morality—a man does what he must despite the personal consequences—and there is suggested her the thought that, without in the least disparaging the courage with which men die, it is the courage with which they live which adorns true greatness.

Kennedy replied that he hoped Evan's glowing description of the book quickened "some advance enthusiasm in the company."[2] He appreciated his editor's kind words, adding, "I have not yet finally determined upon a title."

Kennedy was planning a trip to Europe, leaving Sorensen behind to run his Senate office as well as the work on details of the book. And it was just a matter of time before Kennedy's father weighed in on it with his heavy-handed and unsolicited advice, complete with a famous name drop. What he had to say must have irked Ted—and Thomas, as well.

"I think *Harper's* should have an excellent editorial writer go over the whole book," said the former Ambassador, "with the idea of punctuation and simplifying the structure. It's a fine job as it is but I remember when Lindbergh spoke to me about the real success of his book he said he almost did not recognize it after the editorial writer at *Scribner's* had finished working on it—he brought so much more clarity and punch to it. I think instead of having *Harper's* take this book just as it is, they should have a man of top caliber do this same job on it and, if he is very good, I am sure you will have a worthwhile and profitable piece of literature, and worthwhile financially if properly exploited."[3]

Thomas may have admired Jack Kennedy, but he had no warm feelings for the Senator's father. After the publication of *Profiles*, Kennedy and the editor had a conversation about their fathers. The setting was the *Links Club*, on Manhattan's Upper East Side. Thomas arrived before Kennedy, and when the senator showed up, he seemed to be decidedly unimpressed with the venue. "This is the first and probably the last time

I will have visited this club," he snapped as he and Thomas went upstairs to a "long fancy table."[4] Thomas recalled the food being great, but Kennedy kept complaining about the place, for whatever reason.

Kennedy brought up the subject of fathers. Thomas said, "He knew that I was very mad at his father, but he didn't want me to be noisy about it, so after about ten minutes of saying very little, Kennedy said, 'Now, your father is a controversial man, as I understand it'."

"Yes," Thomas replied.

"But you love him, don't you?"

"Yes."

"Same here," Kennedy said with a slight smile.

If you were able to somehow stand the S.S. *United States* on end, she would be as tall as New York City's Chrysler Building. The majestic vessel was 100 feet longer than the *Titanic* and completely American, having been constructed using all American products and American workers. During its trials in 1951, the majestic vessel broke speed records, knifing through turbulent waters at the speed of more than thirty-eight knots (44 mph).[5]

Jack boarded her on Friday, August 5, 1955, to begin a two-month European trip, leaving the Senate and the book far behind, though never completely out of mind. He wasn't scheduled to return until early October. Jackie had gone head several weeks earlier and was already in London. A few days before leaving, Kennedy wrote to Thomas, "To clear up several items with respect to the book before I leave. Some will require an answer on your part; and I hope you will get in touch with Ted Sorensen concerning these."[6] Among the matters on Kennedy's mind was the issue of how *he* would be dealt with. He had no objection "concerning items in my personal life or military service—and, in that connection, thought you and Nevins might be interested in John Hersey's article which I am enclosing." This was a reference to the piece that appeared in the *New Yorker* back in 1945 dealing with the *PT 109* story.

He enclosed a copy of the bio his office handed out in advance of his various appearances, adding, "Sorensen could supply any details you feel are necessary." He also encouraged Thomas to, in the promotion of the book, make liberal mention of *Why England Slept* from 1940. Kennedy shared a quote from *The New York Times Book Review* about that earlier work: "He has written a book of such painstaking scholarship, such mature understanding and fair-mindedness and such penetrating and timely conclusions, that it is a notable textbook for our times."

Kennedy also told his editor that "I would prefer not to have Schlesinger's comments on the cover," though he did not elaborate. He ended the note, "I should be available in this country shortly after October 1 and have authorized Ted to act in my name until that time."

Thomas replied the day before Kennedy's departure and spoke in glowing terms about his promotion of the book. "I discussed your book at a conference preliminary to our winter sales conference yesterday. We have arranged to make it one of our leading titles with two pages in the catalogue."

The other leading title was *A Democrat Looks at His Party*, by former U.S. Secretary of State Dean Acheson.

Evan Thomas had reminded Kennedy several times that he needed to fill out a simple form—the Author's Information Sheet. It was something required by the publisher for "copyright and for other necessary work on your book." With the senator in Europe, Sorensen filled it out and sent it in on August 24. Where it said "Author's Signature," Ted wrote, "John F. Kennedy, Per Theodore C. Sorensen."[7]

That same month, memos were sent back and forth between Thomas and Sorensen detailing minor corrections, things like word usage and punctuation. Both men apparently ignored the advice of Ambassador Kennedy for a more thorough edit. Their work that August could best be described as the tweaks of proofreaders. Thomas was clearly put off by the elder Kennedy's meddling. He told Sorensen, "This book reads like Jack Kennedy, and damn good, too. I'd just as soon it continued to read that way. Hell, I suppose we could get it rewritten by a poet or whatnot, but then it would be a different book. I think you will agree that the book has had a certain amount of editorial attention. It was not as implied in Kennedy Sr.'s note, taken on 'just as is (or was)'. We're fairly well known as publishers who do what we can to help, but we also want the book to be the author's own creature—unless of course he's an adventurer or some such who is really inarticulate."[8]

In other words, the manuscript was solid, no matter what Joe Kennedy thought.

A few days later, the galleys were ready for author review. "I understand that you will read galleys and that the Senator will not need to," Thomas wrote to Sorensen. He asked that they be turned around quickly so as to "get them back in five or six days."[9]

Ted was on his own.

When Evan Thomas wanted the Senator to weigh in on something— for example, the drawings for the book's jacket—Sorensen covered as best he could. "I have passed on to the Senator the rough jacket drawings," he wrote. But he acknowledged that Kennedy was "traveling in various parts of Europe now; so that I am never certain how quickly my communications reach him."[10]

Thomas was once again frustrated by Joe Kennedy in early October. He received a call from "a Mr. Racine of the Ambassador's office," regarding the book jacket.[11] "Apparently one of these must be flown up to the Cape for Ambassador Kennedy's approval before they reach my palsied grip." The elder Kennedy was also pressuring Sorensen and the Senator. Still in Europe, Jack got word to his assistant that he was less-than-impressed with the book cover proposed and that his wife "drew four alternative covers which I think are preferable." Sorensen told Thomas, "Although I assume that his father's recommendation will have some influence here."

Many cooks were now tending the soup.

Meanwhile, Thomas asked Sorensen, "When is the Senator coming back? I am particularly anxious to know."[12]

Copies of the galleys were also sent to several Kennedy friends, including Adlai Stevenson. It was no secret that Jack was already part of a short list of potential vice-presidential possibilities on a ticket with Stevenson for the next year, so he must have been pleased with what Adlai wrote about his book: "Few men have ever been so richly entitled to write about courage as Senator Kennedy, and none that I know of have ever written so well about the heroic side of American politics. This book should be an inspiration to everyone in public life."[13]

CHAPTER 42

"The Lost Introduction"

Four strange men called upon me in my hospital room in the winter of 1954. I did not think them strange because they had stepped from the past—a step which required no pass, no approval by the head nurse, not even a knock at my door—for those who doze in hospital beds with the aid of various medical devices are accustomed to enjoying frequent obliteration of those walls that separate the past from the present, that distinguish fantasy from fact and that divide the dreams of the sleeping imagination from the realities of room 1032.[1]

READING THOSE WORDS, ONE CAN ALMOST HEAR THE VOICE OF ROD Serling introducing an episode of the 1959 television series *The Twilight Zone*—complete with its eerie theme music. But the words were not written for a television fantasy program, nor did they appear in a novel.

The passage was written as part of the original introduction to *Profiles in Courage*. It continues: "Despite the differences in their ages, manners, and styles of dress—they were, I realized, all United States Senators from Massachusetts."

Kennedy's original plan was to begin his nonfiction book with a *fictional* story.

The rest of the "lost" introduction featured a series of conversations in eleven letters back and forth with the ghostly statesmen, a method reminiscent of C. S. Lewis's *Screwtape Letters*. Most of them involve dialogue between a "Senator L.C. Oldtimer" and Jack Kennedy, who after a few drafts becomes "Edward Youngfellow." It appears intact in several early drafts of the book and was only removed shortly before publication. Sorensen most likely came up with the idea and wrote the original draft.[2]

The eventually deleted section continues: "*Nor did I think my visitors strange because they were that very day the leading characters in books my wife was reading aloud at my bedside.*" It was likely designed to keep the image of Kennedy fighting his own courageous battle before the readers. In fact, during that dark period in late 1954 and early 1955, when Jack was very sick and near death, Jackie did sit at his bedside reading history and biography to him. And she also arranged her own "dream" visitation of sorts.

While her husband languished physically and mentally, Jackie arranged to have the beautiful actress, Grace Kelly, whom she had recently met at a party in Palm Beach, visit him dressed up as a nurse. When the movie star entered the room, Jack didn't recognize her. She breathily whispered in his ear, "I'm the new night nurse,"[3] and then she began to feed the patient. But Jack didn't show any response. Later, Kelly told someone that she was clearly losing her sex appeal. Told about it the next morning, Kennedy replied that he thought the whole thing was a dream.

Likely suggested by Kennedy, but first drafted by Sorensen, the literary device of parliamentary spirits visiting Jack in the hospital, and the following correspondence, serve to explain Kennedy's purpose in writing *Profiles in Courage*. The four senators, particularly Senator L. C. Oldtimer, represent the Senate's paternal leadership. They are older men, and Jack, or "Edward Youngblood," seeks their sage advice about how to handle situations when constituent pressure on a particular issue flies against the conscience of a legislator. The old man, purportedly with the wisdom of years, pushes a get-along/go-along approach. Play ball. Wait your turn. Don't rock the boat. Be pragmatic.

In his first letter to Senator Oldtimer, Jack, writing on January 6, 1955, as "Youngblood," begins, "Dear Senator Oldtimer, Thank you for your very kind congratulatory note concerning my election. . . ."[4] He then poses a question: "Do you have any advice on S. 1636?" It was a fictitious bill. He continues, "Apparently the voters in our state are nearly unanimous in their opposition to the bill. But isn't this being somewhat short-sighted and sectional in outlook? I am sure you have met this problem many times in your career, and the advice of a veteran Senator like yourself would be very helpful."

Oldtimer replies: "My Dear Ed . . . I wouldn't worry much about S. 1636, if I were you. There is no doubt that our constituents are very much opposed to the bill. So why pursue the matter further? I realize that it may be a good thing nationally, but our responsibilities, Ed, are to our constituents. If we don't represent their views, who will? You can be sure that the representatives of the other states will look out for their interests. Don't spoil the pleasure of your first session by worrying your head with this kind of problem. Take it from me, you can vote 'no' and cement relations back home."

In other words, go along with your constituents.

The contrived correspondence incorporated Kennedy's health challenges. Senator "Oldtimer" sent a get-well note dated March 6, 1955, and Kennedy/Youngblood replied: "My doctor, in what I hope was more of professional prognosis than a political promise, assure me that I will be able to return to the Senate by the middle of the session. I look forward to being with you and my other colleagues at that time."[5] He asked again about S. 1636, receiving the same advice as before—vote with your constituents.

In yet another exchange, Youngblood asks, "But do we fulfill that responsibility on a given issue by counting noses in some super-Gallup poll?" He quotes the seventeenth-century British statesman Edmund Burke who represented the city of Bristol in the House of Commons, on the matter: "Your representative owes you, not his industry only but his judgment; and he betrays, instead of serving you, if he sacrifices it to your opinion . . . Parliament is not a congress of ambassadors from different and hostile interests, which interests much maintain, as an agent and advocate against other agents and advocates; but Parliament is a deliberative assembly of one nation, with one interest, that of the whole—where not local purpose, not local prejudices, ought to guide, but the general good, resulting from the general reason of the whole. You choose a member, indeed; but when you have chosen him, he is not a member of Bristol, but he is a member of Parliament."

Kennedy argued that sometimes it was important for a political leader to put national interest above political self-interest. Eventually, the younger Senator wins Oldtimer over to his viewpoint.

At the end of the eventually deleted introduction, Kennedy acknowledges the fictitious nature of the dialogue: "There is, of course, no Senator Old-timer. If a reference is needed, it might be said that he represents the mistaken concept of a Senator almost universally portrayed by Hollywood, Broadway, and fiction writers; or that he is based upon the delightful character in Dickens' Nicholas Nickleby, Member of Parliament Gregsbury—'a thick-headed gentleman, with a loud voice, a pompous manner, a tolerable command of sentences with no meaning in them, and, in short, every requirement for a good member'."[6]

That seemed to describe someone more like Warren G. Harding, the bloviating senator from Ohio whose good looks, charm, and aversion to conflict took him all the way to the White House, even though his intellect and character were no match for that high office, than the senators Kennedy planned to include in his forthcoming book.

Nearly four decades after the publication of *Profiles in Courage*, historian John Hellmann wrote: "The deleted chapter is a backstage look at how the character of the future presidential candidate was being scripted from the actual man's situation."[7] Of course, the fantasy introduction was eventually left on the cutting-room floor, as Hellmann said, "Its essential theme, a potential young hero receiving powerful knowledge from visitors out of the past, was submerged into the controlling narrative of the book as a whole."

In a real sense, the development and presentation of *Profiles in Courage* served to further introduce John F. Kennedy to the country as a name connected to the idea of heroism, "making Kennedy the man over into a universal image, the transcultural figure of the young hero." And to introduce it all, another device was ultimately chosen to begin the book.

Another "old-timer" appears—this one, however, was very real.

Among the hundreds of thousands of documents residing at the John F. Kennedy Presidential Library in Massachusetts is a collection related to a man Kennedy never actually met, though he admired him from afar.

Ernest Hemingway.

There was almost a cult surrounding the famous author at the midpoint of the 1950s. He embodied the dominant male, a fighting risk-taker. Kennedy devoured Hemingway's books and read many of them during downtime in the South Pacific. He was drawn to the fatalistic heroism woven into the narrative.

When he came home from the South Pacific, Jack even penned a letter to his hero. In it, he reflected about the war, politics in America, and the idea of young people risking their lives in the military, his recent experience no doubt in mind. He wrote, "There is no comparable pressure on the politician to sacrifice all for the public good."[8]

For whatever reason, he never sent the letter to Hemingway.

But as he was preparing his final introduction to *Profiles* toward the end of July 1955, he had decided to begin his book with one of his favorite quotes, purportedly from Hemingway. The problem was, he couldn't find the source. So, he wrote another letter to Hemingway.

This one he sent.

On just about anyone's short list for greatest novelist in American history, Ernest Hemingway, affectionately referred to as "Papa," was, in mid-1955, living on his farm called Finca Vigia, located approximately nine miles from Havana in pre-Castro Cuba. He was surrounded by a "domestic staff of nine, fifty-two cats, sixteen dogs, a couple of hundred pigeons, and three cows."[9]

It was said that when Hemingway wrote, "He was the soul of brevity, telling compelling stories in sparse prose that spoke to millions of readers. His central theme was personal courage."[10] He was more than a novelist. He was a superstar, as well as a heroic "role-model" for people around the world.

He was also the man Jack, in many ways, wanted to be.

Hemingway was, at the time, recovering from back-to-back airplane crashes that took place on successive days in Africa the previous year. His most recent book, *The Old Man and the Sea*, had won the Pulitzer Prize. With its theme of courage against all odds, it became a Kennedy favorite.

Jack loved the book and coveted the prize.

He admired "Papa" so much he decided to invoke his name to begin his own book. Hellman suggested that by using Papa to open his own book, Kennedy "furthered his larger strategy for redefining his own public image."[11]

It was all about image. The idea was to connect the kind of courage profiled in the book to that exhibited by, and written about by, Hemingway. And in the 1950s, the image-making medium of choice was the magazine. Long before television became the driving force behind the creation of celebrity, publications such as *Saturday Evening Post*, *Look*, *Colliers*, and, above all, *Life* determined who was in and who was out.

Life was, by far, the most popular magazine of the day, with more than five million weekly readers. The others were imitators, at best. But together, their images defined the times. And it seemed like every time you turned around either Hemingway or Kennedy was featured on a cover. Like bookends, both representing their own generations, yet, strangely similar.

On July 26, 1955, Kennedy wrote a letter to Hemingway, in care of the publisher *Charles Scribner's Sons* in New York: "Dear Mr. Hemingway, I am completing a book on political courage—the stories of Senators who risked their careers by speaking out for principles which were extremely unpopular among their constituents. I am most anxious to use in the text a definition of 'courage' as 'grace under pressure' which I recall was attributed to you. I am planning to open the book by quoting this definition and stating that the book contains the stories of the pressures operating on eight courageous Senators, and the grace with which they endured those pressures . . . Unfortunately, I am unable to find the source of this quotation or verify your authorship of it. I wonder if you might recall the phrase and would be kind enough to let me know so I might use it in the manner suggested."[12].

Hemingway's publisher wrote to Evan Thomas on August 5, "That quotation has been variously ascribed to Hemingway, but we don't know where he said it. Certainly not in his principal books."[13] Thomas forwarded the note to Sorensen with his handwritten recommendation scribbled on the bottom of the page: "Dear Ted Sorensen, I'd go ahead and use this quote as it stands in view of this, Evan." But Thomas eventually managed to track the source down in August, writing to Kennedy, "Found that 'grace under pressure' thing in a book I'm editing. Seems that Hemingway said it in conversation with Dorothy Parker."[14] Indeed, Papa Hemingway had been interviewed in 1929 by Parker for the *New Yorker*, during which he used the phrase.

Problem solved.

Originally buried on page 22 of early drafts of the book, once the whole "Senator Oldtimer" introduction was deleted, Hemingway's gem was used for the very first sentence of *Profiles in Courage*: "This is a book about that most admirable of human virtues—courage. 'Grace under pressure,' Ernest Hemingway defined it."

CHAPTER 43

"Sorensen Was a One-Man Promotion Machine"

EARLY ON IN THE MAKING OF *PROFILES IN COURAGE*, TED SORENSEN seemed to develop a sense of ownership. He took pride in his work and offense at criticism. In a letter he wrote to Kennedy on Valentine's Day 1955, Sorensen mentioned a message, one that deeply discouraged his hard-working wordsmith. "One of your dicta-phone records which Mrs. Lincoln had not yet transcribed was played back today, and I thus received the message you sent me upon the receipt of the Benton and Lamar drafts." Kennedy had suggested that "a book produced at such speed is bound to be second-rate."

Ted pushed back, "I am not certain the final product will be second-rate even though these drafts, which we need to get started, are rushed and admittedly not great literary works." He reviewed his work in detail for the Senator, "with this impassioned plea for my own work (made more emotional by fatigue), I close for the defense with the statement that I will, of course, abide by your final judgment in the matter."

He couldn't resist, however, advocating for the book, in light of his already-extensive research and writing. "I do sincerely believe this book has a contribution to make." He saw the book as filling a niche, "It tells stories never, to my knowledge, previously told in full, in complete context and without interruption." Sorensen believed "this book will be, in my biased judgment, greatly superior to William O. Douglas's *Almanac of Liberty*," a reference to the bestseller written a year earlier by the Supreme Court Justice. He continued, "As prejudicial as I am, I really feel this is going to be a damned fine book."

Sorensen looked forward to Kennedy's return to Washington, "when we can talk things over. It will not be too long now, I trust, before your triumphant return from Elba, when you will gather with you as your proceed all men of spirit and courage ready to do battle with the forces of evil." Then, he added, "So I can't write, eh? That's right!"[1]

A week later, he told Kennedy, "I am working on my thoughts for the introductory and concluding chapters." With those, he said, "we will at least have a complete book of the proper length in rough draft form."[2]

The picture is clearly one of Ted as the writer and Jack as the editor.

Sorensen was initially impressed with Dr. Jules Davids, and he was the primary connection between the professor and the project. "With respect to the presentation of material, Dr. Davids suggests a catchy title for each chapter and variations in chapter beginnings." But "on the whole, Dr. Davids was most impressed" with Sorensen's drafts.[3] However, less than a month later, Sorensen wrote to Kennedy that he was "disappointed in Dr. Davids"[4] most recent memoranda, though acknowledging "it was wise to obtain a professional historical perspective."

Possibly, Ted was becoming a bit territorial.

Meanwhile, *Collier's* magazine had reached out to Sorensen—they were "interested in publishing as an article some portion of the book prior to its publication date." He told the Senator "the chapter on Edmund Ross, possibly combined with the material on the six who stood with Ross, could be worked into an excellent feature article of interest to *Collier's* readers."[5]

Dr. Davids visited the senator's office on March 9. He and Sorensen discussed the book, and Ted reported to his boss that the professor was satisfied that the material he had helped with was in great shape and ready for "finishing touches."[6] A month later, Davids was back in touch with Sorensen about a sensitive matter. It seems that a typist he had hired for his part of the project "had not yet received his check." Ted wrote to Jack, "I said I would mention it to you if there is a slip-up for any reason."[7]

A couple of weeks after Easter 1955, Ted sent his boss an update on the book. "I am enclosing a suggested chapter on John Quincy Adams,"[8] he wrote. "My final chapter on Lamar has also been completed and will be forwarded to you as soon as it is retyped. I am presently working on the prologue on the history of the Senate which will precede the chapter on John Quincy Adams; and hope to send this as well as a new draft on Norris." He also updated Kennedy on the work being done by James Landis and Jules Davids. Then he added, "My thought is that I ought to go ahead and try a full chapter on Taft and the war crimes trials. What do you think, after reading the enclosed?"

A couple of days later, Ted sent "a suggested draft on Lamar."[9] "The other historical prologue, the miscellaneous chapter and the chapter on Norris I hope to complete in the near future," he wrote, with a personal appeal: "I assume I will be talking with you on the phone as per my last letter regarding the Taft, introductory and concluding chapters."

The indication being that rather than the kind of frenetic and nonstop dialogue between Sorensen and Kennedy that has been suggested, their actual contact with each other was sporadic, with Ted having to rely on writing letters and memos. Kennedy comes off as less-than-engaged in "his" project.

Sorensen seemed to be driving things, asking all the questions, posing all the suggestions, with Kennedy in the role of gatekeeper, someone making final decisions about material he did not write. For example, it is Sorensen who seemed to be the one to pick Evan Thomas's brain about the book. "I think we will want to ask Evan Thomas for his suggestions as to a format by which these many small stories can be best pieced together; and further, whether some of the very brief references might not better be omitted entirely . . . I hope to have both Dean Landis's and Dr. Davids' suggestions for the introductory and concluding chapters by the time I have revised Norris. So I think we are moving ahead fairly well."[10]

In early May, Ted sent Jack the promised draft of the chapter on Senator George Norris.[11] By that time, Sorensen had drafted 47,000 words and told his boss that the "introductory and concluding chapters" he was finishing, "will bring this total to 63,000 words or more."[12]

By mid-July, the book was almost finished, having been reviewed by Kennedy, Evan Thomas, Arthur Schlesinger, Arthur Holcomb, and Walter Johnson. But Sorensen still wrestled with a title. "Personally (and based upon a fairly literate circle of friends)," he wrote to Kennedy on July 17, "I can't see 'The Patriots' or 'Courage in the Senate'; and I will string along with 'Eight Were Courageous' unless something better appears. I think devotion of several hours or days to reading quotations, Shakespeare and the Bible could turn up something better."

Abe Moses was an intern in Kennedy's office in the summer of 1955. Sorensen described him as "a good fellow, a good worker . . . quiet and respectful."[13] Sorensen told Moses, "That yet to be famous literary masterpiece continues to occupy a good deal of our attention. We're terribly pleased by the fact that *Life*, the *Reader's Digest*, *Collier's*, and *Harper's Magazine* have already decided to publish various portions of it."[14]

Sorensen had also come up with his own idea for a title, one he said was "both interesting and indicative—with both mystery and meaning: *'Call the Roll'* by John F. Kennedy." He even wrote a poem to support it:[15]

> *Now has come the time for action,*
> *Clear away all thought of faction,*
> *Out from ventilating shame—*
> *Let him answer to his name—*
> *Call the roll—Call the Roll.*

Sorensen was a one-man promotion machine when it came to pitching the book to magazines for serialization, a process he began early in 1955. He was excited that March after a lunch meeting with Jim Derieux, the Chief of the Washington Bureau of *Collier's* magazine. Ted had given him his early drafts and Derieux was "extremely enthusiastic about them."[16] He suggested that the magazine would be interested in publishing an excerpt of the book in the magazine. Sorensen told Kennedy, "*Collier's* has about 3,800,000 readers."

By August, several publications were on board. *Life* magazine committed to publish an article based on "the first and last chapters of the book," paying a fee of $5,000 for the privilege.[17] Sorensen told Kennedy that Harper & Brothers would receive 10 percent, per their contract. *Harper's* magazine (affiliated with the book's publisher) was on board to reprint the chapter on Edmund Ross, and the *Reader's Digest*, with its circulation of more than ten million, also committed to reprint a section of the book.

Sorensen's aggressive negotiations bothered Evan Thomas, especially the pitch to *Reader's Digest*. Ted clearly saw the book, as least somewhat, as his baby. But in his communications with his boss, he indicated that all was well between him and the editor. "All is going smoothly," he wrote.

In September, Sorensen told the Senator that he planned to have the completed manuscript to the magazines by October 1. He then asked, "Do you want to review the revised manuscript?"[18] He was excited by the fact that, according to some friends he had been talking to in the publishing world, "they have never heard of any book receiving so much pre-publication treatment in all the big magazines." He added, "More people will have heard of this book by January than any other." Then he mentioned other magazines he intended to approach, including *Saturday Evening Post* and *Look*.

Because of his efforts, the book had already earned fees "around the $11,300 level." Thomas also mentioned that the 10 percent of these fees, assigned to Harper & Brothers, would be "entirely used for advertising over and above the large-scale promotion."

Life Magazine was asking for a picture of the senator on the Capitol steps, but Sorensen said, "Unfortunately, this will probably only be for the first page of the article, not the cover." He added, "Can you give me any date as to when you might plan to be in Washington soon after your return?"

As he had been throughout the process, Jack Kennedy was clearly functioning more as an editor than a writer. "All of the corrections which you have suggested in your various letters, as well as some based upon suggestions by your father, have been incorporated," Ted wrote. He had also made "several minor corrections," those having apparently not been seen by Kennedy.

He told the senator that Evan Thomas felt "quite strongly about not having the book edited any further for style." The editor was confident that "all major items of syntax have already been taken care of." Thomas also asked Sorensen to check with Kennedy about how many copies of *Why England Slept* had sold.

Sorensen end his letter with this post script: "I hope to hear from you soon."

Ted drafted a memo for the Senator on October 20: "Summary of Negotiations for Serialization of the Book."[19] It listed the publications committed to covering *Profiles in Courage*. In addition to *Life, Collier's, Harpers,* and *Reader's Digest,* the *Boston Globe* agreed to "serialize the entire book." This would begin on January 3, 1956, the book's publication date. The fee was $2,000. Another $750 was forthcoming from *This Week Magazine,* a Sunday supplement appearing in newspapers across America, for "an article based upon Norris, Taft, and miscellaneous chapters." *Look Magazine* was also close to a deal. And Hearst expressed interest "in serializing the entire book."

CHAPTER 44

"With a Little Help from His Father"

Evan Thomas told Sorensen on September 16 that he had settled on the cover and title. Ted shared it with his boss:

PROFILES IN COURAGE
by John F. Kennedy
Foreword by Allan Nevins
Americans who risked their careers, reputations, and happiness to do what they thought was right.[1]

He added: "Being rather uncertain as to your present whereabouts, I am sending copies of this to all the various addresses which you have been using . . . Regards to your wife—and happy second anniversary from an old-timer of six years."

Several days later, Sorensen still had not heard from the Senator. He sent Kennedy a couple of options for the rough jacket drawings. The cover jacket needed to be approved before the end of September. "Evan Thomas pleads that they have little time remaining on this, it will be expensive to make too many major changes but that it is important to be very specific now because of the even greater expense in making changes once the actual plates have been prepared."[2] He again told the Senator that he was sending "this letter to your other addresses."

In fact, issues with the book's cover would continue to trouble Thomas, even threatening the book's January publication date.

The editor was once again frustrated by Joe Kennedy in early October. He received a call from "a Mr. Racine of the Ambassador's office," regarding the book jacket.[3] "Apparently of these must be flown up to the Cape for Ambassador Kennedy's approval before they reach my palsied grip." The elder Kennedy was also pressuring Sorensen and the Senator. Still in Europe, Jack got word to his assistant that he was less-than-impressed with the book cover proposed and that his wife "drew four alternative covers which I think are preferable." Sorensen told Thomas, "Although I assume that his father's recommendation will have some influence here."

The publicity department at Harper & Brothers, led by Ramona Herdman, worked hard to get *Profiles* early notice in the media. In late October, Herdman wrote to Senator Kennedy to solicit his participation.

"The Dave Garroway 'Today' show would like to have you on publication date. We could arrange to have this interview in Washington if you do not care to come to New York."[4] The publicist also mentioned a book and author luncheon sponsored by the *Cleveland Press* scheduled for January 19, as well as a similar event sponsored by the *Washington Post* in February. "I realize that January is a busy time for you," she wrote, "and I would be grateful if you could tell me how much time you can spare for publicity appearances in connection with the book and when you could be available."

Evan Thomas was actively involved in all of this, particularly the early advertising campaign for what he called "one of our leading winter titles."[5] Five hundred copies were being sent to reviewers and booksellers in the Boston area, alone. And he planned "announcement ads in the *New York Times Book Review*, Washington, Boston, and TV in Los Angeles and San Francisco." His goal was to see "an estimated advance sale of 6,500 copies." This promotion was apparently being paid for out of what Harper's had received from Kennedy—a percentage of the fees paid to him directly for serialization. On point, Thomas thanked Kennedy specifically for a recent $750 check.

Upon his return from Europe, Kennedy renewed his interest in the details of the book. In late October, he proofread the final manuscript and had Sorensen contact Thomas with eleven minor changes in the text. They were simple things, such as changing the word "probably" in one place to "possibly," and "the same day" in one spot to "not long ago."[6]

He wrote to Evan Thomas about the book's promotion, "I wonder if the appropriate department would send to me a list of all of those to whom you intend to send advance copies of the book for promotion purposes. I might have some additions to suggest to your normal list, such as all of the syndicated columnists, all Massachusetts editors, and others."[7]

A few days later, Kennedy followed up with questions about the kind of investment the publisher was making in *Profiles*. "Although I can understand the general reluctance of a publisher to reveal promotion costs to an author or anyone else, I would appreciate very much receiving from you a detailed budget as to how much you are going to spend on newspaper and television advertising, in which newspapers in which cities, the size and nature of the advertisements, and the costs which would be involved in larger and more extensive advertisements in the different media."[8] He indicated to Thomas that he was "interested in the possibilities of supplementing this on my own."

With a little help from his father.

Harper & Brothers Publishing Company had been at least partly responsible for the creation of the largest and most influential book review service in the publishing industry—but not on purpose. Virginia Kirkus was the head of their Department of Books for Boys and Girls, when she was informed by her bosses that both her department and her job were going away. The year was 1932, and the Great Depression was taking its toll on every facet of the global economy.

So, Virginia sailed to Europe for a vacation.

One night, on her way back to America, she had a dream. It was so clear "that it seemed to be an outline written on a blackboard."[9] That dreamed fueled a business, one the gutsy gal started while all around her other businesses were closing their doors. It was called the *Virginia Kirkus Bookshop Service*, know these days simply as *Kirkus Reviews*.

On November 3, Thomas wrote to Kennedy sharing the just released *Kirkus* review of his forthcoming book, adding, "I know the enclosed will please you as it does me."[10]

Senator Kennedy's book on the courageous stands made by those who have stood their ground on the Senate floor from the day John Quincy Adams spoke for the Embargo Act to the days of Robert Taft is a stirring and effective tribute to the nature of office as well as character. Basic to the principles the concept of representative office of whether the elected man's duty is to represent by acquiescence to the desires of his constituency or by exercising his own judgment, whether his first witness the battles waged and the men who faced the dissonant music of opposition and censure, we see the growth of the United States and its changing conception of unity. In the mid-nineteenth century, we see the attempts of Daniel Webster, Thomas Hart Benton, and Sam Houston to build a bridge, each in a differing way, across the widening chasm that ended in secession. Edmund Ross, the man who despite party pressure and a new constituency voted against Johnson's impeachment, was politically dead afterwards. Senator Kennedy hails other stalwart men and considers the problems that faced them in a book that will certainly give the constituents and congress men a greater sense of pride—and understanding in their connections.

Foreword by Allan Nevins.

One week before Christmas 1955, the *New York Times Magazine*—part of the paper's massive Sunday edition—featured a lengthy article titled "*The Challenge of Political Courage: A Senator Analyzes the Pressures Confronting the Conscientious Lawmaker*, by John F. Kennedy."[11] The article was adapted from the first chapter of the forthcoming book. It also served as a notice to readers of the newspaper of record that a major new book would make a splash in the new year. The article followed a two-page spread titled "Pressures on Berlin"—a reminder that the world remained a very divided and dangerous place. Of course, Berlin and its issues would be centerstage in a few years when the author of *Profiles in Courage* occupied the Oval Office.

CHAPTER 45

"Jack Kennedy Called Evan Thomas on Christmas Eve"

LESS THAN SIX WEEKS PRIOR TO THE BOOK'S SCHEDULED RELEASE DATE, the cover remained a sticking point.[1] The people at *Harper's* had tried hard to make one of Jackie Kennedy's concepts work, but to no avail. Thomas wrote in an almost apologetic tone to Kennedy, "The enclosed will explain why I have gone back to the hand-lettered jacket with the blue and white background which you reluctantly approved as a last-ditch alternative in the event that we should come up with no successful adaptation of Mrs. Kennedy's idea."

Thomas acknowledged that what they had come up with was "about the crummiest, cheapest, and most unimpressive-looking execution that one could imagine, so I am taking the responsibility of having these plates scrapped"—this on November 23. Thomas told Kennedy, "It's really too late to be doing all this, but we are doing it anyhow, disregarding the logistics, mechanics, and cost. You see, as I told you on the phone, I had approved the idea for this bloody thing, but the execution looks so much like a fourth-rate juvenile that, with Cass's approval, I am turning the Manufacturing Department inside out." He then added, "If we sound un-businesslike, it's because we are."

A few days later, Thomas told Sorensen, "On account of all of our fumbling around, we will only just get this in time for publication. I will send you a proof when it arrives."[2] He then added a caveat: "but it won't do any good if you don't like it."

All matters seemed to be settled in early December, and Thomas sent a *Western Union Telegram* to Kennedy at his Senate Office: "As of now we will make publication date of January Second. Complete with Illustrations. EVAN THOMAS."

But another shoe was about to drop.

Jack Kennedy called Evan Thomas on Christmas Eve with an unusual and urgent request. Thomas, who was enjoying the evening with his family at their Long Island home, recalled, "My wife was filling stockings, children's stockings, at the fireplace, to make a corny scene of it—we were very sentimental about that.[3] In my childhood and her childhood and our children's youth, we always had gone through the ceremony of filling stockings after supper on Christmas Eve and hanging them from the fireplace. Well, on this occasion, the date I forget, I had a phone call from

Senator Kennedy, and he said, 'Now, I've really got to get this book out this year'."

Both the timing and nature of the request startled Thomas. He later recalled that it seemed "incredible that he would know so little about book publishing as to think that on the 24th of December you could have it published in that calendar year." So, he pushed back, "Well, we've announced it for mid-January of next year and there's nothing we can do about it."

But Kennedy was adamant: "We've got to get it out before the year turns."

So, Thomas asked the obvious question. Why?

"Well," he said, "I've just been talking to Arthur Krock, and I understand it would win the Pulitzer Prize this year."

Thomas replied, "Well, there's nothing we can do about changing the publication date. It's going to be reviewed in the mid-January issue of the *Times Book Review* and it's got a good review, and I can't do anything for you, and besides that I'm busy, I'm filling stockings."

Kennedy was not pleased. Nor was Thomas. He was uncomfortable with Kennedy giving him orders he was unable to obey.

The day after Christmas, the *Boston Globe* carried a front-page story about Kennedy's forthcoming book, referring to it as "an exciting tale of how many great Senators—from John Quincy Adams to Robert A. Taft—risked their careers to do what they thought was right, regardless of the consequences."[4] The paper announced that the next Sunday they "will begin publishing the book in serial form."

The article, written by John Harris, featured an interview with Evan Thomas, describing him as the man "who got the Senator to write the book." Harris had interviewed Thomas a few days earlier in the editor's New York office.

Harris told his readers that "Thomas knows good books." He then listed several titles connected with the Harper's editor, including "William White's '*Taft Story*' that won the Pulitzer Prize, '*The Day Lincoln Was Shot*', '*The African Hunter* 'and many others'." Evan recounted for Harris a visit he had made to the Hospital for Special Surgery in New York, where Kennedy was laid up after "an operation to cure a World War II back injury." "The Senator was on the flat of his back," Thomas said, "and read to me from his own longhand notes." Thomas told Harris that he was greatly impressed and "suggested that Kennedy include more Senators and expand the proposed magazine into a full book."

The article was a flattering and effective promotion for the book, which Thomas said, "reflects Kennedy's own character. He's quite a courageous guy." He added, "The book is unusual, too, because its non-partisan though it comes from a man with a great position and future in the Democratic Party." Thomas suggested the book would be successful because, "a reader can associate himself with the events and gets a sense of being right there."

For Kennedy's part, when interviewed by Harris, he told the writer about reading Herbert Agar's *The Price of Union* as a catalyst for his own work, which started as a potential magazine article. "When I showed the magazine article to Thomas he asked me if I'd have time to turn it into a book. Since I was in the hospital, I said I'd have a lot of time." Kennedy said that, as part of the research, "I must have read between 300 and 400" books.

The reporter pressed him on that reading. Kennedy qualified his claim, "Some I read all the way through, and some I used just to read a chapter. I can read pretty fast." He then made a reference to something that eventually became the stuff of Camelot legend: Speed reading. "I once took a course, at night in Baltimore, on fast reading," Jack said. "It was given by an industrial firm there. I'd say I'm a fast reader . . . can do a book in a day. I had plenty of time to read from the middle of December until the end of May . . . I'd read from nine in the morning until noon; break for lunch, then go outdoors and read again. I'd lie down for a while and then work until 5:30. I worked every night, too. I'd write in longhand or dictate into a machine. Then a stenographer would type this out."

The classic puff piece chronicled Kennedy's earlier writings, including his 1940 book, as well as his newspaper work for Hearst. Kennedy acknowledged the help of his wife, as well as professors Johnson, Nevins, Holcomb, and Schlesinger.

There was, however, not a single word about his assistant Ted Sorensen who, in fact, wrote the book's complete first draft. Sorensen likely chalked this up to business as usual. He had already received compensation (via his serialization negotiations) equal to nearly half of his salary as a Senate staffer, and he stood to make so much more from the book's actual royalties over time. But he was sensitive about the lack of public credit he was receiving. In fact, when he did a final proofread of Kennedy's preface to the book—where the author thanked this person and that one, Ted noticed the conspicuous absence of his own name. Kennedy had even thanked Ted's father in Nebraska.

In a memo to JFK written several weeks earlier, titled "Possible Changes in Preface," item number four was: "TCS?"[5] It was a reference to the fact that the Senator had not written a single word about his assistant. Kennedy addressed his aide's concern at the last minute, adding words he hoped would assuage him: "The greatest debt is owed to my research associate, Theodore C. Sorensen, for his invaluable assistance in the assembly and preparation of the material upon which this book is based."

Better late than never.

CHAPTER 46

"The Book Was Quickly Captivating America"

WHILE MUCH OF BOSTON—THE ENTIRE COUNTRY, FOR THAT MATTER— participated in various expressions of New Year's Eve revelry as 1955 gave way to 1956, more than 5,000 stone-cold sober Protestants filled the aged Mechanic Building's Grand Hall in the city's Back Bay section. And they were captivated by the fiery oratory of world-famous evangelist Billy Graham. He thundered, "Every night club and hotel in Boston is filled to capacity tonight," but he issued a call for a spiritual awakening. "I believe," he said, "that this is God's hour in Boston." The minister had made a name for himself preaching a blend of revivalist gospel and anti-Communist Americanism. "America tonight is in the night clubs, but that's not where the Communists are. The past six years, I have listened to the tramp of their feet, encircling, encroaching, and even now the noose is being made and drawn for America. We are sleeping while the world is on fire. Let's take our heads out of the sand and away from the television sets and turn to God."

It was all right there on the front-page of the *Boston Globe* on Sunday, January 1, 1956. But for those readers swallowing aspirin with their coffee and looking for something in the paper that didn't shout judgment at them, there was a picture just to the left of the Graham story, one that featured Senator and Mrs. John F. Kennedy.

Though *Profiles in Courage* would not be for sale in bookstores for two days, the *Globe* was scooping all competitors, publishing the first chapter of the book in its entirety. "Senator Kennedy has transferred cold facts of history into dramatic personal stories. There is suspense and inspiration here, but first of all there is an extraordinary understanding of that intangible thing called courage," the article said before adding, "Turn now, for Senator Kennedy's opening chapter, to page 12."

Sorensen had handled the serialization details while Kennedy was in Europe. "The *Boston Globe* (largest newspaper in Massachusetts and New England on Sunday, with circulation well over one-half million) wants to serialize the entire book, at the earliest date prior to publication," he wrote to Kennedy, who was staying at the Hotel Du Cap D'Antibes in France, the previous September.[1]

Other serializations of *Profiles* negotiated by Sorensen included:[2]

LIFE MAGAZINE—paid Kennedy $5,000 "to base an article of 5,000 to 6,000 words on the first and last chapters" of Profiles.

COLLIER'S MAGAZINE—paid Kennedy $2,000 for "an article on the seventh of March speech" by Daniel Webster, this being Sorensen's suggestion to the executive editor.

READER'S DIGEST—paid $1,000 for a condensed version of the chapter on Edmund Ross.

HARPER'S MAGAZINE—paid $300 (magazine owned by Harper & Brothers), also for the Ross chapter.

THIS WEEK MAGAZINE—paid $750 for "an article based on Norris."

And so, it went. All in all, Kennedy received nearly $14,000 for these and other serialization deals before the book was even published. Ten percent went to *Harper's*, per their contract, with 50 percent of the remaining going to Sorensen, in keeping with his long-standing agreement with his boss. But that agreement would eventually be revisited and replaced.

By *Joe* Kennedy.

"One of the reasons that the profession of politics suffers from such low public esteem is that it is constantly being run down by politicians themselves," wrote Cab Phillips, his newspaper's Washington correspondent, in his review of *Profiles in Courage* published the first day of 1956 in the *New York Times Book Review*. Phillips continued, "In this unfortunate state of affairs it is refreshing and enlightening to have a first-rate politician write a thoughtful and persuasive book about political integrity."[3]

Kennedy's book was set to make a big splash.

It was on prominent display in bookstores across the county on Tuesday, January 3. The book was light blue cloth with a black spine and gold letters. The jacket cover had the title against a white backdrop, with the word "*Profiles*" in blue, and the words "*in Courage*" in red. The backdrop of the bottom third of the jacket cover was blue, with black lettering for the words: *Decisive Moments in the Lives of Celebrated Americans*. At the bottom of the front cover, also in black, it said, *Foreword by Allan Nevins*.

Just above that, it said: *Senator John F. Kennedy* in white letters.

Profiles contained 266 pages and retailed for $3.50.

It immediately made bestseller lists, including at the *New York Times*, where it would become a fixture for ninety-five weeks in 1956–1957. It received glowing reviews in newspapers and periodicals around the country.

Kennedy made sure that all of his colleagues in the Senate received autographed copies. Richard Nixon received one, as well, and wrote Kennedy a warm thank-you note. A few years later, Kennedy would tell Nixon, "There's something about being an author which really builds the reputation of a politician."[4]

And it was working for Jack Kennedy.

Charles Poore, who would review books for the *New York Times* for four decades, wrote the rare contrarian view of *Profiles*. He saw his role as a book critic akin to "describing a mountain. The mountain is made of books, 10,000 new ones, at a venture, every year. If you concentrate on taking outstanding or representative sample from its forests and mines and peaks and valleys and settlements and streams, you may manage to give the public a true view of the mountain."[5]

Poore, a "gray-haired, gray-eyed man" who was "addicted to pin striped suits," preferred to write his reviews from the quiet confines of his office at home. His first review in 1956 was of *Profiles*, and he had an interesting take. Writing on January 7, for his regular column, *Books of the Times*, he challenged the notion that courage was an unqualified virtue and questioned Kennedy's failure to think it completely through:

> *In writing about Senator George Norris of Nebraska, Senator Kennedy says: "It is not now important whether Norris was right or wrong. What is important is the courage displayed in support of his convictions." The observation comes at the end of a paragraph on Norris' opposition to President Wilson's 1917 proposal to arm our*

merchant ships against attacks by the Kaiser's U-boat. It almost urges us to admire courage as courage, no matter where it appears. And this has its repugnant aspects. For it would be rather difficult for many of us to admire the courage of men who advocate crimes against civilization, wouldn't it?[26]

CHAPTER 47

"The Book Has Taken Off Like a Bird"

As he had with *Why England Slept* in 1940, Jack threw himself into promoting *Profiles in Courage* in 1956. Only this time, he wasn't a recent college graduate and novelty as an author. He was a U.S. senator, married to a beautiful socialite, and on a career path that could possibility take him to the pinnacle of political power in the years to come.

Kennedy became the hottest ticket in America in early 1956.

He clearly relished being a celebrity author. Newspapers around the country ran large advertisements calling *Profiles* "The All-American Best Seller!"—complete with Kennedy's image and blurbs from glowing reviews:

> As fine a book as we are likely to get all year—*Cleveland Plain Dealer*
> Absorbing and valuable—*Providence Journal*
> Easy to read, hard to forget, and as non-political as the chaplain's opening prayer—*Washington Post*
> Stirring, packed with drama, suspense, high purpose—*Houston Chronicle*
> A heartening and extremely spirited book—*Wall Street Journal*
> We hope *Profiles in Courage* becomes a national best seller—*St. Louis Post-Dispatch*[1]

A week after the book's release, Evan Thomas made a deal with the Book-of-the-Month Club "to do a condensation of *Profiles in Courage*."[2] It would appear in their April edition, "along with three other best-selling books." The royalty was small, "four cents a copy with an advance payment of $2,000, to be equally divided between publisher and author." But Thomas defended it, "This doesn't make anyone rich, but it gives distribution to some material that should be read as widely as possible, and does it in a tasteful form."

Thomas excitedly told Kennedy, "As they say in the advertising business, the book has taken off like a bird." In just a week, he told the Senator, "sales have climbed to nearly 11,000, and we'll soon have 20,000 books in print." The first printing totaled 15,000 copies. But while the various advertisements and advance reviews had yielded a successful launch, he told Kennedy that he was going to offer "some quiet prayers that the word-of-mouth gets going . . . that's what really sells books."

Although Harvard historian Arthur Schlesinger had helped Kennedy some with the book, he still wrote a glowing letter to Kennedy a couple of weeks after its release. "As a writer myself," he wrote, "I admire the book's architecture, which I am sure was difficult to arrive at, and the text itself is thoughtful, stimulating, and wise. You not only write fluently but convey a sense of holding back a great deal not directly relevant to your theme."[3]

The professor then mentioned a typo in chapter eight.

With his book front and center in the nation's consciousness, Kennedy also received more speaking invitations than he could handle, so he chose those that would help his book the most. One of the first he accepted was announced in newspapers across the country. "Senator John F. Kennedy will be the speaker at the seventh annual National Book Award presentation ceremonies in New York City on February 7 it has been announced by the award committee. Virginia Peterson will act as master of ceremonies."[4] Peterson, herself the author of two well-regarded books, was a well-known literary critic and radio personality.

Sorensen wrote the first draft of the speech and sent a copy to Thomas in New York on February 3, with an eye on pitching it to magazines. He said, "Like most speeches, this would have to be considerably reorganized and reoriented, with some additions and deletions, before we were satisfied that it was suitable for publications as a magazine article."[5] Sorensen thought it might be a good fit for what he called "one of the 'egg-head' magazines."

Historian Craig Fehrman has described the scene: "On the day of the National Book Awards, the Commodore Hotel pulsed with cheery enthusiasm. About a thousand literary types filed in, past the famous lobby, with its functioning waterfall, to the Grand Ballroom. The editors wore red carnations, the authors wore white, and everyone was making predictions."[6]

After the winners were announced, and the awards given—John O'Hara for fiction (*Ten North Frederick*), Herbert Kubly for nonfiction (*An American in Italy*), and W. H. Auden for poetry (The *Shield of Achilles*), Virginia Peterson introduced Kennedy.[7] "It is not often," she declared, "even in this land of opportunities, that a man can crowd into such relatively few years so many achievements," which she then recited. She told the audience that Kennedy's new book was "already climbing the bestseller lists."

Kennedy began his address with a humorous anecdote.[8] Referencing those who had won awards that day, he said:

> *The judges have decided both wisely and well, demonstrating the superiority of this method over the method occasionally suggested of permitting the authors themselves to pick the winners. Perhaps you know that a similar idea for the political sphere was advanced by the late Speaker of the House, Thomas B. Reed, more than 60 years go. Mr. Reed prophesied—somewhat sarcastically—that the time would eventually come when the people, weary of second-rate Presidents, would amend the constitution so as to provide that the President should always be chosen by the Senate, out of the Senate. The American people, as Reed described the situation, awaited with the tensest excitement the result of this first trial of "The choice of the wisest man by and out of the wisest body of men. When the time came for the announcement of the first such vote, 'Reed went on,' the presiding officer's hesitation and caller indicated that something unexpected had happened. He shouted to the vast multitude the astounding result: 96 Senators had each received one vote!*

Kennedy then proceed to deliver an eloquent speech titled "The Politician and the Author: A Plea for Greater Understanding." In the course of his Ted-talk-length remarks, he told the literati assembled in the ballroom, "I have not come through the enemy's lines today to accentuate our differences, but to plead for recognition of our similarities, of all we have in common, of all we share and should share." And concluded with an appeal, "Let us forget our petty quarrels of the past and present—and unite our talents for the challenge of the future."

The next day, back in Washington, Kennedy addressed a gathering of fellow authors sponsored by the *Washington Post*. "In the course of my research on political courage," he told the group, "I learned a lot about responsible—and irresponsible—journalism. Some of the harshest and most abusive attacks on Senators described in my book came not from opposing politicians, not from intellectual constituents, but from newspapers."[9]

But the next day in many of those newspapers, there was a mention of Kennedy as a potential vice-presidential candidate in 1956. "Democratic leaders are saying the Senator John F. Kennedy of Massachusetts looks more and more like a good bet for the party's vice-presidential nomination. They point to these factors: Adlai Stevenson is reportedly favorably inclined toward Kennedy as a possible running mate. Kennedy would be geographically 'right' on the ticket. He has an excellent war record—to balance Adlai's World War II civilian status. He is a Roman Catholic—and the Democrats want to lure back the Catholic voters who voted for Ike in 1952. He is only 38 now."[10] Kennedy's best-selling book was doing more than just earning financial rewards. It was already boosting his political career and putting him on the national stage.

Profiles sold 3,016 copies in the last week of February, bringing the total sold in its first two months of release to 23,833.[11]

CHAPTER 48

"The Star of the Night"

As Democrats from across the nation converged on Chicago in mid-August, the nomination of Adlai Stevenson—their standard bearer in 1952—was hardly a sure thing. He was the front-runner, by far, but there was a strong Stop-Stevenson push led by former President Harry S. Truman. He backed New York's governor, Averell Harriman, who had been his Secretary of Commerce.

But the real drama would have to do with the number two spot on the party's ticket to run against President Eisenhower and Richard Nixon. Several prominent Democrats were interested in the spot: Hubert Humphrey, Robert Wagner, Estes Kefauver, Albert Gore, and Frank Clement—and John F. Kennedy. Stevenson had played coy with the potential candidates, as well as the media.

The first night of the convention featured two possible vice-presidential contenders—the young men of the group. There was Kennedy from Massachusetts, a thirty-nine-year-old senator and best-selling author, and Clement, the thirty-six-year old governor of Tennessee, who had been tapped by Paul Butler, the Democratic National Chairman, to deliver the coveted Keynote Address on Monday evening.

In 1948, Kentucky Governor Alben Barkley had pretty much won a spot on the ticket with President Truman on the basis of his Keynote Address that year. And decades later, a young U.S. senator from Illinois would become a national political star in 2004 via a rousing Keynote speech to the Democrat faithful. Four years later, that same senator, Barack Obama, would win the White House.

So, a great Keynote speech could be a ticket to much bigger things.

Clement, like Kennedy, was a young man in a hurry and a gifted orator of the evangelical revivalist type. His friend, the Reverend Billy Graham, coached him. One newspaperman said Clement "has studied the techniques of Liberace, Billy Graham, and Elvis Presley . . . He is at once Demosthenes and a little old country boy."[1]

His platform skills had "caught the attention of national party leaders."[2] And he had a dream that he might just electrify his fellow Democrats the way another young politico had sixty years earlier, when William Jennings Bryan, also just thirty-six years old at the time, pontificated his way to the presidential nomination with his famous "Cross of Gold" speech.

Jack Kennedy clearly had some talented competition for the convention spotlight.

Fortunately, for Kennedy, he had also been tapped for an important role for the first night of the convention. He was chosen to narrate a film chronicling the history of the Democratic Party. Called "The Pursuit of Happiness," the documentary had been created by a veteran Hollywood producer named Dore Schary. It would turn out to be a huge break for Kennedy on a night that turned out to be beauty contest of sorts featuring two young party stars.

The film traced the story of the party from the days of Thomas Jefferson. Described as "an expertly edited and interesting documentary,"[3] the images were enhanced by Kennedy's voice. The producer worked with Kennedy beforehand, dubbing his voice onto the finished product. Schary, who was an old Hollywood hand, with credits such as *Mr Blandings Builds His Dream House*, *The Bachelor and the Bobby-Soxer*, and *The Farmer's Daughter*, coached Kennedy on his timing. He later said that Kennedy "grasped his lines quickly . . . and was very good at it."[4] He added, "All of us who were in contact with him immediately fell in love with him because he was so quick and so charming and so cooperative, and obviously so bright and so skilled." He said that Jack's personality "jumped at you on the screen."

As the film was shown to the convention, Kennedy talked about Woodrow Wilson, and events such as the Bonus Army, and built to highlights from the days of Franklin Roosevelt and Harry Truman. Kennedy's voice filled the large room. The film and Jack's narration were broadcast beyond the Chicago Amphitheater into homes across America via the television networks.

At least, that was what was supposed to happen.

As it turned out, CBS ignored much of the video and focused instead on interviews from the floor of the hall as well as Stevenson's headquarters at the Hilton Hotel. They didn't show any of the movie until the story was up to the Truman years. Paul Butler was made aware of this and his anger grew as he waited for the film to end. He was next up and scheduled to introduce Senator Kennedy to the crowd and thank him for the narration.

After the film, Butler, "looking grim headed" unloaded on "one of the major networks that failed to carry" the documentary. And lest there be any doubt, he told the crowd, "I want to express my thanks to NBC and ABC for keeping their commitments . . . we had no idea any network would edit this convention." The chairman then regained his composure and introduced "one of the new, young, brilliant giants, Senator John F. Kennedy of Massachusetts."

The crowd went wild for "the star of the night."[5]

Next up, Frank Clement did his best to eclipse Jack Kennedy. His very best. He was fiery and focused. He attacked Vice President Nixon, calling him "vice hatchet man." He even mocked Eisenhower as one staring down "the green fairways of indifference." And, in an almost sermonic manner, he several times defaulted to a cry: "How long, America? O, how long?"

But his effort fell short.

Press coverage back home in Tennessee was positive. The *Nashville Banner* said that Clement "became Tennessee's serious fighting candidate for the Democratic presidential nomination."[6] But others saw his effort differently. Journalist Red Smith, writing in the *New York Herald Tribune*, said the speech was akin to "slaying the Republicans with the jawbone of an ass." One observer said Clement's speech was "overwrought, his emotive manner more appropriate to a nineteenth-century evangelist's tent that a mid-twentieth-century political arena."[7]

Billy Graham, who had strongly advised his friend to take a moderate tone and not criticize Eisenhower or Nixon, distanced himself from Clement. In fact, the episode turned out to be "a bitter and traumatic experience" for the man from Tennessee, one from which "he never completely recovered."[8]

As soon as Clement finished, a demonstration began, but it was not for the young Tennessean. Banners appeared bearing the words "*Kennedy for President*." In fact, that evening was when Jack Kennedy became "a major presence in national politics."[9]

Meanwhile, Adlai Stevenson was so impressed by Kennedy's performance that he asked the Senator to give the speech nominating him to the convention. With Sorensen's significant help, working around the clock, the speech was prepared, which Kennedy then delivered skillfully.

And Governor Stevenson was nominated on the first ballot.

Of course, there was much scuttlebutt about Jack's book that week. It was part of his celebrity attraction. It might have been more of a boost for his VP prospects had he been able to persuade Evan Thomas to release it the last week of December 1955, qualifying it for 1956 Pulitzer consideration. But it was obvious that some had heard rumors questioning his authorship of *Profiles*. One Kennedy friend, Harvard classmate Blair Clark, who eventually became a vice president at CBS News, recalled a luncheon that week. While a group including Kennedy and newspaper columnist Joe Alsop shared a meal at the Blackstone Hotel, Kennedy's book came up and there was discussion about the "flap," apparently already extant, about "whether Jack had actually written *Profiles in Courage*."

Clark, who had helped Kennedy significantly with the book based on his senior honors thesis at Harvard, years earlier, remembered trying to inject what he thought was humor into the moment. He said to Jack, "Well, of course, you remember when you and I met at Widener Library [Harvard], and you asked me to rewrite sections of *Why England Slept*." He said Jack became defensive, even "furious."[10] Kennedy denied that Clark had ever helped him. "What do you mean?" Kennedy asked, indignantly. "You never did a goddamn thing on it. You never saw it."[11] But Clark, who had been editor of the *Harvard Crimson*, had indeed helped Kennedy back in the day.

That, however, had become an inconvenient truth.

CHAPTER 49

"It Was the Perfect Trial Run"

THEN STEVENSON DID SOMETHING SURPRISING—HE THREW THE choice of the party's vice-presidential nominee to the convention floor, setting the stage for a day of frenetic activity. It quickly became a race between Senator Estes Kefauver from Kentucky, Hubert Humphrey from Minnesota—and John F. Kennedy. When Jack decided to let his name go forward he told his brother Bobby to call their father, who was vacationing in the south of France. The old man was "livid," and he referred to his son as "an idiot."[1]

Joe Kennedy was convinced that such a move would ruin Jack's career.

But he didn't need to worry. Though Kennedy came very close to winning—just thirty-eight votes short—the convention chose Kefauver, setting the stage for one final Kennedy "moment" that week. With the outcome of the vice-presidential poll no longer in question, Kennedy went to the platform. House Speaker Sam Rayburn, who was moderating the session, was informed and he said from the rostrum: "If there is no objection, the chair will recognize Senator John Kennedy of Massachusetts."

Jack walked to the podium and waved to the audience. He seemed unsettled, even sad, like he hadn't slept. The right collar on his wrinkled shirt was pointed up. As he spoke, he had the gavel in his hands and twirled it nervously. He spoke without notes:

I want to take this opportunity first to express my appreciation to Democrats from all parts of the country, north and south, east and west, who have been so generous and kind to me this afternoon. I think it proves, as nothing else can prove, how strong and united the Democratic party is. Secondly, what has happened today bears out the good judgment of our Governor Stevenson in deciding that this issue should be taken to the floor of this convention. Because I believe that the Democratic party will go from this convention far stronger for what we have done here today. And therefore, ladies and gentlemen, recognizing that this convention has selected a man who has campaigned in all parts of the country, who has worked untiringly for the party, who will serve as an admirable running mate to Governor Stevenson,

I hope that this convention will make Estes Kefauver's nomination unanimous. Thank you.

Jack turned to walk away, while the audience roared its approval. He met Sam Rayburn a few steps away, who told him, "Go back and make a motion." So, Kennedy turned back and made his motion. Rayburn then called for the vote.

It was Kennedy's third appearance before the convention that week—a week that, in effect, was the beginning of his own quest for the presidency four years later. Gracious in defeat, it wasn't lost on many that Jack Kennedy had demonstrated the kind of "grace under pressure" he wrote about in his best-selling book, which had just moved past the 50,000 mark in hardcover sales.

Profiles, the big winner of the week, was poised for a fresh post-convention bounce.

Although he hated to lose, it didn't take long for Kennedy to realize that by losing he had actually won. It was "a stroke of luck."[2] He later told reporters, "Like everything in life, you cannot tell how it will be reflected in the future. After all, we came much closer than I thought we were going to."[3]

Stevenson wrote to him, "If there was a hero, it was you, and if there has been a new gallantry on our horizon in recent years, it is yourself." Kennedy's office received a ton of mail indicating that Jack had touched a political nerve. Much of the mail was from people under twenty years of age, but who would be voting in their first election four years later.

Historian James MacGregor Burns, writing about Kennedy's 1956 loss, said, "As things turned out, it was his great moment—the moment when he passed through a kind of political sound barrier to register on the nation's memory. The dramatic race had glued millions to their television sets. Kennedy's near-victory and sudden loss, the impression he gave of a clean-cut boy who had done his best and who was accepting defeat with a smile—all this struck at people's hearts in living rooms across the nation. In this moment of triumphant defeat, his campaign for the presidency was born."[4]

Kennedy traveled the country for Stevenson that fall, but he had his own agenda, targeting areas that would be important to him in any future race. He also promoted his book. The tour was actually better than being on the ticket, "it was the perfect trial run."[5]

By mid-November, as the nation readied itself for another four years of Ike and Dick, sales of *Profiles* reached 69,936 mark.[6] It remained a fixture in the number two spot on the *New York Times* bestseller list for nonfiction.

While his political future looked bright in the wake of the Democratic convention in 1956, his personal life—particularly his marriage—told a different story. Jackie was pregnant that summer, but Jack decided he needed a vacation, apparently one from her. He chartered a sailboat and crew for some time in the Mediterranean, while his wife, who was due in October, went to stay with her mother in Rhode Island.

This was her second pregnancy, having lost a baby back in 1954. She "asked Jack not to leave her, but he decided to go anyway."[7] And while Kennedy was cruising and cavorting with friends on a forty-foot boat, his wife suffered another miscarriage on August 23, requiring an emergency cesarean section.

A baby girl was stillborn.

When Jack was reached, "he took the news calmly, and after hearing that Jackie was in good condition, he initially intended to resume his leisurely sail." But a friend sailing with Kennedy—Senator George Smathers—told him: "If you want to run for president, you'd better get your ass back to your wife's bedside or else every wife in the country will be against you."

So, Jack made the trip.

Then, after a few days at his wife's bedside, he took off again, this time to make speeches for Stevenson and promote his book, and "for the next two months Jackie seldom saw him."[8] He received more than 1,000 speaking invitations in the weeks following the convention. And by the end of 1956, *Profiles in Courage* had sold 79,869 hard-cover copies, generating $40,290.27 in royalties.[9]

In a deal with Pocket Books, Harper and Brothers authorized the publication of a soft-cover edition of *Profiles* that went on sale in January 1957. Retailing at just thirty-five cents, 400,000 copies were printed in the first run. There would be twenty-four more soft-cover printings by the end of 1963. But the availability of a copy at one-tenth the price of the hardcover version didn't have much impact on sales. Evan Thomas reported to Jack in March 1957 "that we now have over 100,000 copies of our edition of *Profiles* in print. 103,000 to be exact. Our total sales are now 89,714. The softcover book doesn't seem to have hurt us so far."[10]

CHAPTER 50

"Pulitzer Prize"

It was likely because he was an immigrant, having come to America from Hungary at the age of seventeen to fight for the Union during the waning days of the Civil War, that Joseph Pulitzer took up the cause of raising money to ensure the Statue of Liberty would become a fixture in New York Harbor. Work on the statue's pedestal had been suspended in the early 1880s, and there was a strong possibility that France's great gift to America might wind up on permanent display in—perish the thought—*another* city. So, the wealthy publishing magnate threw his weight, and that of one of his newspapers, the *New York World*, behind a massive fundraising effort to finish the job.

He even made Lady Liberty the new logo for the masthead of the popular paper.

A few years after the monument's dedication, Pulitzer built what at that time was the tallest building in the world for his headquarters. He also commissioned an artist to design a massive stained-glass window bearing the image of the iconic statue. It was called "Liberty Lighting the World."

But by the 1950s, the *New York World* was defunct, and the once-great building was vacant and had an appointment with the wrecking ball as part of the city's plan to expand access to the nearby Brooklyn Bridge.

John Hohenberg, a 1927 graduate of Columbia University's School of Journalism, a school that was originally funded by a bequest from Pulitzer, had the vision to try to rescue the large window. He negotiated with the Mayor of New York, Robert Wagner, and managed to make a deal for one dollar. But he had to raise about $8,000 to have the window salvaged and moved to the Morningside Heights campus. It was installed in room 305 of the journalism building.

The space was renamed—The World Room.[1]

You can almost draw a straight line from The Yellow Kid, "a sardonic Irish ragamuffin who lived on the streets of New York,"[2] to the annual awarding of coveted honors called Pulitzer Prizes. You see, The Yellow Kid, dubbed so because he wore a yellow nightshirt, was a character in a comic strip called Hogan's Alley, popular in the last decade of the nineteenth century, created by Richard F. Outcault, who also gave us the first dialogue balloons used in the funny papers ever since.

In 1896, Outcault, who had been running his work exclusively in Pulitzer's *New York World*, struck a deal with a rival paper, the *New York Journal*, and its powerful owner, William Randolph Hearst, to run his work there, as well. This set up a fierce war between the media moguls, one that led to increasingly sensational reporting to win readership. Such writing was soon dubbed "Yellow Journalism," the color drawn from, you guessed it, The Yellow Kid.

After a few years in the gutter and as he began to face his own mortality, Pulitzer made the decision to play it straight and became a vocal advocate for journalistic responsibility. Trying to chisel this in stone as his legacy, he offered $2 million to Columbia University for the establishment of a school of journalism, the first of its kind in the country. They rejected the offer because the newspaper profession was then viewed by academia as just a step or two above the sordid vice written about in the papers.

Eventually, the university rethought this, establishing the Columbia School of Journalism in 1912, the year after Pulitzer died. The wealthy newspaperman provided generously for the university in his will, including a provision establishing prizes in his name for excellence in journalism. The first awards were given in 1917, and the process has evolved since then, adding categories and increasing the size of the cash benefits.

Any work within an official category could be submitted for a fee, with all submissions going to a jury of experts in that field, those jury members being appointed by the Pulitzer Board. The board then made the final decisions.

By 1957, John Hohenberg was the "secretary and day-to-day administrator" for the Pulitzer Advisory Committee, the group tasked with making final decisions about the annual awards.[3] He had been given the job in the wake of the death of Joseph Pulitzer II, a couple of years earlier. Pulitzer's son, Joseph Pulitzer III, or Jr., as he preferred, served as the new chairman, following in his father's footsteps.

Hohenberg had spent several months in 1956 away from his duties on sabbatical leave, something offered to tenured members of the Columbia faculty "every seventh year" of their service to the school.[4] On his return after the holiday break in early 1957, he said that one of the first books he picked up was "Senator Kennedy's *Profiles in Courage*, an entry for the biography award."[5] Harper and Brothers had filed an application with the committee and sent the four copies required with the submission. He recalled not only reading it, but also taking the additional step of researching "the tremendous amount of work he'd done on it."

He knew that other members of the Pulitzer board were aware of the book, as it was already a bestseller and its author a ubiquitous presence in the news. Hohenberg was also aware of some talk about the possibility that Kennedy may have used a ghostwriter. So, "as a matter of caution," he "looked into the manner in which Kennedy had gone about researching and writing the book."

He wrote about this in his diary: "Make sure that *Profiles in Courage* is Kennedy's work before the verdicts of the Biography Jury and the board. Every author I know of who does nonfiction needs help with sources, but make sure the Senator did the writing." Decades later, when writing his book about the history of the Pulitzers, he quoted the entry from his diary and then added two words.

"I tried."[6]

Regardless of any doubts he had about Kennedy's authorship, even months before the decision had to be made, Hohenberg "was reasonably sure" the book would be in contention for the prize in biography.[7]

He was wrong.

Professor Hohenberg was in The World Room for the annual meeting of the Pulitzer Advisory Committee one day in the spring of 1957. The fifteen men of the committee sat around an oval table in front of the Liberty window inset in the wall. Thirteen of them were distinguished journalists, editors, or publishers. The other two were from Columbia University, including its president. It was their job to weigh the recommendations passed to them by others who made up juries tasked with sifting through several hundred entries from the world of journalism and literature. By the time the best entries were sent to the Advisory Committee, there were only a few still standing in each category.

That year, they would give out fourteen prizes, including a Special Citation Award. The members making up the 1957 Pulitzer Advisory Committee were:

Barry Bingham, Sr., editor-in-chief and president, *Louisville Courier-Journal*

Hodding Carter II, editor, *Delta Democrat-Times*, Greenville, Mississippi

Turner Catledge, managing editor, *The New York Times*

Norman Chandler, president and publisher, *Los Angeles Times*

Robert Choate, editor and publisher, *The Boston Herald*

Gardner Cowles, editor and publisher, *Des Moines Register-Tribune*

J. D. Ferguson, president and editor, *Milwaukee Journal*

John Hohenberg, executive secretary, The Pulitzer Prizes, Columbia University

Grayson Kirk, president, Columbia University

John S. Knight, editorial chairman, *Knight Newspapers*, Inc.

Benjamin M. McKelway, vice president and editor, *The Washington (DC) Evening Star*

Paul Miller, president/chairman of the board, *Gannett Newspapers*, Inc.

Joseph Pulitzer III, president and publisher, *St. Louis Post-Dispatch*

Louis B. Seltzer, editor, *Cleveland Press*

The two judges tasked with overseeing the review of submissions published in 1956 in the genre of biography and autobiography in early 1957 were Julian Boyd, the editor of the Jefferson papers at Princeton University, and Professor Bernard Mayo, who worked with Boyd on the Jefferson project, but who also was a biographer of Henry Clay.[8] Both were highly regarded historians. Having weeded out the unworthy titles, they settled on five works, listed in their order of preference:

Harlan Fiske Stone: Pillar of the Law, by Alpheus T. Mason
Roosevelt: The Lion and the Fox, by James MacGregor Burns

James Madison: The President, 1809–1812, by Irving Brant
John Quincy Adams and the Union, by Samuel Flagg Bemis
Old Bullion Benton, by William N. Chambers

There was no mention of *Profiles in Courage*.

Boyd and Mayo described Mason's biography of Chief Justice Stone as "the product of a searching mind that is also capable of clear analysis." Regarding Burns' book, they referred to it as "a brilliant performance, and its literary quality is in our opinion superior to that of Mason's *Stone*." But they thought it fell short of having the "definitive quality" of Mason's work. Though they had managed to dispense with awards in history and literature with relative ease, "the board deadlocked over biography."[9] There were enough votes for Mason's book, but little enthusiasm.

The chairman of the committee was Joseph Pulitzer, grandson of the original benefactor. Described as "rather small and distinguished in appearance, with a handsome face set off by a mass of curly brown hair," he was ready to call for a vote on the Mason book, when he saw a hand being cautiously raised by a member of the committee member. It was Donald Ferguson from the *Milwaukee Journal*.

Hohenberg described the scene in his diary:

The white-haired veteran of many a journalistic conflict sighed deeply, then murmured of the Kennedy book, I read it aloud to my 12-year-old grandson and the boy was absolutely fascinated. I think we should give the prize to Profiles in Courage. Then, suddenly, the atmosphere changed. Others who had read the book agreed with Ferguson.

There was some discussion. Hohenberg later recalled that "at that particular point, Kennedy was so much in the news, and his book so much admired by the editors around the table, most of whom had read it, that they overruled the biography jury."[10]

Chairman Pulitzer later said, "It wasn't great distinguished history in that sense. It was a book that showed a great understanding of the American political figure and how these people operated, and I think it just appealed to the board."[11] He added, "The appeal of this young man writing a very lively book about political figures . . . It's a funny thing, they picked this fellow. Nobody had any idea of what would happen in later history."

There was, however, more to the story.

CHAPTER 51

"I Worked as Hard as I Could to Get Him That Prize"

"THE INSIDIOUS INFLUENCE OF JOE KENNEDY VIA HIS FRIEND ARTHUR Krock, who did lobby behind the scenes for *Profiles in Courage*, has long been assumed," wrote British Historian Mark White more than five decades after Kennedy won the Pulitzer Prize.[1] This opinion is widely shared by those well acquainted with the story, but admittedly, there isn't much of a paper-trail. The evidence is anecdotal.

Krock, who had been the driving force back during the *Why England Slept* project, continued his side job as media consigliere for Joe Kennedy. Himself a three-time Pulitzer Prize honoree, the *New York Times* Washington Bureau Chief had earned the nickname "Dean of Washington newsmen."[2] Krock had only recently finished serving for fifteen years on the Pulitzer Advisory Committee.

And he remained on very good terms with its members.

His newspaper published a highly laudatory notice when Krock stepped down in 1955: "The Advisory Board on the Pulitzer Prizes has again cited Arthur Krock of *The New York Times* for distinguished correspondence from Washington. It called him a 'great newspaper man' and an example to the world of journalism."[3] At that time, John Hohenberg wrote in his diary: "I'm told that Arthur Krock of the *New York Times*, the most influential member of the board as well as the White House Press Corps, intends to retire after this year."[4]

Krock's influence in Pulitzer matters apparently did not end with his retirement.

Early on during the research phase of *Profiles*, Jack reached out to Krock, who lobbied hard for the inclusion of the chapter about Robert Taft. In his *Memoirs*, Krock wrote: "He consulted me, among others, and I strongly urged the inclusion of Robert A. Taft. I cited Taft's lone courage, as a politician, in opposing the ex-post-facto guilt thesis of the Nuremberg trials."[5] He added, "Kennedy accepted my nomination, but with considerable reluctance." Kennedy later told Krock, "One of the things I wish you had never persuaded me to do was to put Taft in the *Profiles*."

Likely, though, Jack was more appreciative of Krock's help with the Pulitzer people.

That Jack had, in fact, discussed the Pulitzer Prize with his father was obvious from a letter he wrote to the Ambassador in January 1957: "Dear

Dad: I am enclosing a list of the members of the Advisory Board for the Pulitzer Prize."[6] We can only speculate about what either Kennedy had in mind with such an exchange, but to rule out the idea that the elder Kennedy, someone well known to find creative ways to fix problems and influence outcomes, wanted to find ways to steer committee members toward his son's book, would be irresponsible.

Winning the Pulitzer Prize was important to John F. Kennedy, personally and professionally. His candid comment to Margaret Coit back in 1953—"I would rather win a *Pulitzer Prize* than be President of the United States"—was more than casual conversation. It was from the heart, something he had obviously thought about. And when he decided to write a sequel-of-sorts to *Why England Slept*, there can be little doubt that it was with an eye on the coveted prize.

This was further confirmed just prior to the publishing of *Profiles*, when Kennedy called Evan Thomas and interrupted a family Christmas gathering to pressure the editor to back date the publishing date to 1955. As he said, "I've just been talking to Arthur Krock, and I understand it would win the Pulitzer Prize this year."[7]

In the 1983 Oral History interview historian Herbert Parmet made for the John F. Kennedy Library, he confirmed Krock's lobbying efforts. "The instrument, the most direct instrument was Choate [Robert Choate], of the *Boston Herald*, who was on the committee. He was the man through whom [Krock] was lobbying."[8] And Joseph Kennedy was known to have great influence with Choate's newspaper.[9]

When Krock reached out to Choate, the committee member was skeptical, at first. "Give me some reasons why the Kennedy book might be considered among the biographies,"[10] he wrote to Krock. But he encouraged Krock to contact the other members of the committee. "I am quite confident that Joe [Pulitzer] would be glad to see that it went to a Democrat," he told Krock. Choate also "expressed his full confidence" that their dealings should be kept "confidential."

Hohenberg recalled Krock's lobbying efforts, writing that Arthur "had been recommending it widely."[11] In fact, later in life, Krock would "claim credit himself for convincing the jurors of the book's merit."[12] He said that he "worked like hell" toward this end.[13]

A few years later, Krock told William Manchester, who was writing a book about Kennedy, "I worked as hard as I could to get him that prize."[14]

The fix was in.

Jack Kennedy received notification from the Pulitzer Committee on May 7. "Senator Kennedy: I take very great pleasure in confirming the fact that the Trustees of Columbia University, on the nomination of the Advisory Board on the Pulitzer Prizes, have awarded the Pulitzer Prize in Biography or Autobiography, established under the will of the first Joseph Pulitzer, to you for '*Profiles in Courage*' for the year 1956. In accordance with that award, I enclose the University's check for $500 as tangible evidence to you of the selection of your work. With renewed Congratulations, I am—Sincerely Yours—John Hohenberg"[15]

Kennedy donated the prize money to the United Negro College Fund.

The senator received congratulations from Evan Thomas, who added, "Our sales are now 96,000. . . We have sent books out all over the country on consignment, plus Pulitzer Prize bands to go around the jackets.[16]

Not to be outdone, the people at *Pocket Books* sent notice to all their vendors, "immediately upon hearing the news of your winning the Pulitzer Prize."[17] They had already printed 400,000 and were planning another printing soon. "We will have a blurb on the cover telling the world."

Hardcover sales soared past the 100,000 mark the first week of June.[18]

To say that winning the Pulitzer was a boost to Kennedy's political career would be a gross understatement. On the heels of his multiple platform appearances at the Democratic convention a year earlier and being a popular Democrat in spite of another Eisenhower landslide (Ike and Dick carried 41 states), he was among the leaders in most polls about the upcoming 1960 presidential election.

Historian James MacGregor Burns, whose book about FDR was an also-ran to Kennedy's *Profiles* for the 1957 biography Pulitzer, wrote a book about Jack in the run-up to the 1960 campaign. In it, he argued that the prize did indeed help Kennedy politically:

In January 1957, the Gallup Poll had asked people their preference if the choice for the Democratic presidential nomination narrowed down

*to Kefauver and Kennedy. The outcome was 38 per cent for Kefauver
and 41 per cent for Kennedy. Four months later, in answer to substantially the same question, the returns split 33 per cent to 45 per
cent in the same order. Since the only relevant and significant event
in the four-month interim was the Pulitzer award, it seems possible
that literary honors carry more weight with the public than has been
commonly thought.*[19]

John F. Kennedy was the complete package in so many ways—handsome, charismatic, and intelligent. But he was still young, not yet forty.
But the Pulitzer seemed to mitigate some of that youthfulness. It "gave
him the stamp of seriousness and even wisdom that Americans saw as
invaluable in meeting difficulties abroad and at home."[20]

In fact, had he somehow been able to persuade Evan Thomas and
Harper and Brothers to have the book published in December 1955, as
opposed to January 1956, and it were to have won the Pulitzer in May
1956 (instead of 1957), months before the 1956 Democratic convention,
it might have made the difference in the race for the spot on the ticket as
Stevenson's running mate.

However, with the award and all of his obvious success came a pre-
dictable amount of envy. And it wasn't long before rumors began to be
noised about that Kennedy had not really written his prize-winning book.
It was also being whispered that sales figures were possibly being "doc-
tored." These smoldered in the shadows for much of the second half of
1957.

John Hohenberg, however, was concerned enough in the wake of
further rumors following the Kennedy award to recommend what he
described as a "modest change in the procedures of the Pulitzer board."[21]
He suggested that in the future the board should "divide itself into small,
informal committees to do more of the necessary investigating" in order
to "backstop its own juries."

CHAPTER 52

"It Was All a Matter of Money"

WILLIAMS COLLEGE OCCUPIES 450 BREATHTAKINGLY PICTURESQUE acres in the Berkshires in northwestern Massachusetts, not far from the New York and Vermont borders. Long a prestigious private liberal arts college, with one president of the United States—James A. Garfield—in its alumni list, Williams has a long history of prominent scholars on its faculty. James MacGregor Burns, Pulitzer Prize–winning historian, was part of the faculty at Williams for nearly four decades.

A year or so after the publication of *Profiles*, Burns hosted Ted Sorensen at the college. The aide to Senator John F. Kennedy was a regular guest at New England schools, using speaking engagements as part of his passion to try to interest students in politics and policy. Following a morning on campus, he and Burns had lunch at the Student Union, where Ted had conversations with several of the schools approximately 2,500 students—those with political careers on their minds.

Later, in the run-up to the 1960 presidential race, Burns wrote his own book, *John F. Kennedy: A Political Profile*. As it was being written, the historian had several heated exchanges with Sorensen, who wanted Burns to pen more of a puff piece, something Burns would never do. Years later, Burns said it was "a painful period" for him.[1]

But after lunch that day and as they walked out of the Student Union, Burns and Sorensen were chatting and Jack's book came up in the conversation. "That was a very good book, *Profiles in Courage*," Burns remarked to his guest.

"Who really wrote it?" he asked with a smile.

Sorensen, with a slight smile of his own, replied, "I did."

Gilbert Seldes was considered by some to be "the closest our time has come to producing a 'Renaissance' man of the communication arts."[2] He was a widely read cultural critic and would one day become the founding dean of the University of Pennsylvania's prestigious Annenberg School of Communications. Among his pursuits in 1957 was a column he wrote for the *Village Voice* in New York.

Seldes kept his eyes and ears on cultural trends and had been picking up some chatter about *Profiles in Courage*. In fact, the story had been going around for a while, but no one thought too much of it, and it didn't get any traction. However, when the book received the Pulitzer, Seldes, who was already less-than-impressed with Kennedy, decided to go public with what he had been hearing. Writing in his column on May 15, he charged that Kennedy had a "collaborator" for *Profiles in Courage*.[3] Adding insult to injury, he told his readers that the book "shows no research. It hasn't a point of view beyond the one indicated in the title: Courage is A Good Thing." In Seldes' opinion, *Profiles* was "the most innocuous book published in a generation."

Fortunately for Kennedy, the Seldes piece had no legs and was little noticed in those long-before-the-Internet days.

Actually, speculation that Kennedy had received significant help with *Profiles* had been around for more than a year. As the book became a publishing phenomenon in 1956, some wondered how a busy senator, who had spent so much time in the hospital, then took off for a lengthy European vacation, could possibly have done so much research and writing.

For more than five decades, Theodore Sorensen regularly denied his *true* role in the authorship of *Profiles in Courage*. But over time and bit by bit, the real story began to emerge from the shadows, a story that had the potential to tarnish his carefully guarded image, not to mention that of his famous boss.

Sorensen published his memoirs in 2009 and continued to shine a light on Kennedy. He wrote, "I did a first draft of most chapters, which he revised both with a pen and through dictation," adding, "JFK worked particularly hard and long on the first and last chapters."[4]

He was being generous.

The picture that emerges from careful investigation of the documentary evidence is that Kennedy functioned more as a *line-editor* for the book, with Sorensen doing the actual writing, helped some by Dr. Jules Davids. He worked full time on the project for much of 1955, sometimes putting in twelve-hour days. There is no evidence that Kennedy worked all that hard on the book, his protestations and carefully staged demonstrations, notwithstanding.

Theodore Sorenson was, indeed, JFK's ghost.

For her part, Jackie Kennedy found the working relationship between her husband and his speechwriter to be "creepy." In her view, Ted had "a crush" on Jack.[5] She was convinced that Sorensen's near-worship "was perilously rooted in feelings of resentment and inferiority" on the aide's part. She also thought Ted was "sneaky."

She was not alone.

Years later, McGeorge Bundy, who served as Kennedy's National Security Advisor in the White House, noted that the relationship between Jack and Ted was "so close and so entangled and so full of repressed worry to both of them."[6] He said that Kennedy "was never entirely comfortable about having much of his product the work of another man."

Bundy remembers Bobby Kennedy describing a moment when the Kennedy-Sorensen relationship was severely strained in the late 1950s. They almost came to "a parting of the ways" over issues involving "the relative roles of the researcher and writer in *Profiles and Courage*." Bundy added, "I don't think either of them ever entirely forgot it."[7]

And when Kennedy won the Pulitzer Prize, Sorensen was apparently loose-lipped about his own role in writing the book, "making noises about town that in fact he had written a good deal of the book for the senator."[8]

About a year after her husband's murder, Jackie told historian Arthur Schlesinger that Jack "couldn't always trust Ted."[9] She added, that when the Pulitzer was awarded, "Ted didn't behave very well that year." She suspected that he was the source of all the rumors that her husband hadn't really written *Profiles*.

In fact, he had become more than a loose end, he was a potential loose *cannon*.

Kennedy's father was already suspicious of certain "New York people," described as "sleuths," who were apparently determined to sabotage Jack's political career.[10] They were trying to prove that Arthur Krock was the real author of *Profiles* and hoped to charge the senator with fraud. The FBI got involved even before Seldes' column hit newsstands. They monitored the activities of the suspected sleuths, "undoubtedly at the Ambassador's prompting."[11] Of course, Joe knew that Krock didn't work on *Profiles*, but he had helped significantly with Jack's first book, and likely that's why early suspicion fell on the *New York Times* journalist. But the elder Kennedy knew that it was only a matter of time before Sorensen's work became public knowledge.

He needed to fix the problem before it became one.

Money was Joe Kennedy's love language. It was not only the path to prosperity, but it was also a powerful weapon. He had long demonstrated a flair for making money and spending it strategically. He knew the right payment to the right person at the right time could make all the difference. And when it came to the potential for a problem with Ted Sorensen, he was determined to make that problem go away.

It was all a matter of money.

While there is no detailed paper trail or smoking gun in the form of a copy of an agreement between Sorensen and the Ambassador extant, there is enough anecdotal evidence to give us a reasonably clear idea of what transpired. Sorensen had worked very hard on the book. Tirelessly so. He wrote the entire first draft and was fully involved in all of the subsequent edits. He organized the research. He worked with the other historians who had been asked for input. He directed the efforts of Professor Jules Davids, the only other person to receive money for the project—a paltry $700.

Yet, despite all his monumental efforts, Ted had to actually lobby his boss for any mention of him to appear in Jack's original preface to the book, where he thanked so many others—including Dr. Davids. Sorensen wrote speeches for Kennedy's speaking tours after the book came out. He was the primary negotiator for the serialization of the book in publications across the country. Sorensen later said: "It [*Profiles in Courage*] was bought by more than two million American readers and by magazines, book clubs, reprint publishers, foreign publishers, television producers, and others, with all of whom he asked me to negotiate."[12]

Frankly, Ted Sorensen would have been superhuman if the idea that someone else was getting all the credit and praise for his gargantuan effort didn't bother him—at least a little.

CHAPTER 53

"Joe Kennedy Made a Deal with Jack's Ghostwriter"

By the middle of 1957, Ted had already profited handsomely from *Profiles*. Owing to their 1953 agreement, he received 50 percent of any fees or royalties for work on Kennedy's writing. So, by the time of the awarding of the Pulitzer Prize, Sorensen had likely already pocketed at least $26,000 from the various serialization payments prior to the book's publication, as well as his "cut" of the 1956 royalties which totaled $40,290.27.[1]

His early cut would be worth about $250,000 today. His earnings from *Profiles* were already exceeding his salary as a Senate staffer. And with 400,000 softcover copies on the market, all signs pointed toward much more money to be made.

Of course, for Jack Kennedy, it was never about the money. Nor was it for his father. The book was part of something bigger—a campaign for the office that eluded the Ambassador in 1940, and that he hoped his son would win in 1960. If somehow the true account of Sorensen's work on the book came to light, they would likely have to kiss dreams of a Kennedy presidency goodbye. And the most likely scenario for the story springing a leak would be if Theodore C. Sorensen went rogue.

So, Joe Kennedy made a deal with Jack's ghostwriter, likely with the help of his favored "fixer," attorney James Landis. It would be fifty years before this arrangement came to light in any detail. While long rumored, Sorensen himself would do the reveal.

Though Ted Sorensen had written several books dealing directly or indirectly about John F. Kennedy in the years following the assassination in Dallas, he determined to write one more personal memoir, one that was published in 2009, a year before Sorensen himself passed away. Called *Counselor: A Life Lived at the Edge of History*, he listed three reasons for writing it.

First, he referenced his 1965 tome titled simply, *Kennedy*, as being written so soon after Kennedy's tragic death, he "did not want to offend any of" the family and friends still living and grieving.[2] The indication was that he held some things back, and "the passage of time has made a broader, more candid perspective possible."

Next, he suggested that while "the history community knows a great deal about Kennedy's impact on the nation and the world," little was known about where Sorensen's "ideas and ideals originated."

Finally, he wrote it to counter what he described as the current day "cynicism and mistrust about presidential politics." He thought it would be good to remind people "that it is possible to have a president who is honest, idealistic, and devoted to the best values of the country." In other words, Kennedy was the last of the great hero-presidents.

And he helped.

Largely, a hagiographic work designed to keep Kennedy on his perpetual pedestal, it also had a Forest Gump quality to it, as Sorensen is found at just about every turn putting ideas into Kennedy's head, as well as words into his mouth.

When it came to the part of the Kennedy-Sorensen story that involved *Profiles in Courage*, the former aide still couldn't bring himself to come completely clean about Kennedy's sparse role in the creation of the book, though he did describe his former boss's contributions in more modest language than he ever had to date.

The one item, however, that Sorensen did shed some light on was the financial arrangement made in 1957, just as the Pulitzer Prize was awarded. He described an agreement he made as one developed by "Joe Kennedy's advisors," because apparently they thought "it was necessary to prevent me from leaving his service prior to the next presidential election, or from publicly demanding one-half of the book's direct and indirect proceeds."[3] However, he insisted that, whatever the fears of Kennedy's people, "they were wholly mistaken."

But were they?

Two of the most primal drives in life, drives that seem to become particularly aggressive when mixed with politics, are pride and greed. And when wounded pride meets greed, bad things can happen. Whistles can be blown. Stories meant to be kept secret can be told, even uncomfortable ones.

Joseph P. Kennedy had spent a life in the world of high-finance and power politics. There can be little doubt that, as he heard stories about Sorensen's loose lips, he could read the warning signs. Though Ted Sorensen had worked tirelessly for Jack Kennedy, it was always possible that the devotee could become a detractor, under the right—or wrong—circumstances.

So, Joe decided to assuage Sorensen's pride by appealing to his greed.

Sorensen wrote: "Clearly one-half of his earnings from all the direct, indirect, or prospective *Profiles* royalties would total far in excess of anything either of us had ever contemplated, much less expected, when that fifty-fifty royalty-sharing understanding had been reached a few years earlier. He had no financial need to renegotiate or reconsider that longstanding agreement. I had not worked on the book for monetary reasons, nor had he. I made no financial request, and imposed no conditions . . . In May 1957, he [Joe Kennedy] unexpectedly and generously offered, and I happily accepted, a sum to be spread over several years, that I regarded as more than fair."[4]

The clear indication was that the new agreement was more generous than the previous one.

Speaking candidly in his memoir, Ted tellingly said the agreement he made with Kennedy "diminished any interest I might otherwise have had in public recognition of my role." He told Kennedy so in a letter. "Because of our agreement concerning my work and pay for such publications (which agreement has . . . been extremely helpful to me), I am unwilling to push this point concerning recognition of my participation." Apparently, he had been willing to push it earlier.

Mission accomplished.

But the main takeaway is that Joe Kennedy's instincts were right, and Sorensen needed to be handled. Sorensen elaborated a bit on the agreement: "The letter of agreement was binding on our respective heirs, should either of us die before the agreement's expiration." He added, "I kept the agreement confidential until now [2009], lest it fuel speculative exaggeration of my role in the writing of the book."

So, how much money did Sorensen receive? There are apparently no copies of the agreement extant, or at least available to researchers, so we have to piece it together from other fragments found here and there. The most common dollar figure suggested is that Kennedy paid Sorensen $100,000 in a structured deal paid out over several years. That would translate to nearly a million dollars today. Added to what Sorensen had already earned up to May 1957, the figure swells to nearly $1,250,000 in today's dollars.

Such a payout (or payoff) could reasonably be seen as a tacit acknowledgment that Sorensen was the real author, or ghostwriter, if you please, of *Profiles in Courage*.

Jackie Kennedy, in a 1964 conversation with the historian Arthur Schlesinger, said her husband gave Sorensen *all* the money from the book, "over a hundred thousand dollars."[5] She added, "Ted's gotten every bit of money from that book until the memorial edition with Bobby's preface came out," a reference to the edition published in the wake of President Kennedy's death.

So, the final sum may have *exceeded* $100,000. Sorensen wrote: "By January 1961, when we entered the White House, his total net earnings from *Profiles* had not yet reached a level twice as high as the sum he had promised me but he requested no adjustment. Another reminder of how lucky I was."[6]

Indeed.

With the Sorensen agreement in place and the absence of media coverage after the Seldes column, the story had been pretty much contained. But Jack had to deal with the occasional question. In July 1957, he received a letter from Emma Sheehy, a professor at Columbia University. After congratulating Kennedy on winning the Pulitzer, she mentioned a rumor she had heard that the book was "entirely written by someone else."[7]

Kennedy replied a few days later, calling the rumor "completely and utterly untrue."[8] He added, somewhat defensively, "The false rumors concerning my book did not start until it had been awarded a Pulitzer Prize." Things quieted down.

Until one day in December. . .

CHAPTER 54

"Less Profile and More Courage"

TED YATES WAS THE PRODUCER FOR THE ELEVEN O'CLOCK NEWS ON channel five in New York City in 1956. He would go on to have a celebrated career as a reporter before being killed by gunfire while covering the Six-Day War in Israel in 1967. Mike Wallace was his anchorman. At thirty-eight years of age, Wallace was already an old hand in broadcasting, having worked in radio as an announcer, and even a game show host in the early days of television. Yates had an idea, one that would involve Wallace.

But he had no way of foreseeing that it would ultimately and awkwardly involve the Kennedys.

Originally from Wyoming, Yates was brought up on a ranch. It was a tough life, but he told Kay Halle years later, that the toughest two weeks he ever experienced were when he was with his friend Ted Kennedy in Palm Beach. He remembered the Kennedys as a hard-driven bunch. The days included swimming, tennis, baseball, and sailing—all before lunch. Then he had to join Ted and his siblings in the reading of the Federalist Papers, and even had to take part in a discussion about Madison, Jefferson, and Hamilton.[1]

Yates wanted to create an interview show, one that would air late at night. So that fall they blended elements of the news with interviews and called the show *Night Beat*. It was an instant hit, and Wallace quickly made a name for himself as a hard-hitting newsman, an image he would keep and cultivate for the rest of his life.

Night Beat featured Wallace's "candid, sometimes combative style" of interviewing guests.[2] The program aired weeknights from 11:00 p.m. to midnight on WABD, NYC's Channel Five. At almost the exact same time Jack Kennedy was being awarded the Pulitzer, Wallace was getting an award of his own—a network show, one that would be broadcast every Saturday night coast-to-coast. "Our reputation had preceded us to ABC," Wallace recalled years later, "and more than a few of our prospective interviewees were wary of being grilled on network television by a guy who had been described as . . . The Terrible Torquemada of the TV Inquisition."

Drew Pearson had been a guest the previous October on *Night Beat*. Now, he was scheduled for Wallace's new show. He wrote in his diary, "I had to bone up for the Mike Wallace program . . . The last time he interviewed me, he really put me over the hurdles."[3]

He spent the day of the show, December 7, 1957, on his 279-acre farm in Potomac, Maryland. It was his happy place. He had owned the property since 1936. He had horses and cattle. He even sold fertilizer. One sign near his home said: "Drew Pearson's manure, all cow, no bull, better than the column."[4]

Pearson was to print journalism what Wallace hoped to be for its younger media counterpart. A fixture in Washington, D.C., his column, *Washington Merry-Go-Round*, demonstrated muckraking at its most effective. He invented the whole journo-politico niche.[5] He was loathed and feared, blending rumors and facts in ways that antagonized political leaders. He pulled few punches and had a track record of bringing powerful people to their knees. When he did pull the rare punch, it was due to his well-honed investigatory skills—he made digging up dirt he could use for leverage an art form, knowing just what buttons to push to generate outcomes favorable to his agenda—whatever that was at any particular moment.

His column had been behind the story and ensuing feeding frenzy surrounding General George Patton's slapping of a soldier in Sicily during the war. He was persistent critic of Senator Joseph McCarthy and partiality responsible for bringing him down. And his chronic criticisms of Secretary of Defense James Forrestal drove the navy legend to jump out of a sixteenth-floor window to his death at Bethesda Naval Hospital in Maryland.[6]

In the 1950s, newspapers were the locus of media power. Television had passed radio en route to the top of the information pyramid, but print was still at the top of the heap, with the kings of that heap being syndicated columnists such as Drew Pearson. Wallace described him as "a journalistic throwback to the old school."[7] He had a reputation for finding dirt and knowing just when to use it. This made him "the most feared reporter in Washington." He also had a habit of "shooting from the hip." Wallace looked forward to baiting Pearson to try and get him to blurt out something noteworthy. But he had no idea what that would mean for him, his network, or his young television show.

He planned to bring up comments made from politicians, including two former presidents. Both Franklin Roosevelt and Harry Truman had publicly called Pearson a liar. And one senator, speaking on the floor of the Senate, described him as "an ignorant liar, a pusillanimous liar, a pee-wee liar, a liar during his manhood, a liar by profession, a liar in the day-time, and a liar in the nighttime."

As viewers across America, including Jack Kennedy, watched, Wallace got what we would refer to today as his "soundbite" long before he had the chance to bring up all the quotes calling Pearson a liar. It came during the following exchange about presidential politics:

WALLACE: *The December 6th issue of United States News and World Report says that in Washington, quote "Mr. Nixon often is called the man that nobody really knows. Mr. Nixon has never sought to cultivate a circle of close friends. Members of the White House staff refer to the Vice President as an enigma" end quote. How do you, Drew, dope out this so-called enigma?*

PEARSON: *Well, eh . . . a very ambitious young man, who has been on every side of every political fence. He started out as New Dealer, a member of OPA under Roosevelt. He became a member of the extreme right wing, the Taft wing of the Republican Party, all his votes in the House and in the Senate were against Labor, against the farmer, with big business. Recently he has become a semi-liberal, a member of the Eisenhower wing of the Republican Party.*

WALLACE: *Do you think these changes have come from conviction or rather going . . .*

PEARSON: *I am not sure. I agree with Mrs. Roosevelt. I don't know about his convictions. When a young fellow, and he is relatively young, changes that fast, I just don't know. But I do know, that in time of crisis, or at least I believe that in time of crisis, he would be a pretty good president for this reason: That most of his life he's played for his ambition; now he's realized that ambition, or at least would if he became President, and he would be playing for the history books, to make his name in history and to make this country a great country.*

WALLACE: *We hear about power struggles going on, inside the White House, Drew, among Nixon, Sherman Adams, Jim Hagerty, Secretary Dulles's name is sometimes mentioned. What do you know about that?*

PEARSON: *My best knowledge is that there is a definite power struggle, that Nixon and Dulles are on one side that Hagerty and Sherman Adams are on the other. They have definitely not wanted Nixon in there.*

WALLACE: *For what reason?*

PEARSON: *Well, they feel that perhaps that Nixon is pushing the President, I don't think he is at the present time. They don't like Nixon. They probably share the view that Mrs. Roosevelt has held, that perhaps he isn't a man of conviction. I know that there is a lot of feeling against Nixon inside the White House but not by the President.*

WALLACE: *But how do they feel about . . . how does the President feel about Nixon personally, do you know?*

PEARSON: *I believe I know. The Nixon . . . Mr. President feels very kindly towards . . . the President feels kindly towards Nixon. Whenever Nixon has had a break, given any assignment, it's been through largely the President. Sometimes through Mr. Dulles on his trips abroad, but with the President's blessing.*

WALLACE: *Mr. Nixon would seem to be the glamour boy of the Republican Party, the Democratic glamour boy would seem to be Senator Jack Kennedy. In your column on October 27th, you wrote that Senator Kennedy's, and I quote, "Millionaire McCarthyite father, crusty old Joseph P. Kennedy . . . is spending a fortune on a publicity machine to make Jack's name well known. "No candidate in history" you wrote, "Has ever had so much money spent on a public relations advance buildup" end quote. What significance do you see in this aside from the fact, that Joe Kennedy would like to see Jack Kennedy President of the United States?*

PEARSON: *Well, I don't know exactly what other significance other than the fact that I don't believe he should have a synthetic public relations buildup for any job of that kind. Jack Kennedy is a fine young fellow, a very personable fellow, but he isn't as good as that public relations campaign makes him out to be. He is the only man in history that I know who won a Pulitzer Prize on a book which was ghost-written for him, which indicates the kind of public relations buildup he's had.*

WALLACE: *Who wrote the book for him?*

PEARSON: *I don't recall at the present moment, I . . .*

WALLACE: *You know for a fact Drew . . . ?*

PEARSON: *Yes.*

WALLACE: *That the book?*

PEARSON: *I do know.*

WALLACE: *Profiles in Courage was written for Senator Kennedy, by somebody else?*

PEARSON: *I do.*

WALLACE: *And he got a Pulitzer Prize for it, and . . .*

PEARSON: *He did.*

WALLACE: *And, and he has never acknowledged the fact?*

PEARSON: *No, he has not. There's a little wisecrack around the Senate about Jack who is a very handsome young man as you know, who some of his colleagues say, "Jack, I wish you had a little bit . . . uh . . . less profile and more courage" And they refer to some of his voting records.*

Kennedy called Sorensen the next morning, Sunday December 8. He was very upset. "We might as well quit if we let this stand," the Senator told his assistant. "This challenges my ability to write the book, my honesty in signing it, and my integrity of accepting the Pulitzer Prize."[8]

He was not wrong.

CHAPTER 55

"Perhaps Sorensen Made the Statement When Drinking"

Clark McAdams Clifford was the ultimate Washington Insider. He came to town in 1945, as one of the fellow Missourians President Truman preferred to have close at hand. His initial role was relatively minor—Assistant to the President's Naval Aide—but that changed quickly. Before his first year in the White House was up, he had become one of the president's most trusted and useful staff members. And over the next decade, he built a reputation as the man to see when you had a problem to fix. Jack had met Clifford a decade earlier, but their relationship was just a casual acquaintance.[1] The attorney was a "Democratic party statesman and $1-million-a-year Washington lawyer."[2]

He was the man the Kennedy wanted in his corner to fight ABC. At any rate, the family's normal "fixer"—James Landis—had likely helped with the details of Sorensen's secret payment deal.

On Monday, December 9, he was in Kennedy's Senate office discussing options with the Senator. Then, Jack's father called and told Clifford in no uncertain terms to file a lawsuit as soon as possible. He was certain the whole thing was part of a plot. He had been monitoring the rumor mill for months.[3]

Clifford did his best to calm the old man down and tried to explain that he would go to New York at once to "sit down with the people at ABC," he said. Joe Kennedy exploded, "Sit down with them, hell!" The attorney recalled Jack watching "with a faint air of amusement." The elder Kennedy continued to push for suits to be filed against "ABC, Pearson, Wallace, and anyone else in sight."

Years later, in an Oral History Interview Clifford made for the Kennedy Library, he described Joe Kennedy as "really on the warpath."[4] He waited for the old man to finish his "tirade," then he said: "Well it all depends on what you want to accomplish if you want to drag the matter out for possibly two or three years without getting a conclusion, then that's exactly the best way to do it, and get occasional publicity about it and all." But he had a better idea. "If, on the other hand, you would like to get a retraction—which is what we ought to go with—which would clear it up, then I think we ought to get in touch with them and let's don't talk about suing any more at all."

Jack liked the lawyer's proposed strategy better. He had someone from his office call ABC to request a copy of the show's transcript. Sorensen later recalled: "Room 362 in the Senate Office Building was as gloomy that week as the weather. We rounded up samples of the manuscript in the Senator's handwriting. We prepared a list of possible witness who had seen him at work on *Profiles*—secretaries who had taken dictation, visitors to Palm Beach, publishers and others."[5]

Of course, Sorensen had moved on from wanting any public credit for ghostwriting Kennedy's book. He was on his way to greater financial comfort than he ever imagined as a government employee. He knew that he had been generously compensated for his silence and complete cooperation.

Meanwhile, Wallace called Pearson to find out who specifically had ghostwritten *Profiles*. The columnist wrote in his diary on December 9, two days after the broadcast, "ABC is in a dither over my statement that Jack Kennedy had a ghostwriter for his book. Their lawyers calling up all day. I identified the ghostwriter as Ted Sorensen, Kennedy's assistant."[6]

Wallace recalled that though one day "Sorensen would acquire a certain derivative glory as one of President Kennedy's top advisers and his primary speechwriter, he was unknown to the general public."[7]

Clifford set up a meeting with ABC's Chairman, Leonard Goldenson. He wanted a statement of retraction to be aired the following Saturday, December 14, as part of the Wallace program. They met on December 12 in the ABC offices. Because there was a major snowfall predicted for that day, he took an evening train from Washington the night before. The next morning, as the snow accumulated, he learned that Joe Kennedy, who was supposed to be in the meetings, was unable to travel because of the snow. The lawyer was relieved that he wouldn't have to deal with both the network and the Ambassador, with the latter likely the more difficult party to handle. Jack Kennedy, however, was present. Ted Sorensen was also in town and waiting in a hotel not far from ABC's offices.[8]

"We had, possibly, a day-long conference with the ABC officials," Clifford recalled. "And I think the President of ABC took part in it." Kennedy had brought along some "original notes" for the book. "It seems to me that we needed some additional material which we had to wait for and I have some recollection of possibly waiting over and having another meeting the next day in which we had gotten this material," he said years later.[9]

At one point in the discussion, the network people indicated that they wanted to talk to Sorensen. He was rushed over from his hotel and "expertly rebutted efforts by ABC's lawyers to break down his story." Years later, Ted recalled, "they sought to avoid their own responsibility for publishing an untrue rumor by making a new and equally untrue charge—namely, that I had privately boasted of being the author."[10] He denied this and was moved into another nearby room, but he could still hear the ongoing conversation.

He heard one ABC vice president say to Kennedy, "Perhaps Sorensen made the statement when drinking."

"He doesn't drink," Kennedy barked back.

"Perhaps he said it when he was mad at you."

"He's never been mad at me."

Eventually, Sorensen was brought back into the room, and he agreed to give a sworn affidavit that he "was not the author and had never claimed authorship of *Profiles in Courage*."

He then signed a sworn statement that said:

> *The author of Profiles in Courage is Senator Kennedy, who originally conceived its theme, selected its characters, determined its contents, and wrote and rewrote each of its chapters. The research, and other materials received by him in the course of writing the book from me and the others listed in the Preface were all considered by the Senator along with his own material, and in part rejected by him and in part drawn upon by him in his work. To assert that any one of us who supplied such materials "wrote the book" for the Senator is clearly unwarranted and in error.*[11]

Of course, there was no mention of his million-dollar (in today's value) payoff. Seen now, in light of later investigation, Sorensen's affidavit was somewhere south of the whole truth.

In fact, there is no way to see his statement as anything less than perjurious.

By the conclusion of those marathon meetings, ABC executives indicated that they were satisfied enough to issue a retraction, which was read at the beginning of Wallace's show by an ABC Vice President named Oliver Treyz:

Last Saturday night, December 7, on this same program, Mr. Drew Pearson stated that Senator Kennedy's book, Profiles in Courage, which won the Pulitzer Prize, was not written by Senator Kennedy but was written by some other person, and that Senator Kennedy had never acknowledged this fact. As Vice President in charge of the Television Network of the American Broadcasting Company, I wish to state that this company has inquired into the charge made by Mr. Pearson and has satisfied itself that such charge is unfounded and that the book in question was written by Senator Kennedy. We deeply regret this error and feel it does a grave injustice to a distinguished public servant and author, to the excellent book he wrote, and to the prize he was awarded. We extend our sincere apologies to Senator Kennedy, his publishers, and the Pulitzer Prize Committee.[12]

CHAPTER 56

"The Rumors Still Persist"

MIKE WALLACE WAS LIVID. "THE WAY I SAW IT," he said, "THE ABC apology was a humiliating insult to Pearson, who, for all his reputation as a loose cannon, was a seasoned journalist and no stranger to litigation; through the years he had weathered more than a few libel suits with no serious damage to his career." Wallace was also certain that the Kennedys "were bluffing."[1]

Interestingly, Wallace and Kennedy had lived around the block from each other as kids growing up in Brookline, Massachusetts. The attended the same elementary school, though Wallace was one grade ahead. But the Pearson flap was the broadcaster's last contact with the man who would be President.[2]

Wallace was a guest on Barry Gray's radio show on New York's WMCA a few months after the Pearson controversy. Remembered as "the father of talk radio," Gray was to radio what Wallace was trying to become to television. During the broadcast, Wallace spoke about the retraction. He told Gray, "ABC did not inform me that they were going to apologize on behalf of Drew Pearson and that story I do not believe is finished yet."[3]

He was right.

As for Pearson, he saw Jack Kennedy a month after ABC's retraction. Kennedy had called him for a meeting. Pearson wrote at-length about his impressions in his diary later that day. "Talked for about an hour," he wrote. "He showed me his original notes and unquestionably did conceive the idea of his book *Profiles in Courage*."[4] Kennedy poured on the charm, as Pearson noted, "Sometimes I'm a sucker for a nice guy who presents an appealing story. I'm not sure whether this was the fact in my talk with Kennedy or not. He didn't ask me for a retraction, but I think I shall give him one."

But Pearson noted that Jack "got a whale of help on his book. I'm still dubious as to whether he wrote to much of it in the final draft himself. He showed me rough chapters—some of them worked out by Harvard professors." In the end, though, he acknowledged that Kennedy "showed enough knowledge of the book, had lived with the book, made the book so much a part of him, that basically it is his book."

It was a somewhat tortured acknowledgment.

He was surprised that Kennedy admitted "*Harper* had paid direct royalties totaling $6,000 [equivalent to $57,000 today] to Ted Sorensen of his staff." He quoted Kennedy saying, "Ted did an awful lot of work." Kennedy did not, however, mention the deal made with Sorensen the previous May.

"When I have members on staff working on [articles], I just consider it efficiency. I have to turn out as much as I can," Kennedy told Pearson that day. He added, tellingly, "There is no ghostwriter *outside* my office; Ted Sorensen does a lot of work for me right here in the office."

Pearson rounded out the wordy entry in his diary that day with an assessment of Kennedy as a politician. "Jack Kennedy's leaning more toward the pussyfooting of his old man, trying to please everyone." He concluded that if it were to come down to a choice between Kennedy and Nixon in 1960, he would have a hard time deciding.

A few days later—February 16, 1958—Pearson issued a brief retraction tucked at the end of one of his columns. The piece referred to a sermon by, of all people, Norman Thomas, father of Jack's editor. He quoted the elder Thomas, "It's easy to write profiles in courage about men who are dead—what we need is profiles in courage among men who are living."[5] Then Pearson added: "Author of *Profiles in Courage* is Senator Jack Kennedy of Massachusetts."

After reading that, Kennedy sent a personal note to Pearson, "Dear Drew: I appreciate your comment on the book Sunday—it clarifies the record and I am grateful."

Though Jack Kennedy would never again deal publicly with rumors disputing his authorship of *Profiles*, the story never completely went away, much to his chagrin. His office received regular inquiries about it, asking the senator to comment or be interviewed on the subject, but he refused.

Martha MacGregor was the Book Editor for the *New York Post*. She wrote to Kennedy a few weeks into the new year and told him that "the rumors still persist" even in the wake of the *ABC* retraction.[6] She gave him some details: "There is a rumor that you wrote the first and last chapters and that the rest of the book was worked on various people. Then there's the rumor that Mr. Sorensen did the whole book and that he collects 50% of the royalties."

MacGregor had also reached out to John Hohenberg, who recorded in his diary that "she'd been gumshoeing around Senator Kennedy and the charges that he had a ghostwriter."[7]

MacGregor sympathized with Kennedy, telling him, "It seems to be generally understood that, because of your illness, that you had help with the research and Mr. Thomas at *Harper's* told me he that had batted the ideas around with a few people—certainly a natural thing for an author to do." But she wanted Senator Kennedy to know that "the official denial on Mike Wallace's station has not stopped the rumors." She had an idea: "For your own sake and for the sake of the good reputation of the Pulitzer Prize, would you be willing to tell me for publication exactly how the book was written and what the acknowledgements in the Foreword imply? In other words, exactly what did Messrs. Sorensen, Davids, and Landis do in connection with the book? Is or isn't Mr. Sorensen collecting a royalty? Would it be possible to examine the notebooks?"

She was clearly on to the story and her questions were the ones other investigators should have been asking.

Kennedy's reply a few days later was carefully worded:

I cannot see that anything would be accomplished by another article concerning my authorship of 'Profiles in Courage.' I have on many occasions, directly and indirectly, formally and informally, stated unequivocally that I was the sole author of the book—when I signed a contract with the publishers, filed a copyright, accepted royalties (all of them) and accepted the Pulitzer Prize. My authorship is known to the publishers and to the Pulitzer Prize Committee, which naturally check the matter before the award was given. The question was thoroughly investigated by ABC before the attached statement was issued; and, in addition, I have a recent conversation with Mr. Drew Pearson. Whether or not the rumors still persist, I do not know; but most of us who are active in public affairs have become accustomed to many rumors about many things which have no factual basis whatsoever. The Preface to my book speaks for itself, and I can see no value in attempting to restate those acknowledgements in other words. In short, I do not believe there is anything to be added with respect to this matter, and further speculation on or repetition of the matters in the press would not seem to be worthwhile from your point of view or mine.[8]

Interestingly, Kennedy's insistence that he accepted the royalties from the book ("all of them") contradicts what he had recently intimated to Drew Pearson, that Sorensen had received some royalties direct from *Harper and Brothers*. Nor, of course, did Jack tell MacGregor anything about the lucrative arrangement his father had made with Sorensen.

But Jack did his best to correct the record even when he simply heard someone had repeated the rumor, especially if the person was in the media. One example is when he heard that John Oakes, on the editorial staff of the *New York Times*, said the rumor about Kennedy not being the real author was, in fact, true. In a letter that included language similar to what he used with Martha MacGregor, he sought to "set the record straight."[9] He even invited Oakes to "review the notebook and other evidence" the next time the reporter was in Washington.

And Kennedy's office was not the only one regularly dealing with damage control. Evan Thomas shouldered his share of the burden, responding to similar questions. "There is no truth in the rumor that the book was written by a ghost-writer," he wrote to Mrs. Paul Lynch in Evansville, Indiana.[10] "While Senator Kennedy did receive some help from his own staff with research for the book, he wrote the book himself, and is its author in every sense of the word. Much of the book was written in longhand while the Senator was in the hospital convalescing from a back operation. I am pleased to have the opportunity . . . to rebut this untrue statement."

In fairness to Thomas, there has never been any evidence that he knew anything about Sorensen's complete role in the story—certainly he knew nothing about Ted's financial windfall.

As for Sorensen, he waxed philosophical shortly before he died. He asked, "Is the author the person who did much of the research and helped choose the words in many of its sentences, or is the author the person who decided the substance, structure, and them of the book;

read and revised each draft; inspired, constructed, and improved the work? Like JFK's speeches, *Profiles in Courage* was a collaboration, and not a particularly unusual one, inasmuch as our method of collaboration on the book was similar to the method we used on his speeches.[11] It was a telling comment. As it was with Kennedy's speeches," so it was with the book.

CHAPTER 57

"It's Sort of Sad"

ONE DAY IN MARCH 1958, KENNEDY INVITED HIS SENATE COLLEAGUE, Richard Neuberger from Oregon, over to his office. Neuberger was also a fellow author. One of his books was a biography of George Norris, one of the senators profiled in Jack's book. Jack wanted his friend to "look over the manuscript."[1]

In fact, Kennedy kept writing samples close at hand and was always willing to put them on display as evidence that he, indeed, was the author of *Profiles in Courage*. He was very sensitive about the matter and anxious to convince everyone. But there is history that suggests that Kennedy's efforts may have been *contrived*.

Flash forward to early 1961. . .

President-elect John F. Kennedy, along with a few others, including his speech-writer Ted Sorensen, and *Time* magazine political correspondent Hugh Sidey, were on board *The Caroline*, flying from West Palm Beach to Washington for Kennedy's inauguration as the thirty-fifth president of the United States. The date was January 17.

Kennedy's private plane, a Corsair 240, outfitted with sixteen seats, several tables, a galley for food, and a desk for Kennedy, had taken him around the country, logging nearly 250,000 miles during the recent presidential campaign. The aircraft was now destined for retirement, since Kennedy was getting new ride—government issue.

The speech Kennedy would give on January 20 was finished before that flight, and, "a typed draft" was on the desk in front of him.[2] With Sorensen looking on, Kennedy asked his secretary, Evelyn Lincoln, for a yellow legal pad. He took out his pen and made a note on the first line on the first sheet. It said, simply, "what your country is going to do for you—ask what you can do for your country."

Then, above that, in the unlined section at the very top of the page, he wrote the words: "Ask Not." He wrote a few more sentences on the page. Jack then tore the sheet from the pad and carefully placed it in his desk drawer. He winked at Sorensen and told his aide that part of FDR's first inaugural, in his own hand, had "brought $200,000 at an auction."[3]

Kennedy returned to the legal pad and, working from the typewritten draft of the already-finished speech on his desk, he copied three pages in his own legendary scrawl. Jack then went over to where Sidey was seated.

The journalist was a Kennedy friend and would go on to write, with the President's help, a book called *John F. Kennedy, President*. Sidey's book was very complimentary and came out less than six weeks after the assassination. The writer was part of a large network of journalists who became, in effect, Kennedy insiders, producing a steady stream of material—articles and books— that "celebrated the character, intellect, and political skill of the chief executive."[4]

He was about to witness a revealing ruse.

Kennedy began to read from the handwritten pages, the impression being that he was still writing his speech and working out phrases that had, in fact, already been settled and typed up. Along the way, he "paused for a moment, then murmured some doubts about the long introductory part." He wrote a bit more, "crossed out a few words, then flung the tablet on the desk." Sidey was impressed that he was a witness to history in the making.

But it was pure theater.

After her husband's death, Jackie Kennedy saw to it that the handwritten "first draft" of her late husband's speech would be properly displayed as "his inaugural address in his own handwriting" in what would become the John F. Kennedy Presidential Library and Museum. She clearly believed it was an authentic ancestor to the eventual speech. But it was not. And it is a bit ironic to read her Oral History as she talked about how she felt sorry for her husband's political rival Adlai Stevenson. Jackie said, "He'd carefully take something typewritten and copy it in longhand because he was so proud of everyone saying he wrote all his speeches."[5]

She added, "It's sort of sad."

Yes, it is sad anytime someone we admire is caught being less-than-authentic. We tend to become disillusioned. But all of history's heroes had flaws, some famous, others carefully hidden. Some coming to light at inconvenient moments in their lives. Others not emerging until after they have passed on.

John F. Kennedy was in so many ways a man worthy of admiration. Yet, in other ways, he clearly was not. His protestations, and those from within his tight-knit circle, that he alone was the author of *Profiles in Courage*, can now be shown as a carefully orchestrated deception.

He lied.

If that is hard for some to accept and acknowledge, the idea that the hero of all things Camelot was no different in this matter than Richard Nixon was about other matters, parallels must be sought. There are many, but one will suffice. It was a moment when a falsehood told and retold for years by Jack Kennedy and his entourage was exposed.

On November 22, 1963, President John F. Kennedy was in the emergency room at Parkland Hospital in Dallas, Texas. Doctors were working feverishly to save his life. As they worked on him, his physician, Dr. George Burkley was there and watching. He spoke up and asked the doctors to administer hydrocortisone because Kennedy had Addison's disease.[6]

But the Kennedys had been, for years, denying that Jack had the disease.

In fact, it was first diagnosed in 1947.

The medicines he took contributed to his chronic back problems and led to the surgeries in 1954 and 1955, when he nearly died. But beginning in 1947, whenever there were news accounts about Jack's chronic health issues, usually a flare-up of malaria, which he had contracted during World War II, was blamed.

Political historians Joan and Clay Blair wrote in detail about this disease and the Kennedy cover-up in their 1976 book, *The Search for JFK*. Regarding the cover-up, they said, "It tells something about political technique in mid-century America. It tells some further about Jack and his father."[7]

In 1960, rumors about Jack's health abounded, prompting statements of denial from his staff. A few days after he won the election, during a press conference at Hyannis Port on November 10, 1960, he was asked about reports that he had suffered from Addison's disease:

Q: During the campaign, sir, there was some concern about your physical condition, your back, and I think the reference to Addison's Disease. Could you tell us frankly, sir, now, how you feel and how much of a burden those conditions are to you.

A: Well, in the first place—the first matter was all cleared up some time back in 1955, and is of no problem and has not been for years.

Q: Is that the back, sir?

A: That is the back. The second matter is that I have never had the matter to which you referred, Addison's Disease.[8]

Kennedy biographer, Robert Dallek, wrote: "Looking backwards from today, we can conclude that full disclosure of Kennedy's ailments would, as he believed, have barred him from the White House."[9] This begs the question: Is it all that hard to believe that Jack Kennedy lied about who really wrote *Profiles in Courage?*

CHAPTER 58

"The Prize Was the Problem"

No SERIOUS DISCUSSION OF KENNEDY'S PROBLEMATIC RELATIONSHIP with the prize-winning book bearing his name would be possible without the groundbreaking work of historian Herbert S. Parmet. Born in 1929 and named after the then-new president Herbert Hoover, this less than a month before the stock market crash changed everything, he was like a dog with a bone when it came to research.

It was while he was teaching history at Long Island's Mineola High School in the 1960s that Parmet decided to try his hand at writing about it. His first book, a biography of Aaron Burr, was published in 1967 to favorable reviews and he would go on to write ten more highly successful works, while eventually becoming Distinguished Professor at the City University of New York Graduate School.

He was a Kennedy follower in 1960, having been impressed with James MacGregor Burn's book, *John Kennedy: A Political Profile*. But by the 1970s, he "was becoming fairly saturated with the revisionist views of Kennedy," so he took up the cause.[1] Among his books were two bestsellers about Kennedy, the first of which, *Jack: The Struggles John F. Kennedy* (1980), included the most in-depth analysis of the research and writing of *Profiles in Courage*, to date.

Its more than 500 pages covered Kennedy's life and career up to the point of the 1960 campaign for the White House. In it, the author unraveled much of the puzzle about *Profiles*. He concluded, "Neither the chronology of Jack Kennedy's life in 1954 and 1955 nor the materials accumulated in the preparation of the book even come close to supporting the contention that Jack could have been or was its major author."[2]

He considered what he called "the *Profiles* case" as "the difference between utilizing the prerequisites of office to expedite responsibilities and the manufacturing of a talent to create the image of a young senator distinctively different from conventional politicians and who, while denying that it was principally the work of others, would accept a Pulitzer prize."[3]

The *prize* was the *problem*.

Parmet added, "It was as deceptive as installing a Chevrolet engine in a Cadillac." Regarding the tapes and documents at the Kennedy library, historian Garry Wills said, "Herbert Parmet's investigation of them destroys Kennedy's claim to have written the book."[4]

Parmet was the first serious author to thoroughly examine the records on file at the Kennedy Library in Boston. The files are extensive and contain many examples of passages from *Profiles* in Jack's nearly illegible hand. Of these, Parmet said:

> *The files do show notes in Kennedy's handwriting. Written on letterhead size canary loose leaf paper, they constitute scrawls in his familiar tiny, slanted, almost indecipherable hand, much of the work probably done while on his back. They indicate very rough passages without paragraphing, without any shape, largely ideas jotted down as possible sections, obviously necessitating editing. The portion of the handwritten material, the pages cited by a seemingly endless crew of witnesses ready to testify that they actually watched him write, almost as though he were an author on display at work in a glass booth, in no way resembles the final product. Much of the writing contains notes from secondary sources that were mixed together with the original, creative passages. Almost all of the actual manuscript material rests in eight folders of Box 35 in the Kennedy Library.*[5]

The historian concluded: "There is no evidence of a Kennedy draft for the overwhelming bulk of the book; and there is evidence for concluding that much of what he did draft was simply not included in the final version . . . If the Kennedy Library collection is designed to prove his authorship, it fails to pass inspection. About all the material does demonstrate is Jack's close association with its conception and completion."[6]

The prize was indeed the problem. If you take the Pulitzer out of the story, it defaults to just another ghostwritten book story. In fact, ghostwriting has been around for a long time and it is a quite respectable line of work. One definition of ghostwriting is "the writing of material by one person (the writer) for use by another (the client) who will be credited with its authorship, and where both parties agree that the writer's role will be invisible to readers or hearers of the words."[7]

Politicians and other leaders and celebrities regularly rely on the skill of others for speeches and, yes, even books. It is the norm. In Kennedy's case, however, the issue was different. He wanted the Pulitzer Prize and encouraged Arthur Krock to lobby for it. But as Gary Wills has said, Kennedy was "willing to make claims of authorship that went well beyond the political authorization involved in delivering a speech. Indeed, he made claims, and insisted on them repeatedly, that are not sustainable."[8]

As Craig Fehrman has recently written, "The book's structure, research, first draft, and most of its second came from Ted Sorensen."[9] Then he added the obvious: "The problem came in his quest for literary fame, particularly the Pulitzer."

Jack Kennedy got away with it at the time. It never became a serious problem for him. In fact, winning the Pulitzer for a book largely written by a ghostwriter was an important part of the narrative surrounding his dramatic political rise to ultimate power.

A strong case can be made that if there had been no Pulitzer, there might have been no presidency.

For the rest of his life, John F. Kennedy's political positions on controversial issues would be compared to the heroes in *Profiles*. From his Senate failure to take a stand on issues related to Joseph McCarthy, to his presidential equivocation on civil rights matters, he fell short. Once, his friend Arthur Schlesinger commented that Jack "paid a heavy price for giving his book that title."[10]

Kennedy replied, "Yes, but I didn't have a chapter in it on myself."

Epilogue

THE REST OF THE JOHN F. KENNEDY STORY IS WELL KNOWN. HIS successful run for the White House. The standoff with Khrushchev. His tragic death in Dallas

A new edition of *Profiles* was published—a Memorial Edition—early in 1964, this one with a new Foreword written by Robert Kennedy:

> *Courage is the virtue that President Kennedy most admired. He sought out those people who had demonstrated in some way, whether it was on the battlefield or a baseball diamond, in a speech, or fighting for a cause, that they had courage, that they would stand up, that they could be counted on. That is why this book so fitted his personality, his beliefs. It is a study of men who, at risk to themselves, their futures, even the well-being of their children, stood fast for principle. It was toward that ideal that he modeled his life. And this in time gave heart to others. As Andrew Jackson said, "One man with courage makes a majority." That is the effect President Kennedy had on others.*

There was even a television series based on the book that ran for several months on NBC in 1964 and 1965.

It's hard to believe now, but Jackie Kennedy was only thirty-four years old when her husband was taken from her—and us. Through the decades since that fateful day in Dallas, the Kennedy story has been told and retold. The thousand or so days of his presidency are often referred to as "Camelot," a name pregnant with wonder and magic. In fact, the nomenclature is used so often, that there are some who may assume that was the way people referred to JFK's White House when he lived and worked there. But the truth is that the *Camelot* image began to be associated with all things JFK when Jackie Kennedy met with a famous writer shortly *after* her husband's murder. His name was Theodore H. White.

The day after Thanksgiving in 1963 and one week to the day from the assassination, Jacqueline Kennedy had a late evening meeting with Mr. White at the Kennedy compound in Hyannis Port, Massachusetts. He represented *Life Magazine* and was there for an exclusive interview and feature. Mrs. Kennedy had made it clear to the editors that she preferred White write the primary essay in the special issue they were getting ready to publish. He had covered their wedding for the magazine in 1953, and more recently, he had written sympathetically about Kennedy in his Pulitzer Prize–winning book, *The Making of the President, 1960*.

During their conversation that night, the president's widow talked about how much her late husband had enjoyed the Broadway play, *Camelot*—particularly its music. He regularly played the original soundtrack record in the White House, usually before they drifted off to sleep.

> *Don't let it be forgot,*
> *That once there was a spot,*
> *For one brief, shining moment,*
> *That was known as Camelot.*

White was on deadline. In fact, they were actually holding up publication of the magazine, at a cost of $30,000, to wait for him to file his story. After his conversation with Mrs. Kennedy, he went to another room and spent forty-five minutes composing the essay. Then he went to a telephone in the kitchen to dictate it to an editor.

Jackie Kennedy came in as Theodore White was debating back and forth with an editor about toning down the whole *Camelot* angle. She gave White an angry look, while shaking her head emphatically—"No!"

The story about John F. Kennedy's best-selling book, *Profiles in Courage*, is in many ways a window into all things Camelot. And like so many legends, the myths can actually be seen as superfluous in some ways, because the accomplishments were, on their own and without hype, significant indeed.

A generation later, Jack's son, John F. Kennedy Jr., followed in his father's early journalist footsteps and published a magazine about politics.

Ted Sorensen wrote his own book, a massive tome titled, simply, *Kennedy*, in 1965. And he went on to write several more. His deal with the Kennedys made him financial comfortable, but he did put his law degree to work as an international lawyer.

He remained involved in politics, particularly the Kennedy kind, as an advisor to Bobby Kennedy's presidential campaign in 1968, as well as an advisor to Ted Kennedy during the Chappaquiddick affair.

He was the rather curious nominee for Director of the CIA under President Jimmy Carter briefly in 1977, before withdrawing his name in the face of furious opposition.

He provided some assistance with Barack Obama's inaugural address in 2009. Obama gave him the National Humanities Medal later that year.

JFK's ghostwriter died on October 31, 2010.

Evan Thomas, of course, was not privy to any of the arrangements between the Kennedys and Ted Sorensen and steadfastly defended Jack's authorship for the rest of his life. Years later, he said, "It was written by JFK in the creative sense, as I've said before, but Sorensen had necessarily done all the research because JFK was in the hospital a good bit of the time during the writing for *Profiles*."[1]

But he also said, "Sorensen is not one of my favorite people."[2] He also had problems with other members of the Kennedy family in the years following the President's death. The hard feelings had to do with something called "The Manchester Affair," which soured Thomas on the Kennedys to a point.

A few months after Kennedy's assassination, Thomas got a call from Pierre Salinger, JFK's longtime press secretary. Thomas said that he was inquiring about his company publishing "the official biography of John F. Kennedy." Thomas told him, "We'd just as soon not, because I'm not anxious to make a living on this minor relationship with John F. Kennedy." This was followed by a call from Robert Kennedy, who was still the Attorney General, "asking me to come to Washington that afternoon."

He gave Bobby the same answer: "I don't want to make money off this thing. I'm very sentimental about the subject and I'd just as soon not publish a book about your brother."

"Well, we've selected a writer who may be known to you, by the name of Manchester," Bobby said. It was a reference to the historian William Manchester. Thomas eventually agreed to the project and the writer, but the whole thing turned out to be a nightmare for him

Evan went to visit Manchester at his place near Essex, Connecticut. He remembered, "Manchester was in a terrible emotional state. His fingers were bleeding . . . he'd been writing with a pencil, and he'd gotten himself so involved with the assassination and so on that his fingers were quite literally bleeding." Reading several chapters, Thomas "was disturbed by the fact that Lyndon Johnson was seen as the villain. It was almost as though Manchester were saying that Lyndon Johnson was somehow implicated in the murder."

There was no way Thomas wanted to print such material.

The offending passages were removed, but Thomas said, "From that time on, there was a constant struggle." Eventually, the Kennedy family soured on the book and demanded certain passages containing sensitive personal material be excised from the manuscript. They even filed a lawsuit to get an injunction to prevent publication of the book titled *Death of a President*. The parties came to terms, some offending passages were removed or revised, and the book became an instant bestseller.

"The controversy over *The Death of a President* was a little silly and sometimes it was a little morbid, too," wrote *New York Times* journalist, John Corry.[3] "It joined together celebrated people who rather liked one another and then locked them in something like a tragic embrace, surrounding them at the same time with concentric circles of spokesmen, advisers, sycophants, and reporters."

It certainly put a strain on what had been a good relationship between the editor and the Kennedys. Thomas's son described a chilling moment during the whole Manchester controversy. His father was in a meeting with Cass Canfield and Jackie Kennedy at her Fifth Avenue apartment in Manhattan, and "she leans over and whispers to my father, 'I'm going to ruin you'."[4]

In 1967, Thomas made big news by publishing the memoirs of Josef Stalin's daughter, Svetlana Alliluyeva, paying her an advance of more than a million dollars. He retired in 1983, but lived with the multiple sclerosis first diagnosed in 1950 until 1999 when he died at the age of seventy-eight.

His son, Evan Thomas III, said of his father, "He treated publishing like journalism, and he wanted to get the newsmakers into books as soon as possible." Thomas' work with *Profiles in Courage* helped make John F. Kennedy the president of the United States.

Talk about a newsmaker and a book.

In the early 1960s, Dr. Jules Davids wrote his own highly regarded book, *America and the World of Our Time. The New York Times* called it one of the best books of the year on the subject of foreign affairs. The popular Georgetown University professor served as senior staff member of the Council on Foreign Relations at the time.

A decade later, Davids edited the massive, fifty-three-volume *American Diplomatic and Public Papers: The United States and China*, covering the history of the relationship between the two countries from 1842 to 1905. He was one of the most respected voices in the field of foreign affairs in his time and the founder of the Society of Historians of American Foreign Relations.

He retired in 1968, having been diagnosed with Alzheimer's disease. He had been working on a biography of Averell Harriman, which he never finished.

He died in December 1996. After reading his obituary in the *Washington Post*, President Bill Clinton, one of Dr. Davids' former students, wrote to his widow: "He was a wonderful professor, and I will always be grateful for all that he taught me."

James MacGregor Burns, who had offered early (and solicited advice) about *Profiles*, and whose biography about Franklin Roosevelt was beat out by Kennedy's book for the 1957 Pulitzer, turned his energies to a book about Jack Kennedy in the run-up to the 1960 campaign. He was concerned about his ability to find "authentic information on a candidate running for high office." So, he talked with Kennedy.[5]

He told the senator that he wanted to "do as honest a study of his life as I would try to do if he were a dead statesman." He insisted that the research process "would require his and his family's willingness to be interviewed extensively." And he wanted unfettered access to Kennedy's aides and records.

Kennedy agreed to the terms.

The finished product, *Jack Kennedy: A Political Biography*, was published at the end of 1959. In his Preface, Burns described his book as "neither an authorized biography nor a campaign biography."[6]

But it functioned as one.

Burns sensed that the Kennedys were much more interested "in their image than in historical accuracy." The author let Kennedy and Sorensen review his manuscript. They repeatedly put pressure on Burns to make changes, being "especially sensitive about the McCarthy issue, Jack's relationship to his father, and the depiction of the senator as lacking conviction about specific issues."[7]

The finished product was apparently acceptable to Jack and Ted.

About a year and a half after Kennedy's death, Burns was interviewed as part of the developing Oral History initiative for the John F. Kennedy Library, which would be finished and open to the public years later. He described the time when he was writing his Kennedy book as "a painful period for me."[8] He received a measure of criticism from the professional historian community. "Once word got out that I was working on a biography, a lot of people, a lot of the academic people who I respect and whose respect I want to have, made critical comment that this was to be a puff or campaign biography and all the rest. That probably put me on my mettle, but it is very interesting psychologically that my main constituency was the academic constituency. I did not want to lose face with them." He added, "The problem is to define what is a puff and what is not."

The historian also said, interestingly, "I can't think of any case where Kennedy would have jeopardized his career as the *Profiles in Courage* heroes jeopardized theirs." It wasn't the first time he had said this.

The interviewer—William H. Brubeck—replied: "Well, you know, Ted Sorensen, and I think some of the other people around Kennedy very much resented your comments on this subject on Kennedy."[9]

James Landis continued his legal work for the Kennedy family, acting as a consigliere. When Jack was elected to the presidency, he prepared a detailed report recommending various regulatory reforms, many of which Kennedy adopted. But he fell out of favor when it was discovered that he had not paid his income taxes for several years in the 1950s. He went to jail for a month.

After his release, he went home and drowned in his swimming pool.

Arthur Schlesinger wrote a book about the Kennedy administration, titled *A Thousand Days: John F. Kennedy in the White House*. It won the

Pulitzer Prize for biography in 1966. He went on to help Bobby Kennedy in his run for the presidency in 1968 and was and remained an acerbic critic of Richard Nixon.

But years after Watergate, Nixon moved into the house next door.

As for Arthur Krock, his successful lobbying effort for Jack Kennedy with the Pulitzer Prize committee was the apex of his work for the Kennedy family. By the time Jack entered the White House, Krock was in his mid-seventies. When Joe Kennedy suffered a debilitating stroke in late 1961, Krock ceased to be a family insider. Kennedy assistant McGeorge Bundy recalled, "Krock was a very much of an old man by 1961. And I don't think the President did see him very much, and I think that Krock was sort of sad about it."[10]

Author's Note

President Kennedy inspired me when I was a young boy. I was in elementary school when he was in office. My parents had voted for Nixon, but my mom became a Kennedy fan—particularly of Jackie Kennedy—early on. I remember mom as a "news-junkie." Whenever some big story would break, my phone would ring, and when I answered I would hear the words, "do you have your television on?" In retrospect, I'm sure her passion for current events began with President Kennedy's famous televised press conferences, the First Lady's prime-time tour of the White House, and countless magazines dishing the latest gossip from Washington, Hyannis Port, and Palm Beach—not to mention Berlin and Cuba.

All politicians work hard to project a compelling image. The successful one's work harder.

I was in the second grade on November 22, 1963. My teacher suddenly left a classroom full of, well, second graders. She had never done that before. For good reason. A few minutes later, she returned.

She was weeping.

She wrote on the chalkboard: "President Kennedy has been shot."

Then she left the room—again. A few minutes later, right about the time I had my friend Tim in a chokehold (or was it the other way around?), she came back and went to the chalkboard, this time writing the words: "President Kennedy is dead. You are dismissed. Go straight home."

So, we did.

Those were the days before carpools and long lines in front of schools where helicopter moms hovered. Though we were so young, not much thought seemed to be given back then to any possible dangers on the journey between home and school. So, we walked. Hundreds of kids poured out onto the sidewalks with little security, but for a few fellow students scrambling to get into place while wearing special "safety patrol" belts around their waists and over one shoulder. By the way, becoming a member of that elite "special forces" group was an early ambition of mine.

But I digress.

I remember walking home briskly that day so I could tell my mom what had happened.

Of course, she already knew.

Everyone did.—DRS

Notes

Chapter 1: December 7, 1957

1. "so intimate an acquaintance": *Drew Pearson Diaries, 1949–1959*, edited by Tyler Abell, p. *vii*.
2. "which was ghost-written for him": *Between You and Me*, Mike Wallace, p. 10.

Chapter 2: "A Target on His Back"

1. "Soon after I went to work": *My Twelve Years with John F. Kennedy*, Evelyn Lincoln, pp. 5–6, also in Shaw, p. 71.
2. "Rose Mary Woods": *Evelyn Lincoln, recorded interview by Frederick L. Holborn*, April 2, 1964, p. 7, JFKLOH.
3. "pleasant, tactful, competent": O'Brien, p. 260.
4. "How can you expect me?": ibid., p. 261.
5. "so ill at ease": Evelyn Lincoln, Oral History, p. 5.
6. "something close to totalitarian": *The Best Year of Their Lives: Kennedy, Johnson, and Nixon in 1948*, Lance Morrow, pp. 8–9.
7. Joe kept tabs on things: *John F. Kennedy: A Question of Character*, Thomas Reeves, p. 86.
8. It was Kennedy's father: *Counsel to the President, Clark Clifford*, pp. 306–310; see also Nasaw, p. 714.
9. The FBI even started a file: Dallek, p. 210.
10. a cynical look: *The Selling of the President*, Joe McGinness.
11. "stamp of seriousness": *An Unfinished Life: John F. Kennedy, 1917–1963*, by Robert Dallek, p. 210.
12. Dozens of languages: *Kennedy*, Theodore Sorensen, p. 68.

Chapter 3: "The Idea of Courageous Leadership"

1. a billionaire in our day: Morrow, p. 6.
2. a possible East German spy: See *The Dark Side of Camelot*, Seymour Hersh, pp. 387–398, the woman's name was Ellen Rometsch.
3. Kennedy knew: See *The Kennedy Men, 1901–1963*, Laurence Leamer, p. 690.

4. He told friends: *James A. Reed., recorded interview by Robert J. Donovan*, June 16, 1964, p. 38, John F. Kennedy Library Oral History Program.
5. "Senator Kennedy treats": *Profiles in Courage*, John F. Kennedy, p. xi.

CHAPTER 4: "ONE OF AMERICA'S GREAT POLITICAL WRITERS"

1. "one of America's great political writers": *Theodore Sorensen and the Kennedys: A Life of Public Service*, Michelle A Ulyatt, p. 10.
2. "as a beautiful instrument": *Counselor: A Life at the Edge of History*, Ted Sorensen, p. 136.
3. "in the middle of everywhere": ibid., p. 14.
4. "delinquent Jewish girls": ibid., p. 23.
5. "social work leaders": ibid., p. 24.
6. "as a Don Quixote": *The Peace Ship: Henry Ford's Pacifist Adventure in the First World War*, Barbara S. Kraft, p. 2.
7. "As a winner": *The People's Tycoon: Henry Ford and the American Century*, Steven Watts, p. 231.
8. "I'll give you a million dollars": Kraft, p. 96.
9. He almost missed the boat: ibid., p. 93.
10. "a country boy": *Counselor*, Sorensen, p. 25.
11. "an active prosecutor": Ulyatt, p. 8.
12. "an educated elite": ibid., pp. 11–12.
13. "the issues du jour": *White House Ghosts, Presidents and Their Speechwriters: From FDR to George W. Bush*, Robert Schlesinger, pp. 102–103.
14. "persuasive intellectual": ibid., pp. 102–103.
15. "mental and physical energy": *Grace and Power: The Private World of the Kennedy White House*, Sally Bedell Smith, pp. 54–55.

CHAPTER 5: "THE SECOND SON BORN TO JOE AND ROSE KENNEDY"

1. "bright eyes": *A Life in the Twentieth Century: Innocent Beginnings, 1917–1950*, Arthur M. Schlesinger, p. 383.
2. "by sharp dealing": Morrow, p. 6.
3. early morning call to William Randolph Hearst: *Franklin Delano Roosevelt: Champion of Freedom*, Conrad Black, p. 235.
4. "reading The World Crisis": Kay (Katherine Murphy) Halle interview by William M. McHugh, February 7, 1967, p. 6, John F. Kennedy Library Oral History Program.
5. "History was full of heroes": *A Thousand Days*, Arthur Schlesinger, p. 105.
6. "that admixture of love: *The Kennedy Men 1901–1963*, Laurence Leamer, p. 77.
7. "bemusement": ibid., p. 85.
8. "compatriots": ibid., p. 85.
9. "Attention Deficit Order": *ADD: THE REAL KENNEDY CURSE?* Wade M. Nye—https://thrivewithadd.com/wp-content/uploads/2013/09/the_kennedy_cursewade_nye9.pdf.
10. "in her memoirs": *Joseph P. Kennedy: A Life and Times*, David Koskoff, p. 85.
11. "the mosquito": *Jack: The Struggles of John F. Kennedy*, Herbert S. Parmet, pp. 16–17.

12. "born with a weak back": Dr. Elmer C. Bartels was the doctor, interviewed by Parmet, December 2, 1977.
13. "An unstable back": Blair, p. 25.
14. "the most important fact": *The Dark Side of Camelot*, Seymour M. Hersh, p. 14.
15. "these constant illnesses": Leamer, p. 88.

CHAPTER 6: "THE MUCKERS CLUB"

1. "life lesson being imparted": Leamer, p. 56.
2. "a remarkable closed corporation": *Saturday Evening Post*, October 27, 1962, p. 16, quoted in *Joseph P. Kennedy: A Life and Times*, David E. Koskoff, p. 388.
3. "young generation of Kennedy men": ibid., p. 66.
4. "their family valuables": *Kennedy*, Sorensen, p. 69.
5. "what you can do for Choate": *Document May Shed Light on Origins of JFK Speech*, Michael Melia, November 3, 2011, Associated Press.
6. "The Muckers Club": *Portrait of Troublemaker: A Rare Glimpse of John F. Kennedy's Life at Boarding School*, Alexis Coe, Town & Country Magazine, May 26, 2017.
7. "zest for fun": Parmet, p. 33.
8. And Lem was gay: See *Jack and Lem: John F. Kennedy and Lem Billings, The Untold Story of an Extraordinary Relationship*, David Pitts, pp. 22–23 & 263–268, See also, https://www.dailymail.co.uk/news/article-4566596/Inside-relationship-JFK-Lem-Billings.html.
9. "his loyal company": *JFK: Reckless Youth*, Nigel Hamilton, p. 191.
10. "spit in his eye": Leamer, pp. 53–56.

CHAPTER 7: "THE GATHERING STORM"

1. Jack packed light: Hamilton, p. 178.
2. first up-close and personal look: ibid., pp. 178–179
3. "Would fascism be possible": ibid., p. 190.
4. "insufferable": ibid., p. 193.
5. "He was the first man": Hamilton, p. 254.
6. "the summit of the crisis": *The Gathering Storm*, Winston Churchill, p. 297.

CHAPTER 8: "JFK'S FUTURE GHOSTWRITER"

1. saw FDR: *Counselor*, Sorensen, p. 67.
2. "George Norris' candidacy": *Chief Executive Speaks in Omaha*, The Nebraska State Journal, Sunday, October, 11, 1936, p. 22.
3. "a modest two-story": *Counselor*, Sorensen, p. 49.
4. "This poem is about": ibid., p. 51.
5. "Whatever capacity": ibid., p. 59.
6. "artful combination": ibid., p. 69.
7. "the clarity, quality, and color": ibid., p. 61.
8. "conscientious objector": *Counselor: A Life at the Edge of History*, Ted Sorensen, p. 77.
9. "bravery": *Theodore Sorensen and the Kennedys: A Life of Public Service*, Michelle A Ulyatt, p. 15.

Chapter 9: "A Big Churchill Fan"

1. Dean's List: Harvard Records, JFKL.
2. "answer some definitive": *The Search for JFK*, Joan Blair, p. 75.
3. "masterpiece": *John Fitzgerald Kennedy: As We Remember Him*, Joan Simpson Meyers, p. 23.
4. "through German lines": Parmet, pp. 63–64.
5. "probably the best source": Hamilton, p. 264.
6. "heart-breaking speech": Hamilton, p. 281.
7. "touchstone for his own work": *When Lions Roar*, Maier, p. 222.
8. "We are fighting": *Winston Spencer Churchill: Alone, 1932–1940*, William Manchester, p. 539.
9. "U.S. SURVIVORS IN GLASGOW": *Times of London*, September 8, 1940.
10. "it was a tough situation": Torbert H. Macdonald, recorded interview by Charles T. Morrissey, August 11, 1965, p. 10, John F. Kennedy Library Oral History Program, p. 10.
11. "public crisis": *John F. Kennedy on Leadership: The Lessons and Legacy of a President*, John A. Barnes, p. 188.
12. "As I am now working": Papers of John F. Kennedy, Personal Papers, Harvard, Harvard Records, Academic Records, 1939–1940, p. 29.
13. This media attention: Leaming, p. 95.

Chapter 10: "What's That Limey Been Telling You?"

1. "one of the best talkers": *Jack Kennedy: The Education of a Statesman*, Barbara Leaming, p. 73.
2. He told Jack that Burke's: Leaming, p. 74.
3. to be a writer: *Jack: A Life Like No Other*, Geoffrey Perret, p. 82.
4. "a microcosm": Dallek, pp. 61–62.
5. "a new, big figure": *Moving Picture World*, December 11, 1926, quoted in *The Patriarch: The Remarkable Life and Turbulent Times of Joseph P. Kennedy*, by David Nasaw, p. 100.
6. "a courageous, imperturbable": Hamilton, p. 308.
7. Joe's press secretary: *Hostage to Fortune: The Letters of Joseph P. Kennedy*, p. 391.
8. "SEND IMMEDIATELY": Hamilton, p. 307.
9. "I am checking with Chatham House": ibid., p. 308.
10. "On receipt of this letter": ibid., p. 313.
11. "RUSH PACIFIST LITERATURE": Leamer, p. 147.

Chapter 11: "How's Your Book Coming?"

1. "WANTED": *Jack Kennedy at Harvard: The Four Years that Shaped His Destiny by those Who Knew Him Best*, Coronet Magazine, May 1961. A clipping of this advertisement is on file at JFKL.
2. "He was pretty thorough": Payson S. Wild, recorded interview by Larry J. Hackman, November 25, 1968, p. 9, John F. Kennedy Oral History Program.
3. "There was a library": Hamilton, pp. 314–315.

4. "assembled the paper": The Kennedy Imprisonment: A Meditation on Power, Garry Wills, p. 136.

5. "deeper institutional reasons": *A Question of Character: A Life of John F. Kennedy*, Thomas Reeves, p. 49.

6. "one originally made": Dallek, pp. 63–64.

7. "We must always": Leaming, p. 107.

8. "a close associate": Parmet, p. 70.

9. "In the light of the present day": *Appeasement at Munich*, unpublished honors thesis, John F. Kennedy, Harvard University 1940, Harvard Records, p. 53, JFKL.

10. "Indicate whether the rank": Papers of John F. Kennedy. Personal Papers. Harvard. Harvard Records. Academic Records, 1939–1940, p. 55.

11. "fundamental premise": Papers of John F. Kennedy. Personal Papers. Harvard. Harvard Records. Academic Records, 1939–1940, p. 53.

12. "While Daddy Slept": Parmet, p. 70, also in Dallek, p. 63.

13. "he was pretty thorough": Wild, OH, JFKL, p. 9.

14. "Jack's imagination": Dallek, p. 62.

15. It was likely destroyed: Leamer, p. 125.

16. "cram school": Torbert H. MacDonald, recorded interview by Charles T. Morrissey, August 11, 1965, p. 6, John F. Kennedy Oral History Program.

17. "a well-documented": *The Patriarch: The Remarkable Life and Turbulent Times of Joseph P. Kennedy*, David Nasaw, p. 436.

18. "having successfully prepared": Leaming, p. 104.

19. "the kind of help": Leamer, p. 145.

20. "he and Jack worked together": *A Woman Named Jackie*, C. David Heymann, pp. 173–174. Also, in Hamilton, p. 836*n*.

21. "TWO THINGS": Blair, p. 86.

CHAPTER 12: "WHY ENGLAND SLEPT"

1. "had a way of fixing": *New York Times*, April 13, 1974.

2. "strikingly large family": *Kennedy: A Cultural History of an American Icon*, Mark White, p. 3.

3. "$25,000": ibid., p. 3.

4. "I was not shocked": Blair, pp. 16–17.

5. "solid enough": Perrett, p. 82.

6. "seeking permission": Leaming, p. 104.

7. "I worked two weeks on it": Arthur Krock, Oral History, JFK Library.

8. "a mishmash": *The Kennedys: An American Drama*, Peter Collier & David Horowitz, pp. 477–478. Also in Hamilton, p. 836*n*.

9. "every morning": *JFK'S First Secretary Recalls His Student Days*, Philadelphia Inquirer, August 15, 1971, quoted in Blair, pp. 77–78.

10. "read it, praised it": Hamilton, p. 327.

11. "that would take the wind": Letter from E.C. Aswell to Gertrude Algase, June 18, 1940, HarperCollins Archives, quoted in Hamilton, p. 836*n*.

12. "editing a couple of novels": *Who Wrote Thomas Wolfe's Last Novels?* New York Review of Books, Letter to the Editors, John Halberstadt, March 19, 1981.
13. "The disastrous turn": Hamilton, p. 328.
14. "Wilfred Funk, Inc.": Parmet, p. 72.
15. "Why England Slept": Perret, p. 82.
16. "significant notices for his book": Parmet, pp. 73–74.
17. "mature understanding": *New York Times Book Review*, August 11, 1940.

CHAPTER 13: "HENRY LUCE"
1. "You would be surprised": Wills, pp. 129–130.
2. "his father, not his mother": Nasaw, p. 63.
3. "I have shown your thesis": Papers of John F. Kennedy. Presidential Papers. President's Office Files. Personal Secretary's Files. Books: *Why England Slept*, correspondence and reviews, pp. 13–17.
4. "There are many": Blair, pp. 82–84.
5. "could be found": *Those Angry Days: Roosevelt, Lindbergh, and America's Fight Over World War II*, Lynne Olson, p. 148.
6. "It's outrageous": Leamer, p. 147.
7. an affair with Luce's wife: Leamer, p. 151.
8. "Well, send the manuscript": Henry R. Luce, recorded interview by John L. Steele, November 11, 1965, pp. 5–6, John F. Kennedy Oral History Program.
9. "I cannot recall": *Why England Slept*, John F. Kennedy, from the Foreword by Henry Luce, pp. xiii–xxii.

CHAPTER 14: "A SIMPLE CASE OF MESSAGE MEETING MOMENT"
1. "blood pressure": Letter to Joseph P. Kennedy, August 16, 1940, Joseph P. Kennedy Papers. John F. Kennedy Health File. Quoted in *Endocrine and Autoimmune Aspects of the Health History of John F. Kennedy*, Lee R. Mandel, MD, MPH, History of Medicine, p. 351.
2. "Kennedy prepared": Perret, p. 83.
3. The host began: *https://www.youtube.com/watch?v=qclD4GgIVSE*, Interview transcribed by the Author.
4. "50,000 new planes": *Those Angry Days: Roosevelt, Lindbergh, and America's Fight Over World War II, 1939–1941*, Lynne Olson, p. 98.
5. "Dollars cannot buy yesterday": *The Darkest Year: Britain Alone, June 1940-June 1941*, Herbert Agar, p. 169.
6. "convinced that military": *1941: Fighting the Shadow War*, Marc Wortman, pp. 55–56.
7. "This was what we had": *Special Relationships*, Sir John Wheeler-Bennett, p. 97.
8. "marked the official end": Olson, p. 128.
9. "remarkable for its calm": *Boston Herald*, August 3, 1940.
10. "Jack was downstairs": Charles Spalding, recorded interview by John F. Stewart, March 14, 1968, p. 2, John F. Kennedy Library Oral History Program.
11. "a great argument": Letter from FDR to JFK, August 27, 1940, JFKL.

12. "not only because": *The Kennedys Amidst the Gathering Storm: A Thousand Days in London*, Will Swift, p. 267.

Chapter 15: "Jack Earned More than $40,000 in Royalties"
1. "two scorpions": *The Dark Side of Camelot*, Seymour M. Hersh, p. 79.
2. "had not kept him": ibid., p. 74.
3. "I'm going back": ibid., p. 75.
4. "On October 16": *Memoirs*, Arthur S. Krock, p. 335.
5. "not nearly as full-throated": Nasaw, pp. 494–495.
6. "People call me a pessimist": ibid., p. 499.
7. "I read Jack's book through": Parmet. p. 74.
8. "the creation of Joseph P. Kennedy": Wills, p. 131.
9. "immensely successful young author": Leamer, p. 145
10. "I am sending you herewith": Papers of John F. Kennedy. Presidential Papers. President's Office Files. Personal Secretary's Files. Books: *Why England Slept*, correspondence and reviews, p. 18.
11. "Harold Nicholson": Perret, p. 84.
12. "to send out 250 free copies": Wills, p. 131.
13. "Tell him I am taking the book": Hamilton, p. 333.
14. "that you let him publish": Hamilton, pp. 333–334.
15. "became an instant celebrity": Parmet, pp. 76–78.
16. "I spent a week": *A Woman Named Jackie*, C. David Heymann, p. 173.
17. $40,000 in royalties: Parmet, p. 77.
18. "1 Coventry": *The Splendid and the Vile: A Saga of Churchill, Family, and Defiance During the Blitz*, Erik Larson, p. 298.
19. "fund relief organizations": Swift, p. 260.
20. "would turn on": Wills, p. 131.
21. "the debut of John F. Kennedy": Pizzitola, p. 382.
22. "the crucial first text": *The Kennedy Obsession: The American Myth of JFK*, John Hellman, p. 21, also quoted in Pizzitola, p. 382.
23. Jack was becoming well-known: Pizzitola, p. 381.

Chapter 16: "They Thought She Was a Nazi"
1. there was a photo: Parmet, p. 85.
2. Institute of World Affairs: Blair, pp. 103–104.
3. "IRISH BASES ARE VITAL": Parmet, p. 86.
4. His commission: Parmet, p. 86.
5. love of his life: *JFK and the Nazi Spy*, Washingtonian Magazine, April 1975, p. 90, also in.
6. "I think I told you before": *INGA: Kennedy's Great Love, Hitler's Perfect Beauty, and J. Edgar Hoover's Prime Suspect*, Scott Farris, p. x.
7. "One of Ex-Ambassador Kennedy's": ibid., p. 208.
8. "They shagged my ass": ibid., p. 215, also in Hamilton, p. 439.

9. Ms. Arvad was certainly: *The Vulnerability of the Macho John F. Kennedy*, Daniel Paquette, The Washington Post, January 19, 2017.
10. "move in on targets": Parmet, pp. 95–103; see also *At Close Quarters*, Robert Bulkeley, p. 29.
11. "the steel prow": *PT 109: John F. Kennedy in World War II*, Robert J. Donovan, pp. 106–109.

CHAPTER 17: "THE SKIPPER HERO"
1. "It was involuntary": *John F. Kennedy and PT 109*, JFKL.
2. "the perfect Nordic beauty": *The Surprising Way JFK's Ex-Girlfriends Helped Make Him a War Hero*, James W. Graham, Time magazine, May 26, 2017.
3. "a rapid account": Parmet, p. 117.
4. "a sudden gasp": Collier & Horowitz, p. 137.
5. "I think that if the Kennedy children": *As We Remember Joe*, John F. Kennedy, editor, pp. 3–4.
6. Privately published: Hamilton, p. 704.
7. "Harry, what are you doing?": Collier & Horowitz, p. 145.
8. "one of the most severe": Hamilton, p. 665.

CHAPTER 18: "I ALWAYS SENSED I HAD A LARGER PURPOSE"
1. "a sinister figure": *Roosevelt and Hopkins: An Intimate History*, Robert E. Sherwood, Harper & Brothers, p. 1.
2. "a progressive president": Counselor, Sorensen, p. 60.
3. "a stirring experience": *Counselor*, Sorensen, pp. 82–83.
4. "I loved Lincoln": *Counselor*, Sorensen, p. 89.
5. "With no advance notice": ibid., p. 90.

CHAPTER 19: "KENNEDY WILL NOT BE FILING TONIGHT"
1. "were taken with": Nasaw, p. 173.
2. Joe persuaded Hearst: Parmet, p. 131.
3. "from the point of view": *Jack Kennedy: Elusive Hero*, Chris Matthews, p. 69.
4. "Four times in the modern": *Peace in Their Time*, John Keegan, The Washington Post, December 15, 2002. Also in, *Act of Creation: The Founding of the United Nations, A Story of Superpowers, Secret Agents, Wartime Allies and Enemies, and Their Quest for a Peaceful World*, Stephen C. Schlesinger, p. xv.
5. "the largest international gathering": *United Nations: Shaping Our Future Together*, https://www.un.org/en/sections/history-united-nations-charter/1945-san-francisco-conference/index.html.
6. "Jack, dressed for": *Memoirs: Sixty Years on the Firing Line*, Arthur Krock, p. 351.
7. "There is an impression": New York Journal-American, April 28, 1945, quoted in Hamilton, p. 696.

8. "WORLD COURT": New York Journal-American, May 1, 1945, Papers of John F. Kennedy. Presidential Papers. President's Office Files. Personal Secretary's Files. Articles: By John F. Kennedy in the Hearst newspapers, 1945.

9. "The word is out": *Soviet Diplomacy Gets 50–50 Break*, New York Journal-American, May 3, 1945, Papers of John F. Kennedy. Presidential Papers. President's Office Files. Personal Secretary's Files. Articles: By John F. Kennedy in the Hearst newspapers, 1945.

10. "it would be no exaggeration": Hamilton, p. 688. Also in Stephen Schlesinger, p. 155.

11. "The conference at San Francisco": *Prelude to Leadership: The Post-War Diary of John F. Kennedy*, Deirdre Henderson, ed, p. 5.

12. "the British Labour Party": Chicago Herald-American, May 28, 1945, also quoted in Hamilton, p. 704.

13. "expressed disappointment": Hamilton, p. 705.

CHAPTER 20: "A DIARY HE KEPT FOR A BRIEF TIME"

1. "Britishers will go": *CHURCHILL MAY LOSE ELECTION, John F. Kennedy*, New York Journal-American, June 24, 1945.

2. "defeat poverty": *The Last Lion: Winston Spencer Churchill Defender of the Realm, 1940–1965*, William Manchester & Paul Reid, p. 940.

3. "demonstrated something": Hamilton, p. 709.

4. "My own opinion": Diary, Henderson, ed, p. 37.

5. "the example of young Churchill": Prelude, p. *xxxv*.

6. "a paranoid": ibid., p. 25.

7. "where he found": Perret, p. 132.

8. "there is not a single building": *JFK, Prelude*, pp. 49–50.

9. "it was obvious": ibid., pp. 71–72.

10. "After visit these two places": ibid., pp. 73–74.

11. "fallible men": Dallek, p. 117

CHAPTER 21: "THE NEW GENERATION OFFERS A LEADER"

1. "God! There goes": Collier & Horowitz, p. 145, Dallek, pp. 117–118, and Fay, p. 152.

2. "$2,000 for 20 shares": *JFK, Rhode Island Newspaper Mogul*, Providence Journal, November 22, 1963.

3. "was interested": *James A. Reed., recorded interview by Robert J. Donovan*, June 16, 1964. p. 6, JFKLOH.

4. "used to talk about being President": *The Remarkable Kennedy's*, Joe McCarthy, p. 19, also in Dallek, p. 119.

5. an understanding with Curley: Perrett, p. 134.

6. "Voters of the Eleventh": *John F. Kennedy Pre-Presidential Papers*, box 96, JFKL, quoted in Hamilton, p. 748.

7. "KEEP AN EYE ON HIM": Hamilton, p. 749.

8. "young working-class volunteers": Reeves, p. 78.

9. "Every time a Democrat": *Man of the House,* Thomas P. O'Neill, p. 81, and also in Reeves, p. 435.

10. "after one of the opposing": Blair, p. 476.

11. "met city workers": Hamilton, p. 756.

12. "somewhat scratchy": *The Cape Cod Years of John Fitzgerald Kennedy,* Leo Damore, p. 87, also in Reeves, pp. 77–78.

13. "I can still see the two of them": *The Fitzgeralds and the Kennedys: An American Saga,* Doris Kearns Goodwin, p. 713, also in Reeves, p. 80.

14. "he reminds me of my son": *Times to Remember,* Rose Kennedy, p. 189, also in Perret, p. 137.

15. "may have been in pain": Hamilton, p. 757.

16. "YOUNG KENNEDY ASSURED OF SEAT": Hamilton, p. 770.

17. "a fighting conservative": *A Kennedy Runs for Congress, The Boston-bred Scion of a Former Ambassador is a Fighting Irish Conservative,* Look Magazine, June 11, 1946.

18. "PROMISE KEPT": *Time,* July 1, 1946, p. 23, also in Reeves, p. 83.

19. "To the future President": Reed, OH, JFKL, p. 13.

Chapter 22: "John F. Kennedy and Richard M. Nixon"

1. "I saw a crushed man today": *Kennedy and Nixon,* Matthews, pp. 198–199.

2. NOTE: Nixon's book came out a year later, titled *Six Crises.*

3. "John F. Kennedy and Richard M. Nixon": *Jack & Dick: When Kennedy Met Nixon,* David R. Stokes, pp. 13–17.

4. "the Hollywood Hotel": Shaw, p. 18.

5. "the speech went far": *Truman,* David McCullough, p. 532.

6. "was certainly the most": *Conflict and Crisis: The Presidency of Harry S. Truman, 1945–1948,* Robert J. Donovan, p. 283.

Chapter 23: "They Stayed Up Talking through the Night"

1. "took 400,000 workers": *There is Power in a Union: The Epic Story of Labor in America,* Philip Dray, p. 493.

2. "to have the": ibid., p. 494.

3. "bring not peace": Dallek, p. 145.

4. "I remember that": *Six Crises,* Richard M. Nixon, p. 299.

5. "Soon Dick and Pat": *Richard Nixon: The Life,* John A. Farrell, p. 84.

6. "Ladies and Gentlemen": Stokes, p. 136, [AUTHOR'S NOTE: As a post-script to the McKeesport story, a few years ago this author wrote a dramatized account of Kennedy's first debate with Nixon, and I tried to recreate their conversation on their overnight train ride, based on their speeches and writings on various subjects. The book is titled *Jack and Dick: When Kennedy Met Nixon.*

After my book came out, the Penn McKee Hotel, now abandoned and in woeful disrepair, was declared a historical site, complete with a large sign that says: "KENNEDY-NIXON TAFT-HARTLEY DEBATE, On April 21, 1947, John F. Kennedy and Richard M. Nixon debated the Taft-Hartley Labor Management Relations Act at the

Penn-McKee Hotel. The first debate between the two House Labor Committee members was a precursor to the iconic Kennedy-Nixon presidential debate of 1960."]
7. "was very nice": *Evelyn Lincoln*, Oral History, p. 7, JFKL.
8. "frail, sick, hollow": Parmet, p. 165.
9. "the beginning of a terrible": *The Fitzgeralds and the Kennedys*, Doris Kearns Goodwin, p. 743.
10. "you are one of 435": *Listening In: The Secret White House Recordings of John F. Kennedy*, Ted Widmer, pp. 49–49.

Chapter 24: "He Has a Knack for Alienating"
1. "was not interested": Ulyatt, p. 25.
2. A new poll: *6 Out of 10 Voters Now Think Truman Will Run Next Year*, George Gallup, Washington Post, July 5, 1951, p. 17.
3. "President Truman's Midwestern Liberalism": Counselor, Sorensen, p. 91.
4. "almost all the lawyers": *Counselor*, Sorensen, p. 92.
5. Black Americans: Ulyatt, p. 25.
6. Wallace recalled: Robert A. Wallace, recorded interview by John F. Stewart, April 26, 1968, p. 5, JFKLOH.
7. "We played a game called": ibid., p. 6.

Chapter 25: "The Political Equivalent of Perfect Pitch in a Crooner"
1. "a fish out of water": O'Neill, p. 87.
2. "blanket the map": Shaw, p. 29.
3. "typed the information": ibid., p. 31.
4. "I don't look forward": *No Final Victories: A Life in Politics from John F. Kennedy to Watergate*, Lawrence O'Brien, p. 26, also in Shaw, p. 31.
5. "Lodges's Dodges": Shaw, p. 33.
6. "A lack of integrity": ibid., p. 34.
7. "endorsed Kennedy": Reeves, p. 100, and Parmet, pp. 242–243.
8. "his appearance on behalf: "*Robert Kennedy: His Life*, Evan Thomas, p. 61.
9. "brash, tough, hard-working": Shaw, p. 36.
10. "that family came before": *Bobby Kennedy: The Making of a Liberal Icon*, Larry Tye, pp. 22–23.
11. "I felt rather like": *Kennedy and Lodge: The 1952 Massachusetts Senate Race*, p. 295, also in Dallek, p. 174.
12. "a blooding and a bonding": *Bobby Kennedy: A Raging Spirit*, Chris Matthews, p. 105.
13. "Kennedy was the Frank Sinatra": *JFK: The Man and the Myth*, Victor Lasky, p. 152.
14. "a romance between": Dallek, p. 176.

Chapter 26: "I Would Rather Win a Pulitzer than Be President"
1. "He was the golden boy": Details and verbatim dialogue regarding Margaret Coit and her relationship with JFK drawn from: Margaret L. Coit, recorded interview by Charles

T. Morrissey, June 1, 1966, John F. Kennedy Library Oral History Program; *A Woman Named Jackie*, C. David Heyman, pp. 162–163; *Jack: A Life Like No Other*, Geoffrey Perret, pp. 189–190. And, *My date with President Kennedy: 'He was like a 14-year-old high school football player on the make*, Thomas Maier, at Salon.com, November 2, 2014. [excerpted from *When Lions Roar: The Churchills and the Kennedys*, Thomas Maier, pp. 482–485.]

2. "Modern usage": *When Lions Roar: The Churchills and the Kennedys*, Thomas Maier pp. 62–63.

3. "literary model": *President Kennedy: Profile of Power*, Richard Reeves, p. 41.

4. "This is a book about": Reeves, p. 668*n*.

5. "a version of *Great Contemporaries*": *Ask Not: The Inauguration of John F. Kennedy and the Speech that Changed America*, Thurston Clarke, p. 226*n*.

CHAPTER 27: "ENTER TED SORENSEN"

1. "with him as its chairman": *Progress of a Harvard Man*, Edward B. Lockett, *LIFE Magazine*, February 7, 1944, pp. 17–18.

2. "about money matters": Oral Interview with Robert Wallace," John F. Stewart, John F. Kennedy Library, April 26, 1968, p. 1.

3. statewide on crutches: ibid., p. 3.

4. "ability to write in clear": *Counselor*, Sorensen, p. 96.

5. "ability to write in clear": Oral Interview with Robert Wallace, John F. Stewart, John F. Kennedy Library, April 26, 1968, p. 5.

6. "Sorensen had this flair": ibid., p. 6.

7. "Douglas always paid me": ibid., p. 7.

8. "Our committee was closing": Paul H. Douglas, recorded interview by John New house, June 6, 1964, p. 1, JFKLOH.

9. "tailor made suit": *Kennedy*, Sorensen, p. 11.

CHAPTER 28: "TED BECAME HIS INTELLECTUAL BLOOD BANK"

1. "He went out on my boat": *Joseph P. Kennedy: The True Story*, Irwin Ross, New York Post, January 9, 1960, also in Nasaw, p. 667.

2. "he admired him": Nasaw, p. 667.

3. "soft on Senator": *Counselor*, Sorensen, pp. 98–99.

4. "intellectual blood bank": *JFK in the Senate: Pathway to the Presidency*, John T. Shaw, p. 122.

5. "oddly, even disturbingly": *Jacqueline Bouvier Kennedy Onassis: The Untold Story*, Barbara Leaming, pp. 87–88.

6. "I heard a compliment": *Eunice K. Shriver to Theodore C. Sorensen*, January 31, 1955, TCSPP, box 15, JFKL.

7. "at least one-half": *Counselor*, Sorensen, pp. 144–145.

8. "I think Kennedy gave him all": Oral Interview with Robert Wallace, John F. Stewart, John F. Kennedy Library, April 26, 1968, p. 17.

Chapter 29: "A Kennedy Speech Has to Have Class"

1. "the possibility of becoming": Dallek, p. 182.
2. "broad Massachusetts inflections": *Grace and Power*, Smith, p. 55.
3. "square, wintry, bespectacled": ibid., p. 54.
4. "the hackneyed speeches": *The Crisis Years, Kennedy and Khrushchev, 1960–1963*, Michael R. Beschloss, p. 126.
5. "I never had anyone": *Sounding the Trumpet: The Making of John F. Kennedy's Inaugural Address*, Richard J. Tofel, pp. 86–87, also in Shaw, p. 123.
6. "the most serious liberal": ibid., p. 125.
7. "the senator's willingness": Dallek, p. 180.
8. "after consideration of such": *TCS to JFK*, October 9, 1953, TCSPP, box 15, JFKL.
9. "a most satisfactory": *TCS to JFK*, November 24, 1953, TCSPP, box 15, JFKL.
10. "When I indicated": *TCS to James Landis*, December 18, 1953, TCSPP, box 6, JFKL.

Chapter 30: A Rather Helter-Skelter Relationship"

1. better ratings: *Murrow: One Man, One Microphone, One Murrow*, Katie Bailey, History Link.Org, https://www.historylink.org/File/10224.
2. Friday, October 30, 1953: Description of the Kennedys on Edward R. Murrow's *Person to Person* broadcast drawn from Parmet, pp. 296–298.
3. "that Jack would have married": *John F. Kennedy: A Political Profile*, James MacGregor Burns, p. 127, also in Dallek, p. 192.
4. "having a wife was": Parmet, p. 229.
5. "Shall we go someplace": *Charles Bartlett, recorded interview by Fred Holborn*, January 6, 1965 (page number), John F. Kennedy Library Oral History Program, p. 19.
6. "exquisite features": Burns, p. 127.
7. "Senator Kennedy Goes": LIFE Magazine, July 20, 1953.
8. "a crowd of 3,000": *Notables Attend Senator's Wedding*, New York Times, September 13, 1953, p. 1, also in Burns, p. 128.
9. "an eighteenth-century affair": Parmet, p. 258.
10. "found herself subjected": Parmet, p. 296.
11. "like characters out of Fitzgerald": *The Kennedys" An American Dream*, Peter Collier and David Horowitz, p. 233.
12. "Victorian wife": Lasky, p. 161.
13. "Pretty Mrs. Jack Kennedy": *The Senator's Wife Goes Back to School*, McCall's Magazine, October 1954, p. 50.
14. five-day photo shoot: *Jacqueline Bouvier Kennedy Onassis: The Untold Story*, Barbara Leaming, pp. 57–58.
15. "Jackie asks questions": *McCall's*, October 1954, pp. 50–51.

Chapter 31: "A Quality Book"

1. "who had risked their careers": Perrett, p. 212.
2. "so difficult a surgery": Dallek, p. 196.

3. "performed a double fusion": Burns, p. 156.
4. "weeping in a chair": Parmet, p. 309.
5. "tidbits of gossip": Perret, p. 212.
6. "Jack had dropped maybe 40 pounds": Heymann, p. 171.
7. "Something very important happened": *Jack Kennedy*, Matthews, p. 193.
8. "and a delegation": Burns, p. 169.
9. "On almost every": Burns, p. 141.
10. "a lot of bunk": Parmet, p. 300.
11. "at the other end": Ibid., p. 310.
12. His colleagues did not: Parmet, p. 287.
13. "I also hope to have": *TCS to JFK, December 22, 1954*, TCSPP, box 15, JFKL.

CHAPTER 32: "THE HOUSE OF HARPER"
1. "more than one publisher": Heymann, p. 174.
2. "Cass was born": *A Clash of Camelots*, Vanity Fair, August 31, 2009.
3. "a refreshing presence": *The Time of Their Lives: The Golden Age of Great American Book Publishers, Their Editors and Authors*, Al Silverman, p. 219.
4. "The House of Harper": ibid., p. 215.
5. "Canfield was a working stiff": Ibid., p. 216
6. "A quality book": *Cass Canfield, A Titan of Publishing, is Dead at 88*, New York Times, March 28, 1986, Section D, p. 15.
7. "got rather bogged down": Cass Canfield to JFK, February 15, 1955, Harper & Row Publishers Records, 1935–1973, box 117, Columbia University Libraries, Rare Book and Manuscript Library, quoted in Fehrman, p. 269.
8. "Many thanks": Papers of John F. Kennedy. Personal Papers. Manuscripts: *Profiles in Courage*. Correspondence: Item 2-Harper and Brother, publishers; chronological, 1955: 28 January–31 October, p. 3.

CHAPTER 33: "IT WAS ALL VERY COLLABORATIVE"
1. "only a step or two": Details and description about JFK's recuperative time in Palm Beach are drawn from, Parmet, pp. 312–315, and reporting in the May 22, 1955 edition of the *New Bedford Standard-Times*, by Minna Littmann.
2. "on heavy white paper": Burns, p. 161.
3. "writing almost upside down": Perret, p. 213.
4. "the history of senatorial courage": *Counselor*, Sorensen, p. 145.
5. "monumental work": *John F. Kennedy: A Biography*, Michael O'Brien, p. 285.
6. "the Library of Congress Palm Beach Annex": *Counselor*, Sorensen, p. 146.
7. "Like JFK's speeches": *Counselor*, Sorensen, p. 150.
8. "Though Kennedy dug up": *Elusive Hero*, Matthews, p. 191.

CHAPTER 34: "OUR MONUMENTAL WORK"
1. "the article on": *TCS to JFK*, January 14, 1955, TCSPP, box 15, JFKL.
2. "I literally thought through": *Counselor*, Sorensen, p. 136.

3. ."You may leave your eyes": *Eunice Shriver to TCS, October 17, 1955,* TCSPP, box 15, JFKL.
4. "My present suggestion": *TCS to JFK,* January 25, 1955, TCSPP, box 15, JFKL.
5. "in order to give me": *TCS to JFK,* January 31, 1955, TCSPP, box 15, JFKL.
6. "our monumental work": *TCS to JFK,* February 4, 1955, TCSPP, box 15, JFKL.
7. A few days later: *TCS to JFK,* February 8, 1955, TCSPP, box 7, JFKL.
8. "Drafts sent to you": *TCS to JFK,* February 14, 1955, box 7, TCSPP, JFKL.
9. "We have decided to expand": *Counselor,* Sorensen, p. 146.
10. "endorsement of a contemporary": *Memoirs,* Arthur Krock, p. 355.

CHAPTER 35: "THE PROFESSOR"
1. "one of our great teachers": *Profiles in Humility,* Nancy Frieburg, Georgetown Magazine, Fall 1997, p. 24.
2. She asked Dr. Davids: ibid., p. 25.
3. "did much of the work": Heymann, p. 174.
4. "Since the book": *An Old Letter Backs a Claim of Helping Kennedy Write "Profiles,"* Patricia Cohen, New York Times, October 18, 1997.
5. "to trigger his own contemplation": Parmet, pp. 323–325.
6. Author's note: There is a timeline issue regarding Sorensen's phone call to Jules Davids. Years later, the Professor recalled the phone call coming "several weeks" after his initial conversation with Jackie Kennedy. But then, he described the call as one soliciting his input for a "book" Senator Kennedy wanted write. However, the decision to move the project from article to book was not made until later in the year, after Kennedy's first surgery. Also, Davids mentioned that the book had already been "rejected" by a publisher, which did not happen until December 1954, at the earliest. Possibly there were multiple calls. But a letter written by Davids in August, 1957, more proximate to the actual events, places the call in January 1955.
7. "In January 1955": Freiburg, p. 24.
8. "and the Senator was very anxious": ibid., p. 25.

CHAPTER 36: "DAVIDS WAS PAID A MERE $700"
1. "Evaluation of Draft": Papers of John F. Kennedy. Personal Papers. Manuscripts: *Profiles in Courage.* Correspondence: Item 1-Comments and suggestions on draft by seven historians, 1955: 19 February–7 August, pp. 31–32.
2. "The Meaning of Political Courage": Papers of John F. Kennedy. Personal Papers. Manuscripts: Profiles in Courage. Correspondence: Item 1-Comments and suggestions on draft by seven historians, 1955: 19 February–7 August, pp. 32–45.
3. "not a man interested in fame": Freiburg, p. 27.

Chapter 37: "Some Political Scientists and Historians"

1. "grew to admire Kennedy": *The Legacy of James M. Landis*, Donald A. Ritchie, an article by Ritchie drawn from his book: *James M. Landis—Dean of the Regulations*.
2. "It should be as personal": Papers of John F. Kennedy. Personal Papers. Manuscripts: Profiles in Courage. Correspondence: Item 1-Comments and suggestions on draft by seven historians, 1955: 19 February–7 August, pp. 46–50.
3. "amused by the metaphor": Parmet, p. 326.
4. "It was my first real contact": James MacGregor Burns, recorded interview by William H. Brubeck, May 14, 1965, p. 27, John F. Kennedy Library Oral History Program.
5. "an impressive compilation": Papers of John F. Kennedy. Personal Papers. Manuscripts: Profiles in Courage. Correspondence: Item 1-Comments and suggestions on draft by seven historians, 1955: 19 February–7 August, p. 5.

Chapter 38: "I Should Be Glad to Take a Look at Your Book"

1. "the gossip salon circuits": *Arthur M. Schlessinger Jr, author who shaped lens for viewing U.S. history, dies at 89*, Adam Bernstein, *Washington Post*, March 2, 2007.
2. "Your proposed article": Papers of John F. Kennedy. Personal Papers. Manuscripts: Profiles in Courage. Correspondence: Item 1-Comments and suggestions on draft by seven historians, 1955: 19 February–7 August, pp. 19–20.
3. "Dear Arthur": ibid., p. 23.
4. "I should be glad": ibid., p. 22.
5. "it seems to me": ibid., p. 13.
6. "Many, many thanks": ibid., p. 12.

Chapter 39: "With Something Close to Fascination"

1. "review the manuscript": Papers of John F. Kennedy. Personal Papers. Manuscripts: *Profiles in Courage*. Correspondence: Item 1- Comments and suggestions on draft by seven historians, 1955: 19 February–7 August, p. 7.
2. "it is the kind of book": ibid., p. 6.
3. "Years ago": ibid., p. 8.
4. "at the request of": *Immersed in Great Affairs: Allan Nevins and the Heroic Age of American History*, Gerald L. Fetner, p. 150.
5. "regret that I have": Papers of John F. Kennedy. Personal Papers. Manuscripts: Profiles in Courage. Correspondence: Item 1-Comments and suggestions on draft by seven historians, 1955: 19 February–7 August, p. 27.
6. "Of course, I feel honored": Papers of John F. Kennedy. Personal Papers. Manuscripts: Profiles in Courage. Correspondence: Item 1-Comments and suggestions on draft by seven historians, 1955: 19 February–7 August, p. 25.
7. "will attract wide attention": Papers of John F. Kennedy. Personal Papers. Manuscripts: Profiles in Courage. Correspondence: Item 1-Comments and suggestions on draft by seven historians, 1955: 19 February–7 August, p. 28.

8. "will be extremely influential": *TCS to JFK, August 12, 1955*, TCSPP, box 7, JFKL.
9. "We have no intention": *Evan Thomas to Dr. Allan Nevins*, August 17, 1955, Papers of John F. Kennedy. Personal Papers. Manuscripts: Profiles in Courage. Correspondence: Item 1-Comments and suggestions on draft by seven historians, 1955: 19 February–7 August, p. 43.
10. "suggested that Johnson": *Johnson to Kennedy, October 21, 1953*, Pre-Presidential Papers, Box 481, JFKL, also quoted in Parmet, p. 274.
11. "valuable and important": Papers of John F. Kennedy. Personal Papers. Manuscripts: Profiles in Courage. Correspondence: Item 1-Comments and suggestions on draft by seven historians, 1955: 19 February–7 August, pp. 51–66.

CHAPTER 40: "EVAN WELLINGTON THOMAS II"

1. "The editorial suggestions": *Profiles in Courage*, John F. Kennedy, p. *xx*.
2. "there was something": *Reminiscences of Evan Thomas II*, February 11, 1974, p. 4, Oral History Archives at Columbia, Rare Book & Manuscript Library, Columbia University in the City of New York.
3. "alert quality": https://www.kirkusreviews.com/book-reviews/a/evan-thomas-6/ambulance-in-africa.
4. "well, why don't I": *Reminiscences*, OH, p. 22.
5. "Canfield proved to be": ibid., p. 25.
6. multiple sclerosis: *Author interview with Evan Thomas III*, February 12, 2020.
7. "the best nonfiction editor": Silverman, p. 221.
8. Greek vase: *e-mail conversation with Evan Thomas, III*, April, 15, 2020, see also, The Manchester Affair, John Corry, p. 54.
9. "JFK didn't know": ibid., p. 115.
10. "The publisher, if he thinks": Silverman, p. 221.
11. "a very charming guy": *Reminiscences*, Columbia University, OH, p. 120.
12. he chose the title: *Letter from Thomas to JFK*, August 4, 1955, Papers of John F. Kennedy. Personal Papers. Manuscripts: Profiles in Courage. Correspondence: Item 2-Harper and Brother, publishers; chronological, 1955: 28 January–31 October, p. 27.
13. "I think you have done": *Evan Thomas to JFK, April 14, 1955*, Papers of John F. Kennedy. Personal Papers. Manuscripts: Profiles in Courage. Correspondence: Item 2-Harper and Brother, publishers; chronological, 1955: 28 January–31 October, pp. 8–9.
14. "I would appreciate": *JFK to Evan Thomas, April 18, 1955*, Papers of John F. Kennedy. Personal Papers. Manuscripts: Profiles in Courage. Correspondence: Item 2-Harper and Brother, publishers; chronological, 1955: 28 January–31 October, pp. 10–11.
15. "we think you are wrong": *Evan Thomas to JFK, April 21, 1955*, Papers of John F. Kennedy. Personal Papers. Manuscripts: Profiles in Courage. Correspondence: Item 2-Harper and Brother, publishers; chronological, 1955: 28 January–31 October, pp. 12–13.
16. Kennedy's publishing contract: TCSPP, box 7, JFKL.

CHAPTER 41: "YOUR FATHER IS A CONTROVERSIAL MAN"

1. "stir some advance enthusiasm": *Evan Thomas to JFK, June 14, 1955,* Papers of John F. Kennedy. Personal Papers. Manuscripts: Profiles in Courage. Correspondence: Item 2-Harper and Brother, publishers; chronological, 1955: 28 January–31 October, pp. 18–20.
2. Kennedy replied: *JFK to Evan Thomas, June 23, 1955,* Papers of John F. Kennedy. Personal Papers. Manuscripts: Profiles in Courage. Correspondence: Item 2-Harper and Brother, publishers; chronological, 1955: 28 January–31 October, pp. 21–22.
3. "I think Harper's": *TCS to Evan Thomas,* August 22, 1955, JFKPP, box 31, JFKL, p. 44.
4. "This is the first": *Reminiscences,* Evan Thomas II, Columbia University, OH, pp. 122–123.
5. the S.S. *United States: Once Majestic Cruise Ship,* Fox News, January 26, 2018, https://www.foxnews.com/travel/once-majestic-cruise-ship-the-s-s-united-states-could-be-americas-flagship-once-again.
6. "to clear up several items": *JFK to Evan Thomas, August 1, 1955,* Papers of John F. Kennedy. Personal Papers. Manuscripts: Profiles in Courage. Correspondence: Item 2-Harper and Brother, publishers; chronological, 1955: 28 January–31 October, p. 24.
7. "Author's Information Sheet": JFKPP, August 24, 1955, box 31, JFKL, p. 47.
8. "this book reads": *Evan Thomas to TCS,* August 24, 1955, ibid., p. 51.
9. "I understand that you will read": *Evan Thomas to TCS,* September 1, 1955, ibid., p. 55.
10. "I have passed on to": *TCS to Evan Roberts,* September 23, 1955, ibid., p. 70.
11. "a Mr. Racine": *Evan Thomas to TCS,* October 4, 1955, ibid., p. 78.
12. "when is the Senator coming back?": *Evan Thomas to TCS,* October 10, 1955, ibid., p. 83.
13. "Few men have ever": *Adlai Stevenson says of Profiles in Courage,* October 18, 1955, ibid., p. 88.

CHAPTER 42: "THE LOST INTRODUCTION"

1. "Four strange men": Papers of John F. Kennedy. Personal Papers. Manuscripts: Profiles in Courage. Related papers: Item 4- materials for introduction and conclusion, also in Hellman, p. 2.
2. "Senator L.C. Oltimer": For an interesting analysis of this "lost" intro, see Hellman, pp. 1–6, a chapter titled *A Bedside Visit.*
3.
4. "Dear Senator Oldtimer": Papers of John F. Kennedy. Personal Papers. Manuscripts: *Profiles in Courage.* Related papers: Item 4-materials for introduction and conclusion, pp. 96–97.
5. "My doctor, in what I hope": ibid., pp. 81–82.
6. "There is, of course": Manuscripts—*Profiles in Courage* folder, Item 4 [C] Personal Papers, JFKL, also in Hellman, pp. 63–64.
7. "the deleted chapter": Hellmann, pp. 4–5.
8. "there is no comparable": Papers of John F. Kennedy. Personal Papers. Senator's Notes, 1953–1955, pp. 10–16.
9. "domestic staff of nine": *The Moods of Ernest Hemingway,* Lillian Ross, The New Yorker, May 6, 1950.

10. "He was the soul": *Writer, Sailor, Soldier, Spy: Ernest Hemingway's Secret Adventures, 1935–1961*, Nicholas Reynolds, p. 2.
11. "furthered his larger strategy": Hellmann, p. 64.
12. "Dear Mr. Hemingway": John F. Kennedy's letter to Ernest Hemingway, July 1955. John F. Kennedy Personal Papers, Box 31, Correspondence: Item 2-Harper & Brother, publishers; chronological, 1955: 28 January–31 October, in *JFK & Hemingway: Beyond "Grace Under Pressure,"* by Stacey Chandler, Reference Archivist, JFKL.
13. "That quotation": *Letter from Charles Scribner's Sons to Evan Thomas*, August 5, 1955, Papers of John F. Kennedy. Personal Papers. Manuscripts: Profiles in Courage. Correspondence: Item 2-Harper and Brother, publishers; chronological, 1955: 28 January–31 October.
14. "Found that 'grace under pressure'": *Letter from Thomas to JFK, August 9, 1955*, Papers of John F. Kennedy. Personal Papers. Manuscripts: Profiles in Courage. Correspondence: Item 2-Harper and Brother, publishers; chronological, 1955: 28 January–31 October, p. 35.

CHAPTER 43: "SORENSEN WAS A ONE-MAN PROMOTION MACHINE"

1. "So I can't write, eh": ibid.
2. A week later: *TCS to JFK*, February 21, 1955, TCSPP, JFKL.
3. "With respect to the presentation": *TCS to JFK*, February 28, 1955, TCSPP, box 15, JFKL.
4. "disappointed in Dr. Davids": *TCS to JFK*, March 17, 1955, TCSPP, box 15, JFKL.
5. Collier's Magazine: *TCS to JFK*, March 4, 1955, TCSPP, box 7, JFKL.
6. Dr. Davids visited: *TCS to JFK*, March 9, 1955, TCSPP, box, 15, JFKL.
7. "had not yet received his check": *TCS to JFK*, April 14, 1955, TCSPP, JFKL.
8. "I am enclosing": *TCS to JFK*, April 22, 1955, TCSPP, box 15, JFKL.
9. "a suggested draft on Lamar": *TCS to JFK*, April 25, 1955, TCSPP, box 15, JFKL.
10. "I think we will want": *TCS to JFK*, April 27, 1955, TCSPP, box 15, JFKL.
11. In early May: *TCS to JFK*, May 5, 1955, TCSPP, box 15, JFKL.
12. 47,000 words: *TCP to JFK*, April 29, 1955, TCSPP, JFKL.
13. "a good fellow": *TCS Letter to Roger, July 8, 1955*, TCSPP, box 15, JFKL.
14. "that yet to be famous": *TCS to Abe Moses, August 29, 1955*, TCSP, box 15, JFKL.
15. "both interesting and indicative": *TCS to JFK, July 18, 1955*, TCSPP, box 7, JFKL.
16. "extremely enthusiastic": *TCS to JFK, March 9, 1955, TCSPP*, box 7, JFKL.
17. "the first and last chapters": *TCS to JFK, August 12, 1955*, TCSPP, box 7, JFKL.
18. "Do you want to review?": *TCS to JFK, September 12, 1955*, TCSPP, box 7, JFKL.
19. "Summary of Negotiations": *TCS Memorandum, October 20, 1955*, TCSPP, box 7, JFKL.

CHAPTER 44: "WITH A LITTLE HELP FROM HIS FATHER"

1. Evan communicated with Sorensen: *TCS to JFK, September 16, 1955*, TCSPP, box 7, JFKL.
2. "Evan Thomas pleads": *TCS to JFK, September 20, 1955*, TCSPP, box 7, JFKL.

3. "a Mr. Racine": *Evan Thomas to TCS*, October 4, 1955, ibid., p. 78.

4. "Dave Garroway": *Ramon Herdman to JFK*, October 24, 1955, JFKPP, box 31, JFKL, p. 90.

5. "one of our leading": *Evan Thomas to JFK*, October 28, 1955, JFKPP, box 31, JFKL, p. 92.

6. eleven minor changes: *TCS to Evan Thomas*, October 31, 1955, JFKPP, box 31, JFKL, p. 94.

7. "I wonder if": *JFK to Evan Thomas*, November 1, 1955, ibid., p. 96.

8. "Although I can understand": *JFK to Evan Thomas*, November 3, 1955, ibid., p. 97.

9. "that it seemed": https://www.kirkusreviews.com/about/history/.

10. "I know the enclosed": *Evan Thomas to JFK*, November 3, 1955, JFKPP, box 31, JFKL, pp. 99–100.

11. "The Challenge of Political Courage": New York Times Magazine, December 18, 1955, pp. 13, 32, 34, 35, and 36.

Chapter 45: "Jack Called Evan Thomas on Christmas Eve"

1. Less than six-weeks prior: *Evan Thomas to JFK*, November 23, 1955, ibid., p. 111.

2. "On account of all": *Evan Thomas to TCS*, November 28, 1955, ibid., p. 112.

3. "my wife was filling": *Reminiscences of Evan Thomas II*, February 11, 1974, pp. 117–119, Oral History Archives at Columbia, Rare Book & Manuscript Library, Columbia University in the City of New York.

4. "an exciting tale": *Globe Will Publish 'Profiles in Courage': Editor Tells How Bay State Senator Wrote of Nation's Great Leaders*, Boston Globe, John Harris, December 26, 1955, pp. 1 and 24.

5. "Possible Changes": *Memo from TCS to JFK*, Papers of John F. Kennedy. Personal Papers. Manuscripts: Profiles in Courage. Preface: Item 1-carbon typescript with attached memo, box 27.

Chapter 46: "The Book Was Quickly Captivating America"

1. "The Boston Globe": *TCS to JFK*, September 12, 1955, TCSPP, box 7, JFKL.

2. Other serializations of Profiles: *TCS to JFK*, October 20, 1955, TCSPP, box 7, JFKL.

3. "One of the reasons": *Men Who Dared to Stand Alone: Political Integrity and the Price Paid for It Is Discussed by Senator Kennedy*, New York Times Book Review, January 1, 1956, pp. 1 and 21.

4. "There's something about": *Kennedy and Nixon*, Matthews, p. 199.

5. "describing a mountain": *Charles Poore, Book Reviewer for the Times Till '69, Dies*, New York Times, July 27, 1971, p. 36.

6. "In writing about": *Books of the Times*, New York Times, January 7, 1956, p. 30.

Chapter 47: "The Book Has Taken Off Like a Bird"

1. Newspapers around the country: Holyoke (Mass) Transcript-Telegram, March 28, 1956, TCSPP, box 7, JFKL.

2. "to do a condensation": Evan Thomas to JFK, January 11, 1956, JFKPP, box 31.
3. "As a writer myself": Papers of John F. Kennedy. Presidential Papers. President's Office Files. Personal Secretary's Files. Books: "Profiles in Courage," correspondence, p. 4.
4. Among the first: *Sen. Kennedy to Speak at Book Awards*, Houston Chronicle, undated, JFKPP box 31.
5. "Like most speeches": TCS to Evan Thomas, February 3, 1956, JFKPP, box 31.
6. "On the day of": *Author in Chief: The Untold Story of Our Presidents and the Books they Wrote*, Craig Fehrman, p. 2.
7. Virginia Peterson introduced Kennedy: Find the full audio of this at: https://www. wnyc.org/story/1956-national-book-awards-part-2-senator-john-f-kennedy/
8. Kennedy began his address: *Address of Senator John F. Kennedy, The National Book Award*, New York City, February 7, 1956, JFKPP, Pre-Presidential Papers, Senate Files, box 894.
9. "In the course": *Remarks of Senator John F. Kennedy, Washington Post Book and Author Luncheon*, February 8, 1956, JFKPP, Pre-Presidential Papers, Senate Files, box 895.
10. "Democratic leaders": *Inside Washington March of Events—Kennedy Looks Good Veep Bet to Some Democrats*, Special to Central Press Association, Daily Republican-Register (Mount Carmel, Illinois), February 9, 1956, p. 6.
11. 3,016 copies: Evan Thomas to TCS, March 1, 1956, TCSPP, box 7.

CHAPTER 48: "THE STAR OF THE NIGHT"

1. "he has studied": *Divine, Beautiful, said the Delegates*, John Steinbeck, Boston Globe, August 15, 1956, p. 6.
2. "caught the attention": *Frank Goad Clement and the Keynote Address of 1956*, Robert E. Corlew III, Tennessee Historical Quarterly, Vol. 36, No. 1 (Spring 1977), p. 98.
3. "an expertly edited": *TV NOTEBOOK*, Mary Cremmen, Boston Globe, August 14, 1956, p. 37.
4. "grasped his lines": O'Brien, p. 316.
5. "the star of the night": *Jack Kennedy: Elusive Hero*, Matthews, p. 203.
6. "Tennessee's serious": Corlew, p. 106.
7. "overwrought": Leamer, p. 353.
8. "a bitter and traumatic": ibid., p. 107.
9. "a major presence": ibid., p. 354.
10. "flap": *A Woman Named Jackie*, C. David Heymann, pp. 172–173.
11. "What do you mean?": Thomas Reeves, p. 51.

CHAPTER 49: "IT WAS THE PERFECT TRIAL RUN"

1. "livid": *Elusive Hero*, Matthews, p. 205.
2. "a stroke of luck": Dallek, p. 210.
3. "like everything in life": O'Brien, p. 322.
4. "as things turned out": Burns, p. 190.
5. "it was the perfect": Elusive Hero, Matthews, p. 213.

6. 69,936: Evan Thomas to JFK, November 16, 1956, TCSPP, box 7, JFKL.
7. "asked Jack not": O'Brien, p. 323.
8. "for the next two months": ibid., p. 324.
9. 79,869: *Statement from Harper and Brothers*, December 31, 1956, TCSPP, box 7, JFKL.
10. "over 100,000 copies": *Evan Thomas to JFK*, March 7, 1957, TCSPP, box 7, JFKL.

CHAPTER 50: "PULITZER PRIZE"
1. The World Room: Details drawn from, *Window of the World*, Benjamin Waldman, Columbia Magazine, Spring 2012, https://magazine.columbia.edu/article/window-world
2. "a sardonic Irish ragamuffin": https://www.atlasobscura.com/articles/how-americas-first-popular-comic-shaped-the-19th-century-newspaper-wars
3. "secretary and day-to-day": *The Pulitzer Diaries: Inside America's Greatest Prize*, John Hohenberg, p. 21.
4. "every seventh year": ibid., p. 42.
5. "Senator Kennedy's": ibid., p. 47.
6. "I tried": ibid., p. 49.
7. "was reasonably sure": ibid., p. 48.
8. The two judges: Parmet, pp. 394–397.
9. "the board deadlocked": ibid., p. 50.
10. "at that particular point": Parmet, p. 397, Parmet interview with John Hohenberg, June 18, 1977.
11. "it wasn't great": Parmet, p. 397, Parment interview with Joseph Pulitzer III, August 5, 1997.

CHAPTER 51: "I WORKED AS HARD AS I COULD TO GET HIM THAT PRIZE"
1. "The insidious influence": White, p. 23.
2. "Dean of Washington newsmen": *Lindbergh vs. Roosevelt: The Rivalry that Divided America*, James Duffy, p. 90.
3. "The Advisory Board": *Arthur Krock Cited by Pulitzer Board*," New York Times, May 4, 1955, p. 25.
4. "I'm told that Arthur Krock": Hohenberg, p. 24.
5. "He consulted me": Krock, p. 355.
6. "Dear Dad": *JFK to Joseph P. Kennedy*, January 15, 1957, JFKPP, box 521, JFKL; see also Fehrman, p. 275.
7. "I've just been talking": *Reminiscences of Evan Thomas II*, February 11, 1974, pp. 117–119, Oral History Archives at Columbia, Rare Book & Manuscript Library, Columbia University in the City of New York.
8. "The instrument": *Herbert S. Parmet, recorded interview by Sheldon M. Stern*, August 9, 1983, p. 27, JFKLOH.
9. great influence with Choate's newspaper: *Common Ground: A Turbulent Decade in the Lives of Three Families*, J. Anthony Lukas, p. 485.

10. "Give me some reasons": *Kennedy and Nixon: The Rivalry that Shaped Postwar America*, Chris Matthews, p. 114.
11. "had been recommending it": Hohenberg, p. 50.
12. "claim credit for himself": *The Journalist and the Politician: Former NYT Reporter Arthur Krock had a long friendship with Joe Kennedy—and it showed in his coverage*, Eric Alterman, Columbia Journalism Review, February 14, 2013.
13. "worked like hell": Wills, p. 137.
14. "I worked as hard as I could": *Portrait of a President*, William Manchester, p. 112, also quoted in Thomas Reeves, p. 142.
15. "Senator Kennedy": Papers of John F. Kennedy. Presidential Papers. President's Office Files. Personal Secretary's Files. Books: "Profiles in Courage," correspondence, p. 22.
16. "Our sales are now 96,000": Evan Thomas to JFK, May 8, 1957, Papers of John F. Kennedy. Presidential Papers. President's Office Files. Personal Secretary's Files. Books: "Profiles in Courage," correspondence, p. 24.
17. "immediately upon hearing": *Maurice W. Salomon to JFK*, May 15, 1957, Papers of John F. Kennedy. Presidential Papers. President's Office Files. Personal Secretary's Files. Books: "Profiles in Courage," correspondence, p. 36.
18. 100,000 mark: *Evan Thomas to JFK*, June 6, 1957, Papers of John F. Kennedy. Presidential Papers. President's Office Files. Personal Secretary's Files. Books: "Profiles in Courage," correspondence, p. 37.
19. "In January 1957": Burns, pp. 162–163.
20. "gave him the stamp": Dallek, p. 210.
21. "modest change": Hohenberg, p. 52.

CHAPTER 52: "IT WAS ALL A MATTER OF MONEY"
1. "a painful period": James MacGregor Burns, Oral History, May 14, 1965, JFKL, pp. 30–33.
2. "the closest our time": *Gilbert Seldes*, Television Quarterly: The Journal of the National Academy of Television Arts and Sciences, Vol. IX, Number 4, Fall 1970, p. 5.
3. "collaborator": *The Lively Arts*, Gilbert Seldes, Village Voice, May 15, 1957, also in Shaw, p. 134.
4. "I did a first draft": *Counselor*, Sorensen, p. 146.
5. "a crush": *Jacqueline Kennedy: Historic Conversations on Life with John F. Kennedy*, Jacqueline Kennedy with Arthur Schlesinger, p. 280.
6. "so close and so entangled": MacGeorge Bundy, Oral History: McGeorge Bundy, recorded interview by Richard Neustadt, March 1964 (page number), John F. Kennedy Library Oral History Program, p. 92.
7. "a parting of the ways": ibid., p. 93.
8. "making noises about town": *Jacqueline Bouvier Kennedy Onassis*, Leaming, p. 88.
9. "couldn't always trust Ted": *Historic Conversations*, Schlesinger, p. 59.
10. "New York people": *L.B. Nichols to Clyde Tolson*, May 14, 1957, JFK File, FBI, quoted in Parmet, p. 330.

11. "undoubtedly at the Ambassador's: Parmet, p. 330.
12. "It was bought by": *Counselor*, Sorensen, p. 147.

CHAPTER 53: "JOE KENNEDY MADE A DEAL WITH JACK'S GHOSTWRITER"
1. $40,290.27: *Statement from Harper and Brothers*, December 31, 1956, TCSPP, box 7, JFKL.
2. "did not want to offend": *Counselor*, Sorensen, p. *xv*.
3. "Joe Kennedy's advisors": ibid., p. 148.
4. "Clearly one-half": ibid., p. 147.
5. "over a hundred thousand dollars": *Jacqueline Kennedy: Historic Conversations on Life with John Kennedy*, Arthur Schlesinger, p. 61.
6. "By January 1961": *Counselor*, Sorensen, p. 148.
7. "entirely written by someone else": *Emma Sheehy to JFK*, July 17, 1957, JFK File, U.S. Senate Library, also in Shaw, p. 134.
8. "completely and utterly untrue": *JFK to Emma Sheehy*, July 23, 1957, JFK File, U.S. Senate Library, also in Shaw, p. 134.

CHAPTER 54: "LESS PROFILE AND MORE COURAGE"
1. He remembered the Kennedys: Kay (Katherine Murphy) Halle, recorded interview by William M. McHugh, February 7, 1967, pp. 2–3, JFKLOH.
2. "candid, sometimes combative": *Between You and Me: A Memoir*, Mike Wallace, pp. 5–6.
3. "I had to bone up": *Drew Pearson Diaries 1949–1959*, edited by Tyler Abell, p. 407.
4. "Drew Pearson's manure": *House in Merry-Go-Round Community Lists for $3.65 million*, Kathy Orton, Washington Post, November 24, 2017.
5. "journey-politico niche": *Washington Scribe: The Diaries of the Ultimate D.C. Insider*, Thomas Mallon, in *The New Yorker*, September 21, 2015.
6. "chronic criticisms": *Confessions of a Muckraker*, Jack Anderson.
7. "a journalistic throwback": Wallace, p. 6.
8. "We might as well quit": *Counselor*, Sorensen, p. 149.

CHAPTER 55: "PERHAPS SORENSEN MADE THE STATEMENT WHEN DRINKING"
1. a casual acquaintance: *Clark Clifford: The Wise Man of Washington*, John Acacia, pp. 202–209.
2. "Democratic party statesman": Perret, p. 228.
3. plot: *Counsel to the President, Clark Clifford*, pp. 306–310; see also Nasaw, p. 714.
4. "really on the warpath": *Clark Clifford, recorded interview by Larry J. Hackman*, December 16, 1974, pp. 3–4, JFKLOH.
5. "Room 362": *Kennedy*, Sorensen, p. 69.
6. "ABC is in a dither": Pearson, pp. 407–408.
7. "Sorensen would acquire": Wallace, p. 11.

8. Ted Sorensen was in town: O'Brien, p. 334.
9. "a day-long conference": *Clark Clifford, recorded interview by Larry J. Hackman*, December 16, 1974, p. 5, JFKLOH.
10. "they sought to avoid": *Kennedy*, Sorensen, p. 69.
11. "expertly rebutted": O'Brien, p. 334.
12. "Last Saturday night": Acacia, p. 208.

CHAPTER 56: "THE RUMORS STILL PERSIST"

1. "The way I saw it": Wallace, p. 11.
2. Wallace and Kennedy: ibid., p. 13.
3. "ABC did not inform me": *Excerpt from Interview with Mike Wallace–Barry Gray Radio Show*, undated, TCSPP, box 7, p. 90.
4. "Talked for about an hour": *Pearson Diaries*, January 14, 1958, pp. 420–421.
5. "it's easy to write": Counselor, Sorensen, p. 150.
6. "the rumors still persist": *Martha MacGregor to JFK*, January 20, 1958, TCSPP, box 7, JFKL.
7. "she'd been gumshoeing": Hohenberg, p. 51.
8. Kennedy's reply: *JFK to Martha MacGregor*, January 30, 1958, TCSPP, box 7, JFKL.
9. "set the record straight": *JFK to John B. Oakes*, January 30, 1958, TCSPP, box 7, JFKL.
10. "There is no truth": *Evan Thomas to Mrs. Paul Lynch August 17, 1959*, Papers of John F. Kennedy. Presidential Papers. President's Office Files. Personal Secretary's Files. Books: "Profiles in Courage," correspondence, p. 68.
11. "Is the author": *Counselor*, Sorensen, p. 150.

CHAPTER 57: "IT'S SORT OF SAD"

1. "look over the manuscript": Burns, p. 163.
2. "a typed draft": *Sounding the Trumpet—The Making of the Inaugural of John F. Kennedy's Inaugural Address*, Richard J. Toffel, p. 68.
3. "brought $200,000": *Kennedy*, Sorensen, p. 243.
4. "celebrated the character": Thomas Reeves, p. 2.
5. "he'd carefully take something": *Jackie Kennedy's flawed memory*, Richard J. Tofel, *Washington Post*, September 23, 2011.
6. Dr. George Burkley: *The Kennedy Detail: JFK's Secret Service Agents Break Their Silence*, Gerald Blaine & Lisa McCubbin, p. 232.
7. "It tells something": Blair, p. 568.
8. press conference: New York Times, November 11, 1960, p. 20.
9. "Looking backwards": Dallek, p. 705.

CHAPTER 58: "THE PRIZE WAS THE PROBLEM"

1. "was becoming fairly": Herbert S. Parmet, recorded interview by Sheldon M. Stern, August 9, 1983, p. 1, JFKLOH.
2. "neither the chronology": Parmet, p. 331.

3. "the Profiles case": ibid., p. 323.
4. "Herbert Parmet's investigation": Wills, p. 136.
5. "The files do show notes": Parmet, pp. 331–332.
6. "There is no evidence": ibid., p. 333.
7. "the writing of material": *Ghostwriting and the Ethics of Authenticity*, John C. Knapp & Azalea M. Hulbert, p. 42.
8. "willing to make claims": Wills, p. 135.
9. "The book's structure": Fehrman, p. 278.
10. "paid a heavy price": Michael O'Brien, p. 290.

EPILOGUE

1. "It was written by JFK": *Reminiscences of Evan Thomas II*, February 11, 1974, p. 162, Oral History Archives at Columbia, Rare Book & Manuscript Library, Columbia University in the City of New York.
2. "Sorensen is not": ibid., p. 167.
3. "The controversy": *The Manchester Affair*, John Corry, p. 8.
4. "she leans over": Author interview with Evan Thomas, III, and also quoted in *A Clash of Camelots*, Vanity Fair August 31, 2009.
5. "authentic information": Burns, p. *vi*.
6. "neither an authorized": ibid., p. *vii*.
7. "in the image than in historical accuracy": Thomas Reeves, p. 157.
8. "a painful period": ibid., p. 34.
9. "I can't think of any case": ibid., p. 11.
10. "Krock was very much": McGeorge Bundy, Oral History, November 30, 1970, pp. 18–19, JFKL.

BIBLIOGRAPHY

BOOKS

Abell, Tyler, *Drew Pearson Diaries*, New York, Holt, Rinehart, & Winston, 1974.

Acacia, John, *Clark Clifford: The Wise Man of Washington*, Lexington, The University Press of Kentucky, 2009.

Agar, Herbert, *The Darkest Year: Britain Alone, June 1940-June 1941*, New York, Doubleday, 1973.

Barnes, John A., *John F. Kennedy on Leadership: The Lessons and Legacy of a President*, New York, American Management Association, 2005.

Beschloss, Michael R., *The Crisis Years: Kennedy and Khrushchev, 1960–1963*, Harper Collins, 1991.

Black, Conrad, *Franklin Delano Roosevelt: Champion of Freedom*, New York, Public Affairs, 2003.

Blaine, Gerald, McCubbin, Lisa, *The Kennedy Detail: JFK's Secret Service Agents Break Their Silence*, New York, Simon and Schuster, 2010.

Blair, Joan, *The Search for JFK*, New York, Berkley Publishing Corporation, 1976.

Bulkley, Robert, *At Close Quarters*, Charleston, Arcadia Publishing, 2017.

Burns, James MacGregor, *John F. Kennedy: A Political Profile*, New York, Harcourt, Brace, & Company, 1960.

Churchill, Winston, *The Gathering Storm*, Cambridge, Houghton Mifflin Company, 1948.

Clarke, Thurston, *Ask Not: The Inauguration of John F. Kennedy and the Speech that Changed America*, New York, Henry Holt & Company, 2004.

Clifford, Clark, *Counsel to the President*, New York, Random House, 1991.

Collier, Peter & Horowitz, David, *The Kennedys: An American Drama*, New York, Summit Books, 1984.

Corry, John, *The Manchester Affair*, New York, G.P. Putnam's Sons, 1967.

Dallek, Robert, *An Unfinished Life: John F. Kennedy, 1917–1963*, Boston, Little, Brown & Company, 2003.

Damore, Leo, *The Cape Cod Years of John Fitzgerald Kennedy*, New York, Four Walls Eight Windows, 1967.

Donovan, Robert J., *Conflict and Crisis: The Presidency of Harry S. Truman, 1945–1948*, New York, Norton, 1977.

Donovan, Robert J., *PT 109: John F. Kennedy in World War II*, New York, McGraw Hill, 1961.

Dray, Philip, *There's Power in a Union: The Epic Story of Labor in America*, New York, Random House, 2010.

Duffy, James, *Lindbergh vs. Roosevelt: The Rivalry that Divided America*, Washington, D.C., Regnery, 2010.

Farrell, John A., *Richard Nixon: The Life*, New York, Doubleday, 2017.

Farris, Scott, Inga: *Kennedy's Great Love, Hitler's Perfect Beauty, and J. Edgar Hoover's Prime Suspect*, Guilford, Connecticut, Lyons Press, 2016.

Fehrman, Craig, *Author in Chief: The Untold Story of Our Presidents and the Books They Wrote*, New York, Avid Reader Press, 2020.

Fetner, Gerald L., *Immersed in Great Affairs: Allan Nevins and the Heroic Age of American History*, New York, SUNY Press, 2004.

Goodwin, Doris Kearns, *The Fitzgeralds and the Kennedys: An American Saga*, New York, Simon & Schuster, 1987.

Hamilton, Nigel, *JFK: Restless Youth*, New York, Random House, 1992.

Hellman, John, *The Kennedy Obsession: The American Myth of JFK*, New York, Columbia University Press, 1997.

Henderson, Deirdre, *Prelude to Leadership: The Post-War Diary of John F. Kennedy*, Washington, D.C., Regnery Press, 1995.

Hersh, Seymour M., *The Dark Side of Camelot*, New York, Little, Brown & Company, 1997.

Heymann, David C., *A Woman Named Jackie*, New York, Signet, 1991.

Hohenberg, John, *The Pulitzer Diaries: Inside America's Great Prize*, Syracuse, Syracuse University Press, 1997.

Kennedy, John F., *As We Remember Joe*, Privately Published, 1945.

Kennedy, John F., *Profiles in Courage: Decisive Moments in the Lives of Celebrated Americans*, New York, Harper & Brothers, 1956.

Kennedy, John F., *Why England Slept*, New York, Wilfred Funk, Inc., 1940.

Kennedy, Rose, *Times to Remember*, New York, Doubleday, 1974.

Knapp, John C. & Hulbert, Azalea M., *Ghostwriting and the Ethics of Authenticity*, New York, Palgrave MacMillan, 2017.

Koskoff, David, *Joseph P. Kennedy: A Life and Times*, New York, Prentice Hall, 1974.

Kraft, Barbara S., *The Peace Ship: Henry Ford's Pacifist Adventure in the First World War*, New York, MacMillan, 1978.

Krock, Arthur S., *Memoirs: Sixty Years on the Firing Line*, New York, Funk & Wagnalls, 1968.

Larson, Erik, *The Splendid and the Vile: A Saga of Churchill, Family, and Defiance During the Blitz*, New York, Crown, 2020.

Lasky, Victor, *JFK: The Man and the Myth*, New York, The MacMillan Company, 1963.

Leamer, Laurence, *The Kennedy Men, 1901–1963*, New York, William Morrow, 2001.

Leaming, Barbara, *Jack Kennedy: The Education of a Statesman*, New York, W.W. Norton, 2006.

Leaming, Barbara, *Jacqueline Bouvier Kennedy Onassis: The Untold Story*, New York, Thomas Dunne Books, 2014.

Lincoln, Evelyn, *My Twelve Years with John F. Kennedy*, Philadelphia, David McCay Company, 1965.

Maier, Thomas, *When Lions Roar: The Churchills and the Kennedys*, New York, Crown Publishing Group, 2014.

Manchester, *William, Portrait of a President*, New York, Little, Brown & Company, 1967.

Manchester, William, *Winston Spencer Churchill: Alone, 1932–1940*, New York, Little, Brown, & Company, 1988.

Matthews, Chris, *Bobby Kennedy: A Raging Spirit*, New York, Simon & Schuster, 2017.

Matthews, Chris, *Jack Kennedy: Elusive Hero*, New York, Simon & Schuster, 2012.

Matthews, Chris, *Kennedy and Nixon: The Rivalry that Shaped Postwar America*, New York, Simon & Schuster, 1996.

McCarthy, Joe, *The Remarkable Kennedys*, New York, Popular Library, 1960.

McCullough, David, *Truman*, New York, Simon & Schuster, 1992.

McGinness, Joe, *The Selling of the President*, New York, Penguin Books, 1969.

Meyers, Joan Simpson, *John Fitzgerald Kennedy: As We Knew Him*, New York, MacMillan, 1965.

Morrow, Lance, *The Best Year of Their Lives: Kennedy, Johnson, and Nixon in 1948*, New York, Basic Books, 2005.

Nasaw, David, *The Patriarch: The Remarkable Life and Turbulent Times of Joseph P. Kennedy*, New York, Penguin Books, 2012.

Nixon, Richard M., *Six Crises*, New York, Doubleday, 1962.

O'Brien, Lawrence, *No Final Victories: A Life in Politics from John F. Kennedy to Watergate*, New York, Doubleday, 1974.

O'Brien, Michael, *John F. Kennedy: A Biography*, New York, St. Martin's Press, 2005.

O'Neill, Thomas P., *Man of the House: The Life and Political Memoirs of Speaker Tip O'Neill*, New York, Random House, 1987.

Olson, Lynne, *Those Angry Days: Roosevelt, Lindbergh, & America's Fight Over World War II*, New York, Random House, 2013.

Parmet, Herbert S., *Jack: The Struggles of John F. Kennedy*, New York, The Dial Press, 1980.

Perrett, Geoffrey, *Jack: A Life Like No Other*, New York, Random House, 2001.

Peters, Charles, *Five Days in Philadelphia: The Amazing 'We Want Wilkie' Convention of 1940*, New York, Public Affairs, 2005.

Pitts, David, *Jack and Lem: John F. Kennedy and Lem Billings, The Untold Story of an Extraordinary Relationship*, Philadelphia, De Capo Press, 2007.

Pizzatola, Louis, *Hearst Over Hollywood: Power, Passion, and Propaganda at the Movies*, New York, Columbia University Press, 2002.

Reeves, Richard, *President Kennedy: Profile of Power*, New York, 1993.

Reeves, Thomas, *A Question of Character: A Life of John F. Kennedy*, Roseville, California, Prima Publishing, 1991.

Reid, Paul, *The Last Lion: Winston Spencer Churchill Defender of the Realm, 1940–1965*, New York, Bantam Books, 2012.

Reynolds, Nicholas, *Writer, Sailor, Soldier, Spy: Ernest Hemingway's Secret Adventures, 1935–1961*, New York, William Morrow, 2017.

Ritchie, Donald A., *James M. Landis: Dean of the Regulators*, Cambridge, MA, Harvard University Press, 1980.

Schlesinger, Arthur, *A Life in the Twentieth Century: Innocent Beginnings, 1917–1950*, New York, First Mariner Books, 2002.

Schlesinger, Arthur, *A Thousand Days*, New York, Houghton Mifflin, 1965.

Schlesinger, Arthur, *Jacqueline Kennedy: Historic Conversations on Life with John F. Kennedy*, New York, Hachette, 2011.

Schlesinger, Robert, *White House Ghosts, President and Their Speechwriters: From FDR to George W. Bush*, New York, Simon & Schuster, 2008.

Schlesinger, Stephen C., *Act of Creation: The Founding of the United Nations*, Boulder, Colorado, Westview Press, 2003.

Shaw, John T., *JFK in the Senate: Pathway to the Presidency*, New York, St. Martin's Press, 2013.

Sherwood, Robert E., *Roosevelt and Hopkins: An Intimate History*, New York, Harper & Brothers, 1948.

Silverman, Al, *The Times of Their Lives: The Golden Age of Great American Book Publishers, Their Editors and Authors*, New York, St. Martin's Press, 2008.

Smith, Amanda, *Hostage to Fortune: The Letters of Joseph P. Kennedy*, New York, Viking Books, 2001.

Smith, Sally Bedell, *Grace and Power: The Private World of the Kennedy White House*, New York, Random House, 2004.

Sorensen, Theodore, *Counselor: A Life Lived at the Edge of History*, New York, Harper Collins, 2008.

Sorensen, Theodore, *Kennedy*, New York, Harper & Row, 1965.

Stokes, David R., *Jack and Dick: When Kennedy Met Nixon*, Fairfax, VA, Critical Mass Books, 2015.

Swift, Will, *The Kennedys Amidst the Gathering Storm: A Thousand Days in London*, New York, Harper Collins, 2002.

Thomas, Evan, *Robert Kennedy: His Life*, New York, Simon & Schuster, 2002.

Tofel, Richard, J., *Sounding the Trumpet: The Making of John F. Kennedy's Inaugural Address*, Chicago, Ivan R. Dee, 2005.

Tye, Larry, *Bobby Kennedy: The Making of a Liberal Icon*, New York, Random House, 2016.

Ulyatt, Michelle A., *Theodore Sorensen and the Kennedys: A Life of Public Service*, Switzerland, Palgrave MacMillan, 2019.

Wallace, Mike, *Between You and Me: A Memoir*, New York, Hyperion, 2005.

Watts, Steven, *The People's Tycoon: Henry Ford and the American Century*, New York, Knopf, 2005.

Whalen, Thomas J., *Kennedy and Lodge: The 1952 Massachusetts Senate Race*, New Hampshire, Northeastern University Press, 2000.

Wheeler-Bennett, John, *Special Relationships: America in Peace and War*, New York, St. Martin's Press, 1976.

White, Mark, *Kennedy: A Cultural History of an American Icon*, New York, Bloomsbury Publishing, 2013.

Widmer, Ted, *Listening In: The Secret White House Recordings of John F. Kennedy*, New York, Hyperion, 2012.
Wills, Garry, *The Kennedy Imprisonment: A Meditation on Power*, New York, First Mariner Books, 2002.
Wortman, Marc, *1941: Fighting the Shadow War*, New York, Grove Press, 2016.

ORAL HISTORIES
Bartlett, Charles, John F. Kennedy Library Oral History Program
Bundy, MacGeorge, John F. Kennedy Oral History Program
Burns, James MacGregor, John F. Kennedy Library Oral History Program
Canfield, Cass, Columbia University Oral History
Clifford, Clark, John F. Kennedy Library Oral History Program
Coit, Margaret, John F. Kennedy Library Oral History Program
Douglas, Paul H., John F. Kennedy Oral History Program
Halle, Kay, John F. Kennedy Library Oral History Program
Krock, Arthur, John F. Kennedy Library Oral History Program
Lincoln, Evelyn, John F. Kennedy Library Oral History Program
Luce, Henry R. John F. Kennedy Library Oral History Program
MacDonald, Torbert, John F. Kennedy Library Oral History Program
Reed, James A., John F. Kennedy Library Oral History Program
Spalding, Charles, John F. Kennedy Library Oral History Program
Thomas, Evan, Columbia University Oral History
Wallace, Robert, John F. Kennedy Library Oral History Program
Wild, Payton S., John F. Kennedy Library Oral History Program

NEWSPAPERS AND PERIODICALS
Associated Press
Boston Globe
Boston Herald
Chicago Herald-American
Collier's Magazine
Columbia Magazine
Coronet Magazine
Georgetown Magazine
Harper's Magazine
Holyoke Transcript-Telegram
Houston Chronicle
Life Magazine
London Times
Look Magazine
McCall's Magazine
Moving Picture World
New Bedford Standard-Times

Nebraska State Journal
New York Journal-American
New York Post
New York Review of Books
New York Times
New York Times Book Review
New York Times Magazine
Philadelphia Inquirer
Providence Journal
Reader's Digest
Saturday Evening Post
Television Quarterly: The Journal of the National Academy of Television Arts and Sciences
Tennessee Historical Quarterly
The New Yorker
The Week Magazine
Time magazine
Town & Country Magazine
Vanity Fair
Village Voice
Washington Post
Washingtonian Magazine

WEBSITES

https://www.atlasobscura.com/articles/how-americas-first-popular-comic-shaped-the-19th-century-newspaper-wars

https://www.dailymail.co.uk/news/article-4566596/Inside-relationship-JFK-Lem-Billings.html

https://www.foxnews.com/travel/once-majestic-cruise-ship-the-s-s-united-states-could-be-americas-flagship-once-again

https://www.historylink.org/File/10224

https://www.kirkusreviews.com/about/history/

https://www.kirkusreviews.com/book-reviews/a/evan-thomas-6/ambulance-in-africa

https://thrivewithadd.com/wp-content/uploads/2013/09/the_kennedy_cursewade_nye9.pdf

https://www.un.org/en/sections/history-united-nations-charter/1945-san-francisco-conference/index.html

https://www.wnyc.org/story/1956-national-book-awards-part-2-senator-john-f-kennedy/

https://www.youtube.com/watch?v=qclD4GgIVSE

AUTHOR INTERVIEWS
Evan Thomas III

ACADEMIC RECORDS
Harper and Row Publishers Records, Columbia University
Harvard University, Academic Records
Harvard University, Dean's List

PERSONAL PAPERS
John F. Kennedy Personal Papers, JFKL
Joseph P. Kennedy Personal Papers, JFKL
Theodore C. Sorensen Personal Papers, JFKL

Index

ABOUT THE AUTHOR

David R. Stokes is a ghostwriter, best-selling author, historian, screenwriter, broadcaster, and retired minister. He and his wife Karen have three lovely daughters and seven wonderful grandchildren. They live in beautiful Northern Virginia. David's website is: *www.davidrstokes.com*